THE HU...

CONCISE D...

WORD ORIGINS

THE HUTCHINSON

CONCISE DICTIONARY OF

WORD ORIGINS

Adrian Room

Helicon

Copyright © Helicon Publishing Ltd 1995

All rights reserved

Helicon Publishing Ltd
42 Hythe Bridge Street
Oxford OX1 2EP

Printed and bound in Great Britain by
Cox & Wyman Ltd, Reading, Berkshire

ISBN 1-85986-126-1

British Cataloguing in Publication Data

A catalogue record for this book is available from the British Library

INTRODUCTION

This dictionary contains the origins of just over 2000 words, ranging from the familiar and everyday, such as *happy* and *rabbit*, to the more formal and specialized, such as *dogma* and *repertoire*. It also includes the names of the days and months, and some jargon or slang words, such as *punk* and *swop*.

Where do words come from? Most English words can be traced back to one of two sources, *Germanic* or *Italic*. *Germanic* words, usually regarded as the 'native' ones, often have their counterparts in modern German, as well as related languages such as Dutch, Swedish, Danish and Norwegian. Compare English *house* with German *Haus*, Dutch *huis*, and Swedish, Danish, and Norwegian *hus*. *Italic* words often have their counterparts in modern French, as well as related Italian, Spanish, and Portuguese, and share a common ancestor in *Latin*, spoken in Italy (hence *Italic*). Compare English *poor* with French *pauvre*, Italian *povero*, and Spanish and Portuguese *pobre*, all going back to Latin *pauper*.

Germanic and Italic languages themselves had a common ancestor in *Indo-European*, so that some modern English words have 'relatives' in both branches. This is especially true of the most fundamental words, such as family relationships, numbers, or objects of the natural world. An example is English *mother*, which links up with German *Mutter*, Dutch *moeder*, Swedish *modern*, Danish *moderen*, Norwegian *moren*, French *mère*, Italian and Spanish *madre*, and Portuguese *mãe*, these last four deriving from Latin *mater*.

In general it is the everyday and concrete words that are Germanic in origin, and the more formal and abstract that are Italic. Thus Germanic-based *house* has its equivalent in Italic-based *mansion*, and Germanic *seeing* is at a more basic level than Italic *vision*.

Of course, there are other languages that have also provided English words, albeit to a lesser extent. Two others, each equally ancient, are *Celtic* and *Greek*. Celtic, like Germanic and Italic, is a group of languages today represented, among others, by Scottish Gaelic, Irish, and Welsh. Greek, on the other hand, is a unified language, like Latin.

English words derived from both Celtic and Greek share the qualities of Germanic and Italic in that Celtic-derived words are usually everyday and concrete, and Greek-derived words formal and abstract. Examples are Scottish Gaelic *whisky*, Irish *shamrock*, and Welsh *crag* on the one hand, and Greek *dogma*, *charisma*, and *amnesty* on the other.

Latin, like Greek, has also given many modern learned or specialized words. Just five of those in the dictionary are *dictionary*, *sinecure*, *candidate*, *moratorium*, and *commuter*. These all have precise origins and derivations.

At the other end of the scale, many Germanic words operate at a much more earthy level, appealing as much to the senses as to the mind. Quite often they are in related sound groups. Words beginning with *fl-* often denote something light or transient, for example, such as *flag*, *flake*, *flap*, *fleece*, *flick*, *flight*, *flimsy*, *flip*, *float*, and *flop*. Words with *sl-* denote a gentle downward movement, such as *slack*, *sleek*, *sleep*, *slide*, *slip*, *slither*, *slope*, *slouch*, and *slow*. Words in *wr-* denote a twisting or turning, such as *wrack*, *wrap*, *wreath*, *wrestle*, *wring*, *writhe*, *wrong*, *wrought*, and *wry*.

English as we now understand it was first spoken by the Angles, Saxons, and Jutes who came to the British Isles in the 3rd and 4th centuries AD, when Britain was still part of the Roman empire. These, therefore, were the Germanic peoples who brought their languages with them, and introduced them to the native Celts. The languages that they spoke gradually coalesced into what is known as Anglo-Saxon, or more commonly Old English, and this is the forerunner of the 'new' English we speak today.

As it was forming, Old English itself adopted a number of Scandinavian words imported by the Vikings when they in turn came to Britain in the 9th century. The languages blended fairly readily, since the Vikings also spoke Germanic languages.

The Italic content of English was imported by the Normans, who invaded England in the 11th century. Although themselves of Scandinavian origin, they spoke a form of French, which at first less readily blended with English. Initially it did not blend at all, so that two languages existed in parallel. Hence doublets of the *house* v *mansion* type that still exist. The speech and writing of the Normans also affected the speech and writing of the established inhabitants, with the result that Old English altered significantly. The language it evolved into is now known as Middle English.

Finally, from about the mid-15th century, something like the English of today began to emerge. It was not static, of course, and the growing world of learning frequently coined the new terms it needed from classical Greek and Latin.

One particular development of the new world was an interest in the words themselves. Scholars began to ask the question already asked above: where do words come from? More precisely, what was their original meaning, and how have they evolved? The learned term *etymology* was coined (from Greek) to describe the study of word origins and meanings. Certain scholars set themselves up as specialists and produced either dictionaries with etymologies or purely etymological dictionaries. Many of the etymologies, however, were anything but scientific! Wordsmiths of the 16th and 17th centuries include William Camden, Isaac Casaubon, Richard Verstegan (or Rowlands), Sir Henry Spelman, William Somner, Thomas Henshaw, Stephen Skinner, and John Minsheu. The 18th-century lexicographer Nathan Bailey drew on their etymologies, among others, when compiling his *Dictionarium Britannicum: or A More Compleat Universal Etymological English Dictionary* (1730). Dr Johnson later included etymologies in his own *Dictionary* (1755), but many of them were equally inaccurate.

Dictionaries of word origins in the 19th and 20th centuries have been rather more reliable, as one would hope and expect. They range from W W Skeat's *Etymological Dictionary of the English Language* (1882) to T F Hoad's *The Concise Oxford Dictionary of English Etymology* (1986), taking in on the way Ernest Weekley's *Etymological Dictionary of Modern English* (1920) and Eric Partridge's *Origins: A Short Etymological Dictionary of Modern English* (1958).

Despite the increasingly sophisticated researches of modern etymologists, however, there are still several words whose ultimate or even immediate origins are either uncertain or frankly unknown. Examples are *bar*, *cocktail*, *dog*, *gravy*, *hobo*, *jazz, job, leg, mushroom, pack, pimp, prim, pug, quid, scallywag, scull, shandy, sigh, skiffle, smarm, squiffy, tag, tee, theodolite, toggle, toy, tripe,* and *wherry.*

Such words are mostly omitted from this dictionary's limited selection, since all that can be said about them is *of obscure origin* or *of unknown origin*, which is hardly helpful.

The information that *is* given for almost every word in the dictionary is as follows: (1) its present meaning (unless obvious); (2) its immediate and ultimate languages of origin (in some cases back to Indo-European); (3) its original meaning. Where a word has changed its meaning over the years, as can happen, the different meanings are given. Related words of interest are cross-referred to the appropriate entry.

For the names of the different languages referred to in the entries, such as *Old High German*, see the Language Guide (p. 194).

Examples of popular but incorrect etymologies appear throughout as object lessons and entertainment. These have been gleaned from the works of the writers, mentioned above, as cited by Bailey, as well as from more recent popular works, such as Eliezer Edwards's *Dictionary of Words, Facts, and Phrases* (1901), Basil Hargrave's *Origins and Meanings of Popular Phrases & Names* (1925), and Edwin Radford's *Crowther's Encyclopædia of Phrases and Origins* (1945).

A

abandon The word goes back to the Old French phrase *a bandon*, 'at will', with *bandon* itself related to English *ban*. The idea is that one has things 'at one's will', or under control.

abbey The religious building takes its name from the *abbot* who presides over it. His own title ultimately goes back to Aramaic *abbā*, 'father', as found in the Bible (eg Mark 14:36).

abdicate The literal sense of the verb is 'proclaim away', from Latin *ab*, 'away', and *dicare*, 'to proclaim' (as in English *indicate*). A monarch who *abdicates* proclaims that the throne is 'away' from him, or does not belong to him.

able The word derives, through Old French, from Latin *habere*, 'to have', 'to hold'. If you are *able* to do something you have or hold the power or knowledge to do it.

abominable The ultimate origin of the word lies in Latin *ab*, 'away' and *omen*, 'sign', 'omen'. If something is *abominable* you see it as a bad sign, and 'wish it away' from you. The sense is reflected in the Latin tag *absit omen*, 'may the omen be absent', the equivalent of modern 'touch wood'.

aborigine The word for the original inhabitant of a country (such as the *Aborigines* in Australia or the American Indians in North America) derives from Latin *aborigines*, the name of the inhabitants of Latium in pre-Roman times. The origin of the name is uncertain, but it is probably a tribal name.

abracadabra The magic formula probably derives from the Greek mystical word *abraxas*. This has no meaning, but its letters add up to the magic number 365 (the number of days in a year), with A = 1, B = 2, R = 100, X = 60, and S = 200.

absurd The word has its origin, through French, in Latin *absurdus*, 'dissonant', 'senseless', from *ab-*, here an intensifying prefix, and *surdus*, 'dull-sounding', 'indistinct'.

academy The word originally applied to a gymnasium in Athens where Plato taught in classical times. It in turn was called after the Greek hero *Academus*, since it stood on the site of a shrine sacred to him.

accent The word derives from Latin *accentus*, from *ad*, 'to' and *cantus*, 'song', 'chant'. This was a translation of Greek *prosōidia*, literally 'song added' (English *prosody*), meaning a song added to speech. An *accent* of any sort is added to standard speech.

accident The origin is in Latin *ad*, 'to' and *cadere*, 'to fall'. An *accident* is something that 'befalls' you.

ache The noun has its origin in Old English *æce*, with the same meaning. This gave a word that was pronounced first 'atch' then 'aitch' until as recently as the 19th century. Compare modern *bake* and *batch*, *wake* and *watch*, *speak* and *speech*.

acne The skin condition takes its name from a misreading of Greek *akmas* as *aknas*. The original word was a form of *akmē*, 'eruption', literally 'point', 'edge' (English *acme*).

acorn The word has evolved from Old English *æcern*, 'fruit of a tree', itself probably related to *acre*, as if referring to a tree on uncultivated land. Its present spelling has been influenced by *corn* and *oak*.

FALSE

acorn From Old English *āc*, 'oak', and *corn*, 'grain'.

---

acrobat The word for the agile entertainer derives, via French, from Greek *akrobatēs*, literally 'high walker', from *akros*, 'extreme', 'top', and *bainein*, 'to walk'. The image is of a tightrope walker.

FALSE

acrobat From a blend of *actor* and *bat*, referring to the pole or stick that tightrope walkers usually carry for balance.

---

adamant The word goes back through French and Latin to Greek *adamas*, a term used for a hard metal (probably steel) or a ◊diamond. The Greek word literally meant 'untamable', from a word related to modern *tame*. English *adamant* as a noun meaning 'hard rock' occurs in the Bible: 'As an adamant harder than flint have I made thy forehead' (Ezekiel 3:9).

adder The name of the snake arose from a wrong division of *a nadder* as *an adder*. *Nadder* simply means 'snake', from a word related to Latin *natrix*, 'water snake', and Welsh *neidr*, 'snake'. For words of similar origin, compare ◊apron and ◊umpire.

admiral The word for the naval rank is ultimately of Arabic origin, and represents the first part of the phrase *amīr al-bahr*, 'commander of the sea'. The *-d-* entered the word by association with Latin *admirabilis*, 'admirable'.

adultery The term came into English, via Old French, from Latin *adulterare*, 'to corrupt'. This itself probably evolved from the phrase *ad alterum* (masculine) or *ad alteram* (feminine), 'to another'. *Adultery* is a relationship with someone other than one's spouse.

affray The term for a noisy quarrel or disturbance derives from a conjectured Vulgar Latin word *exfridare*, where *ex* means 'out' and *fridare* comes from a word meaning 'peace' (modern German *Friede*). The literal sense is thus 'out of peace', since people causing an *affray* break the peace.

aftermath The word that now means 'catastrophic consequence' was originally a term for a second crop of grass, literally 'after mowing', from *after* and *math*, 'mowing'. The unfavourable sense came about because the second mowing was rarely as rich or sweet as the first.

agenda The word directly represents Latin *agenda*, the plural of *agendum*, 'thing to be done', from *agere*, 'to do', which also gave English *agent* (whose job is to *do* something).

agnostic The term describes someone who believes that knowledge of God is impossible. It was devised in 1869 from Greek *a-*, 'not' and English *gnostic*, 'relating to knowledge' (from Greek *gnōsis*, 'knowledge') by the biologist T H Huxley, who wanted to express his own stance as opposed to that of contemporary 'Gnostics', who claimed that knowledge of God was possible.

aisle passageway or gangway, as in a church or supermarket, derives from Latin *ala*, 'wing', since in a church an *aisle* runs to one side of the nave or chancel, like a wing. However, the spelling was influenced by *isle*, since the passageway could also be thought of as a detached 'island', separate from the main gangway.

> **FALSE**
>
> **aisle** An altered form of *alley*.

akimbo To stand with arms *akimbo* is to stand with hands on hips, with elbows pointed outwards. The word represents the Middle English phrase *in kenebowe*, literally 'in keen bow', otherwise 'in a sharp bend'. The *in* became *a-* under the influence of words such as *across*. The alteration of *ken* to *kim* may have come about by association with the dialect word *cam*, 'crooked'.

> **FALSE**
>
> **akimbo** From Italian *sghembo*, 'crooked', 'oblique', 'awry'.

alarm The word goes back to Old Italian *all' arme*, 'to the arms', originally used as a military order when an attack was expected. Compare ◊alert.

> **FALSE**
>
> **alarm** From Old French *lerre* (modern *larron*), 'thief', cried as a warning against robbers.

albatross The large sea bird has a name that is an alteration of Spanish *alcatraz*, 'gannet', influenced by Latin *albus*, 'white'. Hence the name of the former United States prison, on the island of *Alcatraz* in San Francisco bay, with the island so named for its gannets. The Spanish word itself represents Arabic *al-ghattās*, 'the sea eagle'.

album Whatever the sense of the word today, it ultimately derives from the identical Latin word meaning 'white', used for a *white* tablet on which records or notices were inscribed. The word has been in general English use since the 17th century.

alcohol The word goes back, through Latin, to Arabic *al-kuhl*, literally 'the eye salve', this being specifically a form of powdered antimony used in Arab countries as a cosmetic to darken the area round the eyes. (Hence *kohl* as the English word for this powder.) In the 16th century, *alcohol* was a term for a fine metallic powder obtained by purification. The term was later extended to liquids so obtained.

alderman The former local council member derives his title from Old English *aldormann*, representing *ealdor*, 'chief' (literally 'older'), and *mann*, 'man'. Historians use *ealdorman* as the equivalent title of the Anglo-Saxon official who was responsible for a shire (see ◊sheriff).

> **FALSE**
>
> **alderman** So called as he was of *all the men* chief.

alert The word goes back to Italian *all' erta*, 'on the watch', that is, on the lookout, with *erta*, 'lookout post', from Latin *erigere*, 'to put up straight' (English *erect*). Compare ◊alarm.

algebra The branch of mathematics ultimately gets its name from Arabic *al-jabr*, 'the reunion', referring to the solving of algebraic equations.

allergy The medical condition has a name of Greek origin, from *allos*, 'other', and *ergon*, 'work', 'activity'. The reference is to a changed reaction in the body, causing hypersensitivity to certain substances.

alligator The word is a corruption of Spanish *el lagarto*, 'the lizard', *alligators* being regarded as a large species of this reptile. The Spanish word is related to *lizard* itself, which means that *alligator* also is.

> **FALSE**
>
> **alloy** From French *à la loi*, 'according to law', referring to gold or silver mixed with other metals according to regulations established by law.

alloy The term for a mixture of two or more metals derives, through French, from an ultimate source in Latin *alligare*, 'to combine', from *ad*, 'to', and *ligare*, 'to bind'. English *ally* has the same source, as a person who is 'bound to' another.

almond The name of the nut goes back, through French, to Latin *amygdala*, itself from Greek *amugdalē*, with initial *a*- becoming *al*- by association with words of Arabic origin such as *alcohol*, and *-mygdala* becoming *-mond* under the influence of Latin *mandere*, 'to chew' (English *mandible*).

alphabet The word derives from Late Latin *alphabetum*, itself from Greek *alphabētos*, representing the first two letters of the Greek *alphabet*, *alpha* and *beta*. English *ABC* is a native equivalent.

altar The word is an adoption of the identical Late Latin word that itself derived from Latin *altus*, 'high'. The native Old English word for an altar was *wēofod*, literally 'idol table', but this did not survive much beyond the 15th century.

amateur The word is French for 'lover', implying someone who is fond of an activity but who is not a specialist or professional.

amber The yellow-coloured fossil resin derives its name, through Medieval Latin *ambar*, from Arabic *'anbar*, 'ambergris' (a waxy substance secreted by the sperm whale). The latter word represents Old French *ambre gris*, 'grey amber'.

> **FALSE**
>
> **amber** From German *anbrennen*, 'to light', 'to catch fire'. Hence German *Bernstein*, 'amber'.

ambiguous The word used for something uncertain or having either of two meanings derives from Latin *ambiguus*, 'shifting', 'doubtful', literally 'leading both ways', from *ambo*, 'both', and *agere*, 'to lead', 'to act'.

ambition The word has its source in Latin *ambitio*, from *ambire*, 'to go round', originally used of a person who went round canvassing for votes. Such a person would have been trying to please. Hence the modern sense, which is used of a person trying to win or succeed.

ambulance The first aid vehicle has a name that originally applied to a field hospital, that is, a medical team which accompanied an army in battle. The present English word evolved from the French term for this, which was *hôpital ambulant*, literally 'walking hospital'. Compare ◊pram.

anathema The word is now used to mean little more than something one dislikes. It is properly a formal ecclesiastical curse of excommunication, deriving, via Church Latin, from the identical Greek word meaning 'thing devoted' (ie, to evil), originally *anathēma*, 'offering', literally 'thing set up', from *ana*, 'up', and *tithenai*, 'to set', 'to place'.

anatomy The word was originally used in English to apply to a dissection of the body. Hence its literal sense of 'cutting up', from Greek *ana*, 'up', and *temnein*, 'to cut'. The English word was formerly taken to represent *an atomy*, so that *atomy* came to be used in the sense 'skeleton'. This occurs in literature down to the 19th century, as in Shakespeare's *Henry IV, Part 2* ('Thou atomy, thou!') and Dickens's *Dombey and Son* ('withered atomies of teaspoons').

anecdote The origin of the word is ultimately in Greek *anekdota*, 'unpublished things', from *an-*, 'not', and *ekdidonai*, 'to publish' (literally 'give out'). The prime source of the term was *Anekdotos*, the title of a work by the 6th-century Byzantine historian Procopius. This contained the previously unpublished memoirs of the private life of the Roman emperor Justinian and his wife Theodora.

anemone The flower is so called because it was believed to bloom under the influence of the wind. Hence the origin of its name in Greek *anemos*, 'wind'.

animal The English word is a direct adoption of the Latin word, which itself literally means 'living being', from *anima*, 'air', 'breath' (related to English *animate*).

anorexia The morbid state of compulsory fasting has a name of Greek origin, representing *an-*, 'not', and *orexis*, 'appetite' (literally 'longing', 'yearning').

answer The literal sense of the word is 'anti-swear', and it actually derives from Old English words related to modern *anti-* and *swear*. An *answer* was thus originally a solemn statement that denied an accusation, as in 'He was quick to *answer* the charges brought against him'.

anthem The word for a religious song derives, through Old English, from Late Latin *antiphona*, 'antiphon' (a hymn sung in alternate parts). The latter word itself derives from Greek *antiphōnos*, 'responsive', literally 'sounding opposite', from *anti*, 'against', 'opposing', and *phōnē*, 'sound'. Church *anthems* still have sections sung by either side of a choir alternately.

> **FALSE**
>
> **anthem** From Greek *anti*, 'opposite', and *humnos*, 'hymn'.

aphis The word for the little insect that feeds by sucking the juices from plants was first used by the botanist Linnaeus in the 18th century. He based it on an identical Greek word that appears to have arisen as a wrong form of *koris*, 'bug', the *kor-* of which was misread as *aph-*. (The Greek letters rho (*r*) and phi (*ph*) are somewhat similar.)

aphorism The word for a short pithy saying derives, through Latin, from Greek *aphorismos*, 'definition', from *aphorizein*, 'to define', ultimately based on *horos*, 'boundary'.

apology The word has its origin in Greek *apologia*, 'verbal defence', from *apo*, 'away', 'off', and *logos*, 'speech'. A person making an *apology* wishes to be dissociated with what has happened, even when taking the blame.

apoplexy The word for a 'fit' or sudden loss of consciousness derives from Greek *apoplēssein*, 'to cripple by a stroke', from *apo*, 'off', and *plēssein*, 'to strike'.

> **FALSE**
>
> **apoplexy** From Greek *Apollōn*, 'Apollo', and *plēssein*, 'to strike', so 'Apollo-struck', alluding to the sun's rays, known to the Greeks as 'Apollo's arrows'.

appal The word originally meant 'grow pale' or 'make pale'. Hence its origin in Old French *appalir*, 'to turn pale'. If you are *appalled* by something it may well make you turn *pale*.

> **FALSE**
>
> **appal** From *pall*, since an *appalled* person loses strength or *palls*.

appetite The word goes back, through French, to Latin *appetitus*, 'craving', from the verb *appetere*, 'to desire ardently', literally 'to aim towards', from *ad*, 'towards', and *petere*, 'to seek', 'to aim at' (English *petition*).

apple The homely fruit has a name that is similar in many languages, such as Welsh *afal* and Russian *yabloko* (though not French *pomme*). It goes back to an Indo-European root element *abl-* which in altered form, as *alb-*, may have given Latin *albus*, 'white'.

apricot The earlier English name for the fruit was *apricock*. This came, via Spanish or Portuguese, from Arabic *al-birqūq*, 'the apricot', which itself derived, through Greek, from Latin *praecox*, 'ripening early' (compare ◊precocious). The *apricot* was known for its early ripening. The word has thus reached its present English form by a rather roundabout route.

April The fourth month has a name that is popularly derived from Latin *aperire*, 'to open', as it is the time of year when flowers bloom and trees bud. But it is possible the name may actually be linked with that of the Greek goddess *Aphrodite*, or with that of some earlier pagan goddess who gave her own name.

apron Like ◊adder, among others, the word is the result of a misdivision of *a napron* into *an apron*. English *napron* evolved from Old French *naperon*, 'little cloth' (related to English *napkin* and *nappy*).

arbour The word for a leafy glade represents a former English word *erber*, which itself came from Old French *herbier*, from Latin *herba*, 'grass' (English *herb*). The present spelling came about by association with Latin *arbor*, 'tree'.

> **FALSE**
>
> **arbour** From Latin *arbor*, 'tree', since it is a leafy bower shaded by trees.

architect The word goes back through French and Latin to Greek *arkhitektōn*, 'head of building', from *arkhos*, 'head', 'chief', and *tektōn*, 'builder' (to which English *technical* is related).

archive The collection of records or documents gets its name, through French, from Late Latin *archivum*, itself from Greek *arkheion*, the term for a repository of official records, based on *arkhē*, 'government'.

arena The word was first used in English for the centre of an amphitheatre. Hence its origin in Latin *harena*, 'sand', referring to a place of combat strewn with sand. The combats themselves were between gladiators or wild animals, and the sand was to soak up the blood of those killed or wounded.

arithmetic The branch of mathematics takes its name from Greek *arithmētikē tekhnē*, 'art of counting', from *arithmein*, 'to count', itself from *arithmos*, 'number'.

arrive The original sense of the verb in English was 'come to the shore', 'land'. The word itself thus evolved from a conjectured Latin verb *arripare*, from *ad*, 'to', and *ripa*, 'shore', 'bank' (related to English *river*).

arrowroot The plant that yields a type of edible starch has a name deriving from Aruak *aru-aru*, literally 'meal of meals'. However, because its *root* was used to treat wounds caused by poisoned *arrows*, the name was perverted to its present form.

> **FALSE**
>
> **arrowroot** So called because its *roots* were used to treat wounds caused by poisoned *arrows*.

arson The act of deliberately setting fire to property derives its name, through French, from Medieval Latin *arsio*, genitive *arsionis*, 'burning', from Latin *ardere*, 'to burn' (English *ardent*).

art The word goes back to Latin *ars*, genitive *artis*, itself from an Indo-European root element *ar-*, meaning 'join', 'fit', which also gave words such as *arm* and *article*.

asparagus The plant, whose succulent young shoots are eaten as a vegetable, has a name of Greek origin but unknown meaning. The name was long popularly corrupted to *sparrowgrass*, as if it described a *grass* eaten by *sparrows*.

> **FALSE**
>
> **asparagus** A mock-Latin form of *sparrowgrass*.

aspirin The well-known medicinal tablet has a name invented by the German scientist Heinrich Dreser in 1899. It represents a short form of *Acetylirte Spirsäure*, 'acetylated spiraeic acid', followed by the chemical suffix *-in*. Spiraeic acid is now known as salicylic acid, and aspirin itself is chemically acetylsalicylic acid.

assassin The word goes back through Latin to Arabic *hashshāshīn*, the plural of *hashshāsh*, 'hashish eater'. The reference is to 12th-century Muslim fanatics, who drugged themselves with hashish when about to murder their victims, usually Crusaders. English *hashish* is thus a related word.

assets The word originates from Old French *asez* (modern *assez*), 'enough', itself representing a conjectured Latin phrase *ad satis*, from *ad*, 'to', and *satis*, 'enough'. If you have *assets* you have enough to meet claims for payment. (The word was originally singular but was taken as plural because of the final *-s*. The modern singular *asset* first appeared only in the 19th century.)

asthma The term for the respiratory disorder was directly adopted from the identical Greek word meaning 'laborious breathing', from the verb *azein*, 'to breathe hard'.

astronomy The word derives from Greek *astron*, 'star', and the suffix *-nomia*, related to *nomos*, 'law'. The term also formerly meant the same as *astrology*, which was itself not only the term, as now, for the study of the stars and planets as they affect our lives but also practical *astronomy*. The two senses of the word were differentiated respectively as *judicial astrology* and *natural astrology*.

athlete The word represents Greek *athlētēs*, a noun formed from the verb *athlein*, 'compete for a prize', itself from *athlon*, 'prize'.

atone The verb was formed from the noun *atonement*, which itself was based on the phrase *at one*. If you *atone* for a sin or crime, you want to be 'at one' with others, or on harmonious terms with them.

attic The topmost room in a house takes its name from what was originally called the *attic storey*. This was one with a façade decorated with pilasters (shallow square columns) in the *Attic* style. *Attic* itself relates to *Attica*, the territory of Athens in ancient Greece.

auction The special type of sale is so called because the prices rise until the object is sold to the highest bidder, from Latin *auctio*, genitive *auctionis*, the noun of *augere*, 'to increase' (English *augment*).

August The name of the eighth month comes from *Augustus*, the title, meaning 'great', adopted by the first Roman emperor, Gaius Octavius (63 BC–AD 14), son of the niece of Julius Caesar. The earlier name of the month was *Sextilis*, 'sixth', as it was the sixth month from March, when the Roman year began.

aunt The term of relationship evolved from Latin *amita* in the same sense. This itself is a 'pet') or diminutive form of a conjectured word *amma*, 'mother'.

automatic The word evolved, through Latin, from Greek *automatos*, 'self-moving', from *autos*, 'self', and a root element meaning 'think' related to modern English *mind* and *mental*.

avalanche The word for a large fall of snow or something similar derives from French. It arose as a misdivision of *la valanche*, with *valanche* from an Alpine dialect word *lavantse*. The ultimate origin of this is uncertain, though it is tempting to relate it to Italian (and English) *lava*.

average The modern word evolved from a former term *averay*, used in the 15th century to denote a loss to shipowners caused by damage at sea. This loss was shared by all concerned. Hence the present sense. The earlier word ultimately came from Arabic *awār*, 'damage'. The *-age* of the modern word may have arisen by association with *damage* itself.

> **FALSE**
>
> **average** From the amount of work done by a lord's *avers*, or draught animals.

avocado The pear-shaped fruit has a name that on the face of it derives from Spanish *avocado*, 'advocate'. However, it is actually an altered form of Nahuatl *ahuacatl*, 'testicle', alluding to its shape. (In this respect, compare ◊orchid.)

away The word evolved from the Old English expression *on weg*, 'on (one's) way'. If you go *away* you are thus 'on your way' from a place.

babble The word has its equivalent in several languages, such as French *babiller*, 'to prattle', Dutch *babbelen* and German *plappern*. These are all ultimately imitative of prattling or 'baby talk'.

baboon The monkey was known in Middle English as *babewyn*, a word that evolved from Old French *baboue*, 'grimace', referring to its face and expression.

bachelor In medieval times the word was a term for a young knight. It came from Old French *bacheler*, which itself represents an conjectured Latin word *baccalarius*, 'farm worker'. This word in turn may have been based on *bacca*, a form of *vacca*, 'cow' (modern French *vache*).

bacon The word is Germanic in origin, from a root element also found in *back*, referring to the part of the pig from which, as well as the sides, the rashers of *bacon* are cut.

badger The animal is probably so named from its *badge*, the white mark it has on its forehead. The name is recorded no earlier than the 16th century. Before this it was known as a *brock* or a *grey*.

balaclava The close-fitting hood, favoured by terrorists, derives its name from the hood covering the ears and neck worn by soldiers in the frequently freezing conditions of the Crimean War, notably during the Battle of *Balaklava* (1854).

balance The word goes back, through Old French, to a conjectured Latin word *bilancia*. This in turn represents Late Latin *bilanx*, from *bi-*, 'two', and *lanx*, 'scale'. Hence a *pair* of scales. (On a modern weighing machine one 'scale' is the platform on which you stand, while the other is the mechanism that gives the reading.)

balcony The origin of the word is probably in Old High German *balko*, 'beam', a word related to English *balk*. Until about 1825 the word was pronounced to rhyme with *pony*.

bald The word is probably based on a root element *ball* meaning 'white patch', as in *piebald* (black and white) and *skewbald* (white and a colour other than black) as applied to a horse. An ultimately related word is Greek *phalaros*, 'having a patch of white', 'white-crested'.

> **FALSE**
>
> **bald** An altered form of *balled*, since a *bald* person has a hairless head, round and smooth like a *ball*.

ballot The word for the voting procedure derives from Italian *ballotta*, a diminutive of *balla*, 'ball'. Voting was originally done by dropping a *ball* into a box. Hence English *blackball*, since a black *ball* in the box indicated disapproval or a veto.

bandit The word represents Italian *bandito*, literally 'banished man'. A *bandit* is lawless, and so has a *ban* imposed on him.

bankrupt The term ultimately goes back to Old Italian *banca rotta*, literally 'broken bench'. If a moneychanger's bench or table was broken it was a sign that he was insolvent. Compare modern English *broke*.

bantam The boxing weight is named for the small breed of chicken, which itself is named for the district of *Bantam* in northwest Java, where the bird was supposed to come from.

barbecue The outdoor meal derives its name from an American Spanish word *barbacoa*, itself from a Taino word for a frame made of sticks on which animals' carcasses were roasted. See also ◊buccaneer.

> **FALSE**
>
> **barbecue** From French *barbe*, 'beard', and *queue*, 'tail', since a *barbecue* was for roasting a whole animal, from head to tail.

bargain The word goes back, through Old French, to a Germanic source related to Medieval Latin *barcaniare*, 'to trade', and Old English *borgian*, which gave modern *borrow*. To *borrow* something is essentially to *bargain* with the lender.

> **FALSE**
>
> **bargain** From *bar* and *gain*, since a *bargain* precludes any significant profit on the vendor's side.

barricade The word ultimately comes from Old French *barrique*, 'barrel' (a related English word). *Barricades* set up in the streets of Paris in the 16th century were formed from *barrels* filled with earth, broken paving stones and the like.

barrister A lawyer is so designated when he or she is 'called to the *bar*', or entitled to plead for clients in the area of the courtroom that is separated from the rest by a partition. The word itself may have been modelled on *minister*.

bassoon The large woodwind instrument has a name that is an English form of Italian *bassone*, the augmentative ('big' form) of *basso*, 'deep', referring to its *bass* range. For a similar name, compare ◊trombone.

> **FALSE**
>
> **bassoon** An altered form of *bass horn*.

bastard An illegitimate child is probably so called because he was known in Old French as a *fils de bast*, 'son of the packsaddle'. He was thus not born legitimately in a bed. Mule drivers and other travelling people used a packsaddle as a pillow. Compare ◊batman.

bat The flying mouselike animal was originally known in English as a *backe*, with this word probably of Scandinavian origin. (The Old Norse name for it was *lethrblaka*, literally 'leather-flapper'.) The creature's native English name was *rearmouse*, although it is not known what *rear-* means. Another name is *flittermouse*, corresponding to modern German *Fledermaus*.

batman The army officer's servant is so called because he originally carried his officer's baggage on a *bat*, or packsaddle. This word is of French origin (modern *bât*), and is also the origin of ◊bastard.

bayonet The weapon is so called because it was originally made in the town of *Bayonne*, in southwest France.

> **FALSE**
>
> **bayonet** Named after *Bayona*, Spain, where swords were made.

beach The word did not appear generally in English until the 16th century. It was originally a dialect term for shingle or pebbles on the seashore. When Shakespeare uses the word, it is not clear whether he meant the general sense or the specific: 'You may as well go stand upon the beach' (*The Merchant of Venice*). The word itself may relate to Old English *bæce*, 'stream' (modern *beck*).

because The form of the word in Middle English was *bi cause*, meaning 'by cause'. If you run when I chase you, then I am the *cause* of your running. Compare French *à cause de*, 'because of'.

beer *Beer* is basically a drink, from Latin *bibere*, 'to drink'. Compare *bevvy* as a slang word for it, from Old French *buvee*, 'drinking'. Both words are related to English *beverage* and *imbibe*.

beetle A *beetle* is so called because it *bites*, with its name deriving from an Old English root element *bit* that gave both words.

behave If you *behave*, you *have* control over yourself. This is the origin of the word, therefore. (The literal sense of *have* is 'hold'. Hence 'to have and to hold' in the marriage service.)

belfry The word was originally the term for a moveable tower for attacking fortifications. Hence its origin in a word that literally means 'protective place of shelter', from Germanic words related to modern German *bergen*, 'to save', and *Friede*, 'peace'. When a similar building was used as a bell tower, the word became popularly associated with *bell*.

> **FALSE**
>
> **belfry** So called because it is a *bell* tower.

belly The original sense of the word was 'bag', from a Germanic root element *balg-* or *belg-* that is related to *bellows* and *billow*. A *belly* swells out, as sails do when they *belly* in the wind.

between The present form of the word evolved from Old English *betwēonum*, 'beside two'. If I stand in the space which separates two trees, I stand *between* them. *Betwixt* has a similar sense. Hence *betwixt and between*.

bias The word for an irrational tendency or 'swing' derives from Old French *biais*, itself either from Latin *bifax*, genitive *bifacis*, 'facing two ways' (from *bi-*, 'two', and *facies*, 'face'), translating Greek *diprosōpos*, in the same sense, or else perhaps via conjectural Vulgar Latin *bigassius* from Greek *epikarsios*, 'oblique'.

Bible The word ultimately derives from Greek *biblia*, the plural of *biblion*, 'book'. The Bible may be published as a single volume, but it contains several individual *books*.

bimbo The (usually derogatory) term for an empty-headed young woman is a direct borrowing of the Italian word meaning 'little child'. Compare Italian *bambino*, 'little boy'.

bishop The English word ultimately derives from Greek *episkopos*, literally 'overseer', from *epi*, 'on', 'over', and *skopos*, 'watcher', 'lookout' (the source of English *scope* and words ending in -*scope* such as *telescope*).

bitter If something is *bitter* it is *biting*. This is the origin of the word, from the Old English element *bit-* that gave both words. The phrase 'to the bitter end', however, is probably of nautical origin, referring to a rope's end fastened to a *bitt*, a post on a ship's deck.

> **FALSE**
>
> **bitter end** From the biblical line: 'But her *end* is *bitter* as wormwood' (Proverbs 5:4).

blanket The word represents Old French *blancquete*, from *blanc*, 'white'. Blankets were originally made from white wool.

blatant The word is related to *bleat*, since something blatant 'cries out' to be noticed. The word was first used (and perhaps even invented) by Edmund Spenser in *The Faerie Queene* (1596), where he describes the monster produced by Cerberus and Chimera as a 'Blatant beast'. The word was based on some adjective formed from a verb and ending -*ant*, such as *rampant*.

blazer The jacket worn by sportsmen, club members and the like is probably so called since in many cases it is brightly coloured, and so *blazes*.

bless The word is related to *blood*. Its precise origin is in Old English *blētsian*, 'to consecrate', referring to a sacrificial rite in which the blood of a slaughtered animal was sprinkled on an object to protect it from evil. (A similar rite is described in the Bible, when lintels and doorposts are streaked with blood in the institution of the ◊Passover, which see in this respect.)

blob The word has a sound that represents its sense. Hence its origin. Other words with similar sounds and senses are *blubber* and *bubble*.

blue The colour has an equivalent name in some European languages, such as French *bleu* and German *blau*. It is probably also related to Latin *flavus*, 'yellow'. Its ultimate origin is uncertain, however.

> **FALSE**
>
> **blue** From French *l'eau*, 'the water', because water reflects the *blue* colour of the sky.

bomb The word was originally used in English in the 17th century to describe a hollow explosive projectile. This made a *booming* sound. Hence the origin of the word, ultimately in Greek *bombos*, which means 'booming' and itself imitates the sound.

bone The word is of Germanic origin and is related to modern German *Bein*. This means 'leg', however, with specific reference to the shinbone (tibia), the thicker of the two *bones* of the leg. The native English word for 'leg' was *shank*, as still in the phrase 'shanks's pony'.

bonfire A bonfire was originally a *bone fire*, that is, a big fire in the open on which bones were burnt (as a forerunner of the modern crematorium). Such fires were spectacular. Hence *bonfire* as a word for a celebratory public fire, as on *Bonfire* Night (itself a symbolic burning of the bones of Guy Fawkes).

> **FALSE**
>
> **bonfire** From French *bon feu*, 'good fire'.

book The word is of Old English origin and is directly related to *beech*, the bark of which was at one time used as a writing surface.

boot Whether meaning 'footwear' or 'luggage compartment', the word ultimately goes back to Old French *bote*, itself of obscure origin. The car *boot* probably got its name from the use of the word for the space on the outside of a coach where the attendants sat (in their *boots*), or possibly from its use for the receptacle for luggage (perhaps including spare *boots*) on such a coach.

> **FALSE**
>
> **boot** So called, in a car, from French *boîte*, 'box'. Compare *box* as a word for the driver's seat in a coach or carriage.

bow The word for the *bow* that fires an arrow is of Germanic origin and related to the other *bow* that means 'bend'. (Compare *bow* legs, which curve like a *bow*.) The ultimate source of the word is uncertain.

> **FALSE**
>
> **bow** From *bough*, because *bows* were originally made from the branches of trees.

box The receptacle is so called because it was originally made from the wood of the *box* tree.

bra The word is a contraction of French *brassière*, which now means 'leading rein' (a harness for a child learning to walk), but which earlier was the term for a type of bodice. Its own origin is in French *bras*, 'arm'. The French word is itself related to English *brace*, in its sense of 'support'.

bran The word for the husks of grain is Old French in origin, and perhaps ultimately derives from a Gaulish source whose basic meaning is unknown.

> **FALSE**
>
> **bran** An altered form of *brown*, referring to its colour.

brand-new Something *brand-new* is so called because it is like iron that is fresh and glowing from the furnace or *brand* (burning place). Hot irons were used for marking goods by *branding* them. Hence *brand* in its modern sense of 'make'.

bread The word has come down from Old English and is of Germanic origin, but its source is unknown. The proper Germanic word for 'bread' is the one that gave *loaf*, so that *bread* may have originally denoted a piece broken from a loaf.

bridle The word for the headgear of a horse's harness is Germanic in origin and is related to *braid*, presumably because of the interweaving of its straps. The ultimate source of either word is unknown.

> **FALSE**
>
> **bridle** So called because it is held by the horse's *bit*.

broadcast In the 18th century the word was an adjective applied to seed that that was *cast* by hand over a *broad* area, instead of being sown by drilling or in rows. In the 19th century *to broadcast* was to sow seed in this way. The present noun evolved in the 20th century. A radio or television *broadcast* disseminates information or entertainment over a wide area.

broom The sweeping implement is so called since it was originally made from twigs of *broom*, the yellow-flowered shrub. There is probably a similar relationship between *brush* and *brushwood*.

buccaneer The word for the pirate derives from French *boucanier*, from a verb *boucaner*, 'to smoke meat', itself from Old French *boucan*, a Tupi term for a frame on which meat was roasted. The original *buccaneers* were French and English hunters of wild oxen in the West Indies. The name was then transferred to pirates of the Spanish Main, whose way of life was similar. A Haitian word related to *boucan* gave the source of modern English ◊barbecue.

budgerigar The popular cagebird has a name of Australian origin said to mean 'good cockatoo', from *budgeri*, 'good', and *gar*, 'cockatoo'. The bird is actually a small parrot.

budget The original meaning of the word was 'pouch', 'wallet', from Old French *bougette*, a diminutive of *bouge*, itself from Latin *bulga*, 'bag', and ultimately of Gaulish origin. The 'pouch' came to be the despatch box in which the

Chancellor of the Exchequer kept the documents for his annual budget statement, and hence for the statement itself. When starting his speech, the Chancellor was formerly said to 'open his budget'.

bugger The word came into English from French *bougre*, itself from Medieval Latin *Bulgarus*, 'Bulgarian'. The East Orthodox Bulgarians who came to France in the 11th century were regarded as heretics and 'deviants'. Hence the use of their name to apply to other heretics, as well as to sodomites, who practised *buggery*.

bulimia The term for a morbidly insatiable hunger derives from Greek *bous*, 'ox', and *limos*, 'hunger'. A person who is ravenously hungry has the appetite of an ox.

bulletin The word for an official statement or news report derives, through French, from Italian *bullettino*, a diminutive of *bulletta*, itself a diminutive of *bulla*, 'papal edict' (English *bull*), ultimately from Medieval Latin *bulla*, 'seal' (as attached to such an edict), from the identical Latin word meaning 'round object'.

bulrush The marsh plant derives its name from a combination of *bull* and *rush*. It is compared to a *bull* because it is relatively large and coarse, unlike most other reeds. Hence also *bullfinch* as a finch that has a large head and stocky body.

bungalow The single-storey house is similar to those in India and *Bengal* (although they usually have a veranda). Hence its name, representing Hindi *banglā*, 'of Bengal'.

burglar The word for a housebreaker is perhaps ultimately from Latin *burgus*, 'castle', 'fortress', itself related to modern English *borough*.

burrow The word for a fox's or other animal's underground home is probably a variant of *borough*, in that it is a fortified or inhabited place. Compare German *Burg*, 'castle', 'fortress', to which are related the *-borough* and *-bury* of many British place-names.

> **FALSE**
>
> **burrow** From *bury*, since an animal's burrow is *buried* underground.

bus The word is a short form of *omnibus*, itself originating in the French name of a new kind of public passenger vehicle. This was the *voiture omnibus*, 'vehicle for all', with *omnibus* the dative plural of Latin *omnis*, 'all'.

bustard The name of the bird is said to derive from Latin *avis tarda*, 'slow bird'. However, the *bustard* is swift in flight, not slow, so that the Latin name may be a corruption of some earlier name.

butcher The word comes from Old French *bouchier*, itself from *bouc*, 'he-goat' (English *buck*). The word was thus originally used of a dealer in goat's meat.

butler A *butler* had charge of the *bottles* in the wine cellar. Hence his name, which came into English from Old French *bouteillier*, literally 'bottler'.

butterfly The winged insect is said to get its name from the popular belief that butterflies stole milk and *butter*. Another theory, however, relates the name to the yellow colour of the insect's excrement.

FALSE
butterfly An altered form of *flutter by*, which is what it does.

buxom The word is a form of what could have become *bowsome*. Its original sense was 'obedient', 'compliant', as applied to someone who was ready to bend or *bow* to another's wishes. (The *-some* is as in *winsome* or *handsome*.) The word then gradually altered its sense, so that today it is used of a plump and pleasant woman (who came to be regarded as easier-going than others).

bylaw The first part of the term for a local *law* comes from a Scandinavian word related to Old Norse *býr*, 'town', itself related to English *borough*. It was later associated with *by*.

C

cab The word for a taxi or driving compartment of a lorry evolved as a shortened form of *cabriolet*, a two-wheeled horse-drawn carriage. Its own name is of French origin, and literally means 'little skip', from *cabriole*, 'caper', ultimately from Latin *capreolus*, 'wild goat', a derivative of *caper*, 'goat'. The carriage was so named for its lightness and springiness when in motion.

cabaret The word is of Norman French origin, with an original meaning 'tavern'. It probably came from Latin *camera*, a term for an arched roof, related to modern English *chamber*. See ◊camera.

caboodle As used in the phrase 'the whole *caboodle*', the word probably arose as a blend of ◊kit (equipment) and *boodle* (possessions). The latter word comes from Dutch *boedel*, used for a person's entire belongings.

caddie The word for a golfer's attendant was originally that for an army *cadet*. It evolved as a Scottish form of the latter word, which itself derives from the identical French word meaning 'younger son', as originally applied to Gascon officers at the royal court who were younger sons of noble families. (The French word comes from Gascon *capdet*, 'captain', ultimately from Latin *caput*, 'head', 'chief'.)

cadge As used for getting money or the like by sponging or begging, the word derives from *cadger*, the person who does this. The origin is uncertain. It may be a Scottish dialect form of *carrier*.

café The word is a straight borrowing of French *café*, 'coffee', since the first English cafés (in the 19th century) were modest restaurants, something on the lines of the coffee houses of France.

calculate The process of solving or computing derives its name from Latin *calculus*, 'pebble', since stones or pebbles were originally used as counters when reckoning. Hence *calculus* as the term for a special branch of mathematics.

calendar The table of months and days gets its name from Latin *calendarium*, the word for an account book. This itself came from *calendae*, 'calends', the first day of the month in the Roman calendar, when interest on debts became due.

callow The word now means 'immature'. It originally meant 'bald', from Latin *calvus* in this sense. The reference was to a young unfledged bird, which lacked feathers.

calm The word goes back to Late Latin *cauma*, 'heat', itself from Greek *kauma* in the same sense. This became associated with Latin *calere*, 'to be hot'. The present sense must have evolved as follows: 'heat of the day', 'rest during such heat', 'peace and quiet during such rest'.

camera The word derives from New Latin *camera obscura*, 'dark chamber', since the modern camera evolved from a darkened room in which images of objects outside the building were projected onto a screen using a convex lens in an aperture. The basic sense of Latin *camera* is 'vault', and the word also gave English *chamber*.

camouflage The word represents the French noun of the verb *camoufler*, thieves' slang for 'to disguise'. This either derived from Italian *camuffare* in the same sense (literally 'cover with a mitten'), or evolved from *camouflet*, used for a puff of smoke in someone's face (from Old French *moufle*, 'muzzle').

camp The origin of the word is ultimately in Latin *campus*, 'field', implying a battlefield or, less militantly, a field where games and military exercises were held. See also ◊campaign.

campaign The word for an army's operations derives from Old French *champagne*, 'champaign', this being a term for level country that itself came from Latin *campus*, 'field'. The military sense of the word came about because an army stayed in its quarters in winter but went into the country when summer came to carry out operations.

canary The bird is so named because it originally came from the *Canary* Islands, where it was native.

cancer The malignant disease gets its name from Latin *cancer*, 'crab', either because the veins round a cancerous growth radiate like crab's feet, or more generally because the disease creeps, as crabs do.

candidate The word for a person applying or nominated for something derives from Latin *candidatus*, 'clothed in white', from *candidus*, 'white' (English *candid*). In Roman times applicants for high office wore a white toga.

cannibal The word comes from Spanish *Canibales*, the name used by Christopher Columbus for the *Caribs*, the people of the West Indies (in the *Caribbean*) who were said to be fierce man-eaters.

canopy The word was originally used for a net over a bed that was a protection against mosquitoes. Hence the ultimate origin of the word in Greek *kōnōps*, 'mosquito'.

canter The easy gait of a horse (midway between a trot and a gallop) takes its name from the *Canterbury trot*, the pace at which medieval pilgrims are said to have ridden to *Canterbury*.

canvas The heavy cloth, made of cotton, hemp, or jute, has a name that ultimately derives from Latin *cannabis*, 'hemp'. Hence also English *cannabis*, the drug.

capital Whatever the sense of the English word, it ultimately goes back to Latin *caput*, 'head', 'chief'. *Capital* punishment is so called because the criminal has committed a crime for which he must be executed by *decapitation*, as is still the case in some countries.

caprice The word for a whim or sudden fancy came into English, through French, from Italian *capriccio*. This means 'shiver', and itself derives from *capo*, 'head', and *riccio*, 'hedgehog'. The image is of a convulsive shudder in which the hair stands on end, like a hedgehog's bristling spines. The modern sense of the word came about by association with Italian *capra*, 'goat'.

captivate If you are *captivated* you are a 'prisoner' of someone or something fascinating or entrancing. Hence the origin of the word in Latin *captivus*, 'captive', itself from *capere*, 'to take', 'to seize'.

caravan The modern vehicle ultimately gets its name from Persian *kārwān*, the word for a company of people and animals travelling through the desert. See also ◊van.

cardinal Whatever the current sense of the word, its ultimate origin is in Latin *cardo*, genitive *cardinis*, 'hinge'. Thus the *cardinal* numbers are those on which the others 'hinge' or depend, and a Roman Catholic *cardinal* was originally attached to a particular church just as a door is attached to a particular building by its hinges.

career A person's *career* is the particular course of his or her professional life. Hence the origin of the word in Latin *carraria*, 'carriage road'. The same idea lies behind the Latin expression *curriculum vitae*, literally 'course of life'.

carnival The general festive occasion takes its name from the specific one that originally preceded Lent (on Shrove Tuesday). Hence its name, which literally means 'removal of meat', from Latin *caro*, genitive *carnis*, 'flesh', 'meat', and *levare*, 'to raise', 'to lift'. Lent was a time of fasting, when no meat was eaten. The term could also be taken to apply to a cessation of *carnal* or fleshly pleasures.

carousal The word for the heavy drinking session has its origin in German *gar aus trinken*, literally 'drink quite out', meaning that every full drink is drunk completely.

carpenter A carpenter was at one time specifically a carriage maker. Hence the origin of the word in Latin *carpentum*, 'carriage', a word related to English *car*.

cartridge The bullet case came by its name as an alteration of French *cartouche*. This was a term for a scroll or tube of paper, which the bullet case resembles. The French word itself comes from Italian *carta*, 'paper', related to English *card* and *chart*.

cash The word originally applied not to money but to the box in which it was kept. It comes from Old Italian *cassa*, 'money box', itself from Latin *capsa*, which also gave English *case*.

castaway The word originally applied to a wrongdoer, a person who had been 'cast away' or rejected by society. It was introduced into English by the translators of the Bible, and specifically in 1 Corinthians 9.27 ('I myself should be a castaway'), where it translates Latin *reprobus* (English *reprobate*) and Greek *adokimos*. The modern sense of the word as 'shipwrecked person' is entirely due to William Cowper's poem *The Castaway* (1799).

castle The word derives from Latin *castellum*, a diminutive of *castrum*, 'fort'. The latter Latin word (or more precisely its plural, *castra*, 'camp') is the source of English town names such as Lan*caster*, Man*chester* and Wor*cester*, referring to the Roman encampment at such places.

catafalque The word for a raised platform on which a coffin rests before a funeral derives, through Italian, from a conjectured Vulgar Latin word *catafalicum*, the source also of ◊scaffold.

catalogue The word has its origin in Greek *katalogos*, 'listing', literally 'laying down', from *kata*, 'down' (in the sense 'completely'), and *legein*, 'to lay', 'to arrange'.

cataract The word for a waterfall derives, through Latin, from Greek *katarrhaktēs*, the noun of *katarassein*, 'to dash down', from *kata*, 'down', and *arassein*, 'to strike'. When used for the eye affliction, the word derives from another sense of the Greek word, which was 'portcullis'. The reference is to the opaque membrane which prevents the image from reaching the retina.

catarrh The nasal condition derives its name from Greek *katarrhein*, 'to flow down', from *kata*, 'down', and *rhein*, 'to flow'. Compare ◊diarrhoea.

category See ◊predicament.

caterpillar The English word probably evolved from the Old North French name for the creature, which was *catepelose*, literally 'hairy cat', from words that have correspondences in modern French *chat*, 'cat', and *poilu*, 'hairy'. Compare *woolly bear* as the nickname of various tiger moth caterpillars. Compare also the current French word for a caterpillar, which is *chenille*, from Latin *canicula*, 'little dog'.

> **FALSE**
>
> **caterpillar** A combination of English *cater* and French *piller*, 'to rob'. The caterpillar *caters*, or provides its food, by stealing from gardens.

caterwaul The word arose as an imitation of the sound it describes: a *cat wauling* (yowling) when on heat.

cattle The original meaning of the word was 'property', implying a holding of livestock. Hence the related English word *chattel*, as in *goods and chattels*. The ultimate source is thus in Medieval Latin *capitale*, 'wealth', to which English *capital* is directly related.

caveat The word for a warning is properly a legal term adopted from the identical Latin word meaning 'let him beware', from the verb *cavere*, 'to beware', the noun form of which is the source of English *caution*.

caviare The delicacy (sturgeon's roe) takes its name from the Turkish word for it, *havyār*. The food is of Russian origin, but the Russian name for it is quite different, *ikra*, perhaps from an Indo-European word for the liver, and so related to the Greek word for this organ, *hēpar*).

celandine The yellow flower ultimately derives its name from Greek *khelidōn*, 'swallow'. The plant's season was at one time believed to match the migration of swallows.

cement The word has evolved from Latin *caementum*, 'quarry stone', from the verb *caedere*, 'to cut'. Chips of stone from the quarry were pounded and mixed with lime and other ingredients to make a strong-binding mortar, otherwise cement.

cenotaph The word is used for a memorial to a person who is buried somewhere else. Hence its origin in Greek *kenotaphion*, literally 'empty tomb', from *kenos*, 'empty', and *taphos*, 'tomb'.

chair The English word ultimately derives, through French, from Latin *cathedra*, 'armchair', itself from Greek *kathedra*, literally 'down seat', from *kata*, 'down', and *hedra*, 'seat'. Hence *cathedral* as the church where the bishop has his seat. French *chaire* is now specifically used for a bishop's throne or a professorial chair, and the everyday word for 'chair' is *chaise*. (The *s* comes from a fashionable 16th-century pronunciation of *chaire*.)

challenge The word originally meant 'accusation'. Hence its origin, via Old French *chalenge*, in Latin *calumnia*, 'false accusation' (modern English *calumny*).

champion The word originally applied to a fighter or warrior on the battlefield. It thus derives, via Old French, from Late Latin *campio*, genitive *campionis*, itself from Latin *campus*, 'field'.

chancellor The ultimate origin of the word is in Latin *cancelli*, 'lattice'. The Late Latin title *cancellarius* was used of a fairly lowly officer whose position was that of an usher *ad cancellos*, 'at the bars', for example in a court. The modern sense of the word as an important title was introduced to England in the 11th century under Edward the Confessor, whose *cancheler* was Regenbald.

chap In the sense 'man', 'fellow', the word is an abbreviation of *chapman*, an old term for a trader or salesman. A *chap* is someone you have to 'deal' with. Compare *customer* in the same sense ('crooked customer') and even *merchant* (as in 'speed merchant'). See also ◊cheap.

charisma The word used for someone's special power or personality was originally applied in a theological sense to a god-given power or talent. It derives, through Church Latin, from Greek *kharisma*, itself from *kharis*, 'grace', 'favour'.

chauffeur The salaried car driver has a rather superior status which was not held by the French *chauffeur* who gave his name. The French word means 'stoker', or literally 'warmer'. Early motorists were so nicknamed as they 'stoked up' the engine to get the vehicle going. (A nickname for a *chauffeur* himself, based on this word, was *shover*: he was the person who *shoved* passengers along!)

cheap The word came from the phrase *good cheap*, where *cheap* represents Old English *ceap*, 'bargain', 'market'. (Compare French *à bon marché*, 'cheap', literally 'at good market'.) The Old English word gave place-names such as *Cheapside*, *Chepstow* and *Chipping Ongar*, all of which had noted markets. It also gave *chapman* (see ◊chap).

checkmate The chess term for a winning position, when one's opponent's king is unable to escape, derives from Arabic **shāh māt**, 'the king is dead'. See also ◊chess, and compare ◊stalemate.

cheque The financial document is so called because it enables one to *check* the amount paid. The French-style spelling of the word (Americans prefer *check*) probably came from *exchequer*. It did not come from French. (French **chèque**, 'cheque', came from English.) For the origin of *check* itself, see ◊chess.

chess The board game derives its name from Old French **esches**, the plural of **eschec**, 'check' (in the game's own sense of the word). English *check*, in any sense, also comes from this word, which itself derives, via Arabic, from Persian **shāh**, 'the king!', as an exclamation when one has put one's opponent's king in check. See also ◊checkmate and ◊cheque.

chestnut The earlier English name of the tree was *chesten nut*. The first word of this ultimately comes from the Greek name of the tree, **kastanea** (which by another route gave *castanets*, so called not because they were made of chestnut wood but because they resembled *chestnuts*).

chicken The name of the bird derives from a root element that also gave *cock*. The final *-en* is a diminutive, and is found in other animals' names, such as *kitten*. The root word itself is probably imitative in origin. Compare *cluck* and *cock-a-doodle-doo* and (although another bird) *cuckoo*.

chiffon The semi-transparent fabric derives its name from French **chiffe**, 'rag', itself of uncertain origin but perhaps related to *chip* in that it is thin, like a *chip* of wood or straw.

chivy The word for chasing or harassing someone was originally a hunting cry, like *tantivy*. It probably came from *Chevy Chase*, the title of a ballad about the Battle of *Chevy Chase* (1388), near the Scottish border, in which the Scots defeated the English.

chocolate The word came to English, through Spanish, from Aztec **xocolatl**, literally 'bitter water', from **xococ**, 'sour', 'bitter', and **atl**, 'water'. The drink was made from cacao seeds, and was the forerunner of modern cocoa. (*Chocolate*, *cacao* and *cocoa* are all related words.)

chopsticks The Chinese eating implements get their name from a combination of Pidgin English *chop*, 'quick' (as in 'chop chop'), from a dialect Chinese word, and English *stick*.

chum The colloquial word for a friend is probably a short form of *chamber fellow*. It was originally Oxford university slang. The equivalent at Cambridge was *crony*, from Greek **khronios**, 'long-lasting', from **khronos**, 'time'.

church The present word evolved from Old English **cirice**, pronounced approximately 'chirichay'. This represented Late Greek **kurikon**, itself from Greek *kuriakon dōma*, 'the Lord's house', from *kurios*, 'lord', 'master'. Scottish *kirk* came from a Scandinavian form of the same word.

cinema The word is a shortened form of *cinematograph*, a 19th-century creation, from Greek *kinēma*, 'movement' (compare *motion picture*, *movie*), and *graphein*, 'to write'.

cipher The word goes back through French and Latin to Arabic *sifr*, 'zero', 'empty'. (The same word gave *zero* itself, as this is an 'empty' number.) The word came to be used of Arabic numerals in general. The modern sense of 'secret writing' came about because early cryptography used numerals in place of letters.

circumstance The literal sense of the word is 'standing round', from Latin *circumstantia*, itself derived from *circum*, 'around' and *stare*, 'to stand'. This itself translated Greek *peristasis*. Some European languages have the equivalent in native words, such as German *Umstand*. Old English had *ymbstandnes*, but this did not survive.

class The word came to English from Latin *classis*, itself used as a term for a division of the Roman people as well as for a similar group of things or objects. Its other prime meanings were thus 'army' (group of soldiers) and 'fleet' (group of ships). Its basic sense is 'summoning', from Latin *calare*, 'to call'.

clerk The word comes from Church Latin *clericus*, which gave *cleric*. This in turn came from Greek *klēros*, 'lot', 'heritage', referring to the biblical Levites, whose inheritance was the Lord (Deuteronomy 4:20). *Clerks* are linked with *clerics* because it was the *clergy* who were the scholars in medieval times. They did the writing and recording that was later undertaken by clerks.

client The word comes from Latin *cliens*, 'retainer', 'dependant', a word that was related to *clinare*, 'to lean' (English *incline*). A client thus 'leans' or depends on another.

cliff The word is of Germanic origin but uncertain ultimate meaning. It may be related to *cleave* in the sense 'adhere to'. The rocks of a cliff can seem to cling or 'stick' to the face, especially when they overhang.

FALSE

cliff So called because it is land that has been *cleft*, or cut off.

---

climax The word is a Late Latin adoption of Greek *klimax*, 'ladder'. A ladder takes you up by steps to a particular height.

clinic The ultimate source of the word is Greek *klinē*, 'bed', meaning a sickbed or one in which a person is bedridden.

clock Many European languages have a word meaning 'clock' that is based on a word for 'hour', such as French *horloge*, German *Uhr* or Russian *chasy*. The English word comes from Medieval Latin *clocca*, 'bell' (compare French *cloche* and German *Glocke*). Clocks were originally thought of as striking the hour rather than showing it.

cloud The original sense of the word in English was 'hill'. Later the word was transferred to clouds, especially cumulus ones, which look like hills. The earlier word for 'cloud' was thus *welkin* or *sky*. The old sense of the word has survived in the names of some hills, such as *The Cloud* on the Cheshire—Staffordshire border. The word itself is probably related to *clod*.

clumber The breed of spaniel takes its name from *Clumber*, the country home of the Dukes of Newcastle, near Worksop in Nottinghamshire, where it was originally developed.

coach The vehicle takes its name from the Hungarian village of *Kocs*, west of Budapest, where coaches (as horse-drawn carriages) were first made in the 15th century. The use of *coach* for an instructor probably came about because he was thought of as 'carrying' his pupils, although there may have been an influence of *coax*.

> **FALSE**
>
> **coach** From Latin *concha*, 'shell', referring to the appearance of the earliest coaches.

Cockney The name for a native of London comes from Middle English *cokeney*, literally 'cock's egg', from *cok*, 'cock', and *ey*, 'egg'. This was a term for a small or misshapen hen's egg, which was out of place, just as a soft townsman was among hardened country folk. The word was thus at first a derogatory nickname.

cockroach The beetle derives its name from Spanish *cucaracha*, altered presumably by association with English *cock* and *roach* (the fish). The Spanish word is said to be based on *cuca*, a children's nickname for a caterpillar.

> **FALSE**
>
> **cocksure** A corruption of French *à coup sûr*, 'for certain'.

cocksure The source of the word, meaning 'over-confident', is uncertain. The original sense may have been 'sure as a cock' (compare *cocky*, which comes from this word).

coconut The name of the nut comes from Spanish or Portuguese *coco*, a term for a grinning face. The reference is to the three holes on the base of the nut, which suggest a monkey's face. The spelling *cocoanut* appears to have originated from Dr Johnson's dictionary (1755), in which by mistake he had the entries for both the coconut palm and cacao ('chocolate nut') under the single heading *cocoa*.

collapse The origin of the word is in Latin *collapsus*, from *collabi*, 'to fall in ruins', literally 'fall together', from *com* (later *cum*), 'with', and *labare*, 'to slip'.

colleague The word for an associate or friend derives, through French, from Latin *collega*, literally 'one chosen with another', from *com* (later *cum*), 'with', and *legare*, 'to choose'. This Latin word is also the source of English *college*, as an institution whose members are *colleagues*.

colonel The military rank has its origin in Old Italian *colonello*, 'leader of a *colonna*', this being a *column* of soldiers. The unusual pronunciation of the word (like *kernel*) derives from the former alternative spelling *coronel*.

coltsfoot The plant with yellow daisy-like flowers is so named from the shape of its leaves, which resemble a *colt's foot*. (The plant grows where horses graze.)

comet The celestial body has a 'tail'. Hence its name, from Greek *komētēs*, 'long-haired', itself from *komē*, 'hair'.

FALSE

coltsfoot A corruption of *cold's food*, since the plant is said to cure colds. Hence its botanical name, *Tussilago*, from Latin *tussis*, 'cough', and *laganum*, 'pastille'.

committee The word was originally used for a person to whom a special charge or trust was *committed*, so that he was responsible for it. The present sense came as an extension of this, as applied to a group of people set up for a special purpose.

commuter The original sense of *commute* was 'exchange', with its origin in Latin *commutare*, 'to replace', literally 'change mutually', from *com* (later *cum*), 'with', and *mutare*, 'to change'. The present sense derives from the American *commutation* ticket (season ticket, sold at a reduced or *commuted* rate) that enables passengers to travel regularly.

companion The word literally means 'fellow bread-eater', from Late Latin *companio*, comprising *com* (later *cum*), 'with', and *panis*, 'bread'. *Company* has the same origin.

concord The word represents Latin *concors*, genitive *concordis*, 'of one mind', literally 'of one heart', from *com* (later *cum*), 'with', and *cor*, genitive *cordis*, 'heart'.

confetti The word came direct from Italian, where it is the plural of *confetto*, 'bonbon' (English *comfit*). The small pieces of coloured paper thrown at weddings are the equivalent of the small sweets thrown at carnivals in Italy.

conkers The children's game played with horse chestnuts on a string was originally played with small shells. The word is thus related to *conch*.

constable The police officer is the descendant of the official who was at one time in charge of stables. The origin of the word is in Latin *comes stabuli*, literally 'count of the stable'. Compare ◊marshal.

conundrum The origin of this word is itself a conundrum. It looks like a fanciful elaboration of some Latin word, and probably arose as a student joke. Earlier spellings of the word include *conumbrum*, *quinombrum*, *quonundrum*, and *quadundrum*.

convent The word has its origin in Latin *conventus*, 'meeting' (compare English *convention*). It originally applied to any religious community, but from the 18th century has usually applied to nuns only. A spelling *covent* existed in Middle Emglish, and this has been preserved in the name of *Covent* Garden, the London fruit and vegetable market that developed from the *convent* garden of Westminster Abbey.

copper The metal ultimately takes its name from that of *Cyprus*, which was famous for it in ancient times. The present spelling evolved by way of Late Latin *cuprum*, from classical Latin *cyprium*.

coral The rocklike growth derives its name, through French and Latin, from Greek *korallion*, itself probably of Semitic origin and related to Hebrew *gōrāl*, 'pebble'.

> **FALSE**
>
> **coral** From Greek *korē*, 'daughter', and *halos*, 'sea', so 'daughter of the sea', a poetical name.

corporal The name of the military rank derives from the identical former French word which was itself a variant of *caporal*, the modern equivalent. This came from Italian *caporale*, from *capo*, 'head', 'chief'. The altered form probably arose by association with *corporal*, 'bodily', as if meaning 'leader of a body of men'.

corpse The word has its origin in Latin *corpus*, 'body'. It was originally used of a living body or person, hence such biblical passages as 'Behold, they were all dead corpses' (2 Kings 19:35). The same Latin word gave *corps* (body of soldiers) and *corpus* (body of writings).

cosmetic The word ultimately goes back to the Greek verb *kosmein*, 'to adorn', 'to set in order', itself from *kosmos*, 'order' (which itself gave *cosmos* as the word for the universe as an ordered system).

costume The word is directly related to *custom*, and originally had this sense, referring to the manners that were associated with a particular time or place. It got its present sense (with French spelling) from the garments customarily portrayed in works of art. Compare *habit* in both the same senses.

council The word evolved from Latin *concilium*, 'assembly', itself literally meaning 'calling together', from *com* (later *cum*), 'with', and *calare*, 'to call'.

county The administrative region historically belonged to a *count*, a French title introduced by the Normans. The native name for such a territory was a ◊shire, which was administered by an earl, and later by a *sheriff*.

courage The word ultimately goes back, through French, to Latin *cor*, 'heart', to which the French suffix *-age* has been added. If you take heart, you are *encouraged*.

coward The ultimate source of the name is in Latin *cauda*, 'tail'. The precise reference is uncertain, although a coward turns tail, or runs away like an animal with its tail between its legs.

> **FALSE**
>
> **coward** A corruption of *cowherd*, as a derogatory nickname given by the Normans to the Anglo-Saxons.

cowslip The wild flower grows well in fields where cows have been grazing. Hence its name, which can be understood as *cow slip*, that is, cow dung (which *slips* or *slops* rather than drops).

cox The helmsman of a boat has a name that is a short form of *coxswain*, from *cock*, a ship's boat, and *swain*, 'young man'. Compare *bosun* as a short form of *boatswain*.

coy The word has ultimately the same source as English *quiet*, since it goes back, through Old French *coi*, to Latin *quietus*, which also gave that word.

crab The creature was probably named for its claws, which *scrabble*. Its name is related to that of the ▷crayfish, which also has claws.

cravat The type of scarf gets its name, through French, from Serbo-Croat *Hrvat*, 'Croat'. Such scarves were worn by Croatian mercenaries in the French army during the Thirty Years War (1618–48).

crayfish The name of the small crustacean goes back through Old French *crevis* to Old High German *krebiz* (modern German *Krebs*), 'crab'. It is thus basically the same word as *crab*, but the second part of the earlier words was altered by association with *fish*. The creature's alternative name, *crawfish*, is of the same origin.

> **FALSE**
>
> **crayfish** A corruption of *crevice fish*, as a creature found among rocks.

creosote The word is a 19th-century creation formed from Greek *kreas*, 'flesh', and *sōtēr*, 'preserver'. The substance was so called from its antiseptic properties.

cretin The term for a fool or idiot originally applied to deformed and mentally deranged people living in certain Alpine valleys in Switzerland. The word is thus of French (or Swiss) origin and goes back to Latin *Christianus*, 'Christian'. Despite their handicaps, such people were simple and kindly, as Christians are supposed to be.

crew The word was originally used for a military reinforcement, that is, a body of men to increase the size of an army. Hence its origin in Old French *creue*, 'increase', 'augmentation', from the verb *creistre* (modern French *croître*), 'to grow', 'to increase', ultimately from Latin *crescere*, in the same sense.

crisp The original meaning of the word was 'curly', from Latin *crispus*. The modern sense, used of something hard yet brittle, may have evolved from the actual sound of the word. At the same time, many *crisp* things are curly or wrinkled, such as lettuce leaves or potato *crisps*.

crocodile The reptile's name goes back ultimately to Greek *krokodeilos*. This literally means 'worm of the stones', from *krokē*, 'pebble', and *drilos*, 'worm'. The reference is to the crocodile's fondness for basking on shingle.

crucial The word originally applied to something that was cross-shaped. Hence its origin in Latin *crux*, genitive *crucis*, 'cross' (with this English word of the same origin). The use of *crucial* to mean 'very important' draws its metaphor from a signpost at a crossroads. If you make a *crucial* decision you must be sure to go the right way. *Crux* has a similar sense.

crucible The word for the vessel in which substances are heated derives from Medieval Latin *crucibulum*, 'night lamp', perhaps itself so called as it hung before a *crucifix*. The reference is to the shape of both vessels, and the heat involved in each.

cubicle The word was originally used for a bedroom. Hence its origin in Latin *cubare*, 'to lie down' (related to modern English *incubate* and *concubine*).

FALSE

crucible From Latin *crux*, genitive *crucis*, 'cross'. When used as melting pots, *crucibles* were marked with a *cross* to prevent evil spirits from spoiling the chemical operation.

---

cuddle The word for a close embrace or hug is of uncertain origin. It may have evolved from the dialect word *couth*, meaning 'comfortable', 'snug', just as *fondle* evolved from *fond*.

cue The term for a signal to an actor to go on stage is said to derive from the letter *Q* marked in his script at the appropriate place. This would stand for Latin *quando*, 'when'.

culprit The word comes from legal Anglo-French and represents *cul. prist*, short for *culpable prist*, literally 'guilty ready'. If the accused pleaded not guilty to high treason or felony, the clerk of the crown replied with the formula '*Culpable: prest daverrer notre bille*', 'Guilty: [and I am] ready to aver our indictment', and noted this in writing as *cul. prist*.

culture The word literally relates to *agriculture*, or the tilling of the fields, and originally referred to a piece of tilled land. Its source is thus in Latin *cultura*, 'tilling', from the verb *colere*, 'to till'. The sense was extended to the cultivation of the mind and of manners in the 16th century.

cunning The word is related to *can*, since a *cunning* person knows how something *can* be done. The word is also related to Scottish *ken*, and may be Scandinavian in origin.

cupboard In medieval times, a *cupboard* was a *board* or table on which *cups* and other vessels were displayed. Hence its name.

cur The word for a dog derives from its snarl or growl. In other words, it is the equivalent of *grrr*.

FALSE

cur A shortened form of '*cur*tailed dog'. Dogs belonging to poor people had their tails cut short.

---

curate The clergyman so designated was originally appointed to have the *cure* or care of souls. Hence his title.

curfew The English word evolved from an Old French word that has its equivalent in modern French *couvrefeu*, literally 'cover fire'. When a curfew was imposed in a town or camp, an evening bell was rung as a signal that fires should be covered up or put out.

curious A *curious* person was originally one who took *cure* (care) over something. The present sense of 'inquisitive' developed only in the 17th century.

currant The fruit gets its name from *Corinth* in Greece. It was originally exported from there as a dried fruit prepared from a dwarf seedless grape, but its name was later transferred to the present fruit (redcurrant or blackcurrant).

curry In the phrase 'to *curry* favour', meaning to ingratiate oneself with a superior, the word probably has its origin, through French, in the conjectural Vulgar Latin verb **conredare**, 'to make ready'. The earliest sense of *curry*, however, was 'rub down with a comb (a *curry*comb) and brush', in the sense of grooming a horse. Hence the phrase, in which *favour* is an altered form of *favel*, the former word for a fallow or chestnut horse. Presumably grooming one's master's horse was a way of getting into his good books.

curtain The word has its origin in Late Latin **cortina**. This was the term for an enclosed or 'curtained off' area, and probably derived from classical Latin *cohors*, 'courtyard'. Hence English *curtain* in the Bible (Exodus 26:1) to translate Greek *aulaia*, a word deriving from *aulē*, 'court'. But *cortina* in classical Latin actually meant 'kettle', 'cauldron'.

cutlery The collective word for eating implements derives from Old French *coutel* (modern *couteau*), 'knife', itself from Latin *culter* with the same meaning (English *coulter* as a blade or disc at the front of a ploughshare).

cutlet The cut of meat from the best end of neck of lamb and the like derives its name from Old French *costelette* (modern *côtelette*), literally 'little rib', from *coste*, 'rib', itself from Latin *costa* in the same sense.

cybernetics The branch of science concerned with control systems gets its name from Greek **kubernētēs**, 'steersman'. The term came into general use only in the mid-20th century.

cynical The original *Cynics* were a group of philosophers in ancient Greece who scorned worldly things and held that self-control was the only good. Their name may derive from the **Cynosarges** gymnasium outside Athens where they taught. It is more likely, however, to represent Greek **kuōn**, 'dog', from their doglike (churlish) attitude.

dachshund The German breed of dog, with its long, low body, has a German name meaning 'badger dog', from *Dachs*, 'badger', and *Hund*, 'dog'. It is so named because it was formerly used to draw badgers out of their burrows.

daffodil The name of the flower has probably evolved, through Dutch, from Latin *asphodelus*, 'asphodel'. This English name has itself been used for the daffodil, among other plants. The Latin name comes from Greek *asphodelos*, a word of obscure origin.

dairy The word was originally that of a person, not a place, and related to bread, not milk. It represents Old English *dǣge*, the term for a servant girl who kneaded bread. (In modern terms it would be *dough lady*.)

dais The term for a raised platform is French in origin, from a word related to English *desk*. It fell out of use before the 17th century, but was reintroduced by historical writers in the 19th century. It is pronounced in two syllables because it is mistakenly thought to be Greek in origin.

daisy The small flower opens in the daytime but closes at night. hence its name, from Old English *dægesēge*, 'day's eye'. (Its 'eye' is its yellow centre.)

damson The small plum ultimately derives its name from Latin *prunum Damsacenum*, 'Damascus plum', referring to *Damascus*, the Syrian city where it originated (as did the fabric known as *damask*).

dandelion The flower has a name deriving from Old French *dent de lion*, literally 'lion's tooth', referring to to its toothed leaves. The modern French name for it is *pissenlit*, literally 'piss-in-bed', from its diuretic properties. This has its equivalent in its English dialect name, *pissabed*.

danger The word was originally used for the power or authority that a lord had in medieval times. Hence its origin in a blend of Latin *dominium*, 'ownership' (from *dominus*, 'lord'), and Old French *dam*, 'injury') (the source of *damage*).

darling The word evolved as a form of *dear* combined with the suffix *-ling*, denoting a person possessing the named quality. A *darling* is thus a 'dear person'. Compare ◊stripling.

date The fruit ultimately derives its name, through French and Latin, from Greek *daktulos*, 'finger'. The reference is to the shape of the date palm's leaves, which are like fingers.

dawn The word is a shortening of *dawning*, which is itself another form of *daying*, since dawn is the time when *day* breaks. (There actually was a verb *to day*, but it did not survive beyond the 15th century.)

deadline The word for a time limit was originally, in American usage, the term for a *line* drawn round a military prison, beyond which a prisoner was liable to be shot *dead*.

dean The head of a cathedral chapter or college has a title that goes back to Late Latin *decanus*, itself the title for a person in charge of ten others, from Latin *decem*, 'ten'. In an ecclesiastical sense this would have been a person in charge of ten monks in a monastery.

debt The origin of the word, via Old French (and modern) *dette*, is in Latin *debitum*, the noun form of *debere*, 'to owe', literally 'to not have', from *de-*, 'un-', and *habere*, 'to have'. The original English spelling was without the *b*, as the French is. However, the earlier French spelling was *debte*, after the Latin, and the English followed this.

December The last month of the year has a name deriving from Latin *decem*, 'ten'. It is now the twelfth month, but in the Roman calendar, which started in March, it was the tenth. Compare ◊September, ◊October, ◊November.

decimate The word originally applied to the putting to death of one person in ten, and derives from Latin *decimus*, 'tenth', from *decem*, 'ten'. In the Roman army, it was the practice to execute one soldier in ten in cases of mutiny.

deck The word is of Dutch origin and originally applied to the roof or covering overhead, not the floor. It is thus related to *thatch*.

decoy The word was originally a specific term for a pool with netted approaches where wildfowl were captured. Hence its probable origin in Dutch *de kooi*, 'the cage', with the noun here derived from Latin *cavea*, which also gave English *cage* itself.

> **FALSE**
>
> **decoy** An altered form of *duck coy*, with *coy* in its old sense of 'allure'.

deer Although now the name of a specific animal, the word originally meant 'animal' in general. Compare related German *Tier*, which still has the general sense. See also ◊reindeer.

defeat The origin of the word is in Old French *desfait*, 'undone', a form of the verb *desfaire*, 'to undo', 'to ruin', itself from Medieval Latin *disfacere*, from Latin *dis-*, 'un'- and *facere*, 'to do'.

> **FALSE**
>
> **defeat** From the fact that a *defeat* amounted to a disfigurement of the *features*. Compare 'to lose face'.

delight The verb comes from Latin *delectare*, 'to allure', a word that also gave English *delectable* and *delicious*. The literal sense of the Latin is 'to draw aside', from *de'-* 'aside', and *lacere*, 'to draw gently'. The spelling of the English word was influenced by *light*.

delirious The word is the adjective of *delirium*, from the identical Latin noun meaning 'madness', itself from the verb *delirare*, literally 'to go out of one's furrow', from *de*, 'out of', and *lira*, 'furrow'. Compare modern English 'off one's rocker' and 'off one's trolley'.

democratic The origin is in Greek *dēmokratia*, 'government by the people', from *dēmos*, 'people', and *kratos*, 'power', 'strength'.

denim The material from which modern *denims* are made is a development of the fabric known in French as *serge de Nîmes*, 'serge of Nîmes', so called after the city in the south of France where it was originally made.

depart The original meaning of the word was 'divide into parts', as if *de-part*. If you *depart*, you are separating yourself from someone or something. The well-known phrase from the marriage service, 'till death us do part', was originally 'till death us *depart*', that is, 'till death divides us'.

describe The literal sense of the word is 'write down', from Latin *describere*, representing *de-*, 'down', and *scribere*, 'to write'.

desert The tract of waste land is so called as it is a region that has been *deserted* or abandoned because it is barren, and so unfit for living in or growing things in.

dessert The sweet course of a meal is so called from the French verb *desservir*, 'to clear the table', from *des-*, 'un'-, and *servir*, 'to serve'. The course was the last one, served after the main course had been cleared away.

detest The word comes from Latin *detestari*. This could mean 'to loathe', as the English word does. Its prime sense, however, was 'to curse', from *de-*, a prefix here indicating a bad sense, and *testis*, 'witness'. The verb implied cursing while calling on a god as a witness.

deuce The term for a score of 40-all in tennis derives from Old French *deus* (modern *deux*), 'two'. When the players reach deuce, one of them must score *two* more points to win the game.

develop The literal sense of the word is 'unwrap', from Old French *developer*, representing *de-*, 'un'-, and *veloper*, 'to wrap' (hence English *envelope*). If something *develops*, it gradually unfolds or unwraps.

devil The word goes back through French and Latin to Greek *diabolos*, 'enemy', 'slanderer', itself from the verb *diaballein*, 'to slander'. This has the literal sense 'throw across', from *dia-*, 'across', and *ballein*, 'to throw'. Compare English *traduce*, literally 'lead over'.

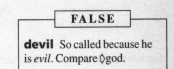

FALSE

devil So called because he is *evil*. Compare ◊god.

dial The earliest sense of the word was for the sun*dial*, which told the time by the changing shadow of the sun as it went on its *daily* course. Hence the word's ultimate origin in Medieval Latin *dialis*, 'daily', from *dies*, 'day'.

diamond The name for the precious stone is of the same origin as ◊adamant, with a spelling influenced by words beginning *dia*-, such as *diaphanous*.

diaper The word for a fabric with a diamond pattern (also the American word for 'nappy') derives, through French and Medieval Latin, from Medieval Greek *diaspros*, 'pure white', from *dia*, 'through', and *aspros*, 'white', 'shining'.

> **FALSE**
>
> **diaper** From French *d'Ypres*, 'from Ypres', as the Belgian town where the fabric was first made.

diarrhoea The disorder has a name of Greek origin that factually describes it, from *dia*-, 'through', and *rhein*, 'to flow'. Its German name is similar, as *Durchfall*, literally 'falling through'. Compare ◊catarrh.

diary A *diary* is properly a *daily* record. Hence its name, from Latin *diarium*, originally 'daily allowance', then later 'journal'. The basis of this is *dies*, 'day'.

dice The word is really a form of *dies*, so that a single numbered cube is a *die*. The ultimate source of this is Latin *dare*, usually 'to give', but here having a special sense of 'to play'.

difficult The adjective was formed from the noun *difficulty*, itself from Latin *difficultas*, in turn a noun formed from the adjective *difficilis*, literally 'not easy', from *dis*-, 'not', and *facilis*, 'easy'.

dilapidated The word has its origin in Latin *dilapidare*, 'to demolish', literally 'to throw stones apart', from *dis*-, 'apart' and a verb formed from *lapis*, genitive *lapidis*, 'stone'.

dilemma The word came into English, through Latin, from the identical Greek word, which literally means 'double premise', from *di*-, 'two', and *lemma*, 'premise'. A *dilemma*, strictly speaking, involves a choice between two equal alternatives.

diligent The word, meaning 'careful and persevering', has its origin, through French, in Latin *diligere*, 'to value', literally 'to read apart', from *dis*-, 'apart', and *legere*, 'to read'.

dinner The name of the meal comes from a French word that itself represents a reduced form of a conjectured Latin verb *disjejunare*, 'to break one's fast', from *dis*-, 'not', and *jejunare*, 'to fast'. This gave modern French *déjeuner*, 'lunch', also *petit déjeuner*, 'breakfast'. The latter English word has the same literal sense as the Latin.

diphtheria The disease particularly affects the throat. Hence its name, which was devised only in the 19th century. It is based on Greek *diphthera*, 'leather', with reference to the tough membrane that forms in the throat.

diplomat A *diplomat* handles confidential matters. Hence the origin of the word, from Greek *diploma*, literally 'letter folded double' (so that no one can see it), from *diploos*, 'double'.

disaster The word came into English from French, which got it from Italian *disastro*, itself from Latin *dis-*, 'not', and *aster*, 'star'. A *disaster* thus occurred when the stars were unfavourable. In Shakespeare's *Hamlet*, Horatio tells of the 'disasters in the sun' just before the murder of Julius Caesar.

disco The dance club or nightclub has a name that is a short form of French *discothèque*, a word modelled on *bibliothèque*, 'library', itself from Greek *bibliothēkē*, literally 'book case'. A *discothèque* is thus a 'disc case'. (The word works because *disc* is also of Greek origin.)

dismal The word was originally a noun, used in medieval times for what were regarded as the two unlucky days in each month of the calendar. The origin is thus in Medieval Latin *dies mali*, 'bad days'. The association with *day* led to the adjectival use of the word.

dismantle The word originally meant 'uncloak', in the sense of removing a *mantle*. Hence the present meaning of 'strip', 'take to pieces'. The origin is in Old French *desmanteler*. from Latin *dis-*, 'un'-, and *mantellum*, a diminutive of *mantum*, 'cloak'.

display The word came into English, through French, from Late Latin *displicare*, 'to scatter', from *dis-*, 'un'-, and *plicare*, 'to fold'. *Display* itself gave *splay*.

district The administrative territory gets its name from Medieval Latin *districtus*, itself from the verb *distringere*, 'to stretch out'. Compare legal English *distraint* (used in seizing property), from the same source, itself related to *stringent* and giving *strain*.

ditto The word comes from the identical Italian dialect word meaning 'said' (standard Italian *detto*), originally used in English when repeating the name of a month in documents.

dive The origin of the word is in a Germanic root element *dup-* that also gave English *deep* and *dip*.

divorce This is basically the same word as *divert*, and both words go back to Latin *divertere*, 'to separate', literally 'turn aside', from *di-*, 'apart', and *vertere*, 'to turn'.

doctor The word derives from the identical Latin word meaning 'teacher', from *docere*, 'to teach'. The sense development goes: 'teacher', 'knowledgeable person', 'knowledgeable person specializing in medicine'. See also ◊dogma.

dodo The extinct bird of Mauritius could not fly and was clumsy and easy to catch. Its name comes from Portuguese *duodo*, 'stupid'.

dog The source of the word is obscure. It may originally have applied to a specially large or strong dog. The general word for the animal was formerly *hound* (compare German *Hund*), which in English has now itself become specialized.

dogma The word for a *doctrine* derives, via Latin, from the identical Greek word meaning 'opinion', 'belief', from *dokein*, 'to seem good'. It is thus actually related to *doctrine*, which in turn is related to ◊doctor.

doldrums The word for a state of depression may have originated in a form of *dull* that was influenced by *tantrum*.

doll The child's toy probably derives its name from *Doll*, the pet form of *Dorothy*. The original meaning of the word, when it emerged in the 16th century, was 'mistress'. Hence the use of the name by Shakespeare for *Doll* Tearsheet, Falstaff's mistress in *Henry IV, Part II*. A mistress was then regarded as a sort of 'pet woman'. Hence the adoption of the name for the toy.

> **FALSE**
>
> **doll** From *idol*, as an object representing a real person, and one that is 'worshipped' by its child owner.

dollar The coin derives its name from Low German *daler*, a form of German *Thaler*. This was short for *Joachimsthaler*, as the original coin was made from metal minted in *Joachimsthal* ('Joachim's valley'), now Jáchymov in the Czech Republic.

dome The word comes from Italian *duomo*, 'cathedral', a form of *domo*, 'house' (ie, of God). Italian cathedrals are famous for their domes, as best seen in St Peter's, Rome.

dominoes The popular pub game is said to derive its name, through French, from Italian *domino*, 'master', a word called at the end of a game by the winner.

donkey The name of the animal is probably a blend of *dun*, meaning 'grey', and the latter half of *monkey*, with which it originally rhymed.

> **FALSE**
>
> **dominoes** From the Latin sentence formerly recited by a monk on winning a game: '*Dixit Dominus*', 'The Lord hath said', the opening words of the vesper service.

down The word has its origin in Old English *dūn*, 'hill' (as in the *downs* that are hills or upland today). To go *down*, you first need to be up, as on a hill.

dragon The word is Greek in origin, and is perhaps related to the root *drak* that lies behind *derkesthai*, 'to see clearly'. Dragons usually spied out their prey.

drama The word comes from Greek *drama*, 'play', itself from the verb *drān*, 'to do'. A play is something *done* on the stage. Compare *actor*, which literally means 'doer', from Latin *agere*, 'to do'. See also ◊drastic.

drastic The word originally applied to medicines that were effective. They *did* something. Hence the word's origin in Greek *drastikos*, 'active', from *drān*, 'to do'.

drawer A *drawer* is so called because you *draw* or pull it out of the table, chest of drawers, or the like. For the same reason, *drawers*, as an undergarment, are so called because you *draw* or pull them on.

drawing room The main sitting room of a house was originally called a *withdrawing room*. It was the room to which ladies *withdrew* after dining with the men in the adjacent dining room.

dress As a noun, the word is first recorded in English only in the 17th century. It derives from the verb meaning 'put straight', ultimately from Latin *dirigere*, 'to direct'. A *dress* is a garment in which the wearer is properly attired.

dromedary The type of camel is famous for its speed, and is thus used for racing. Hence its name, from Late Latin *dromedarius camelus*, 'running camel', itself from Greek *dromas*, 'running' (the *-drome* of *aerodrome*, *hippodrome*, etc).

drowsy The word is based on the root element that gave Old English *drēosan*, 'to fall'. If you are *drowsy*, you are likely to *fall* asleep.

drug The word is of disputed origin. It directly came into English from Old French (and modern) *drogue*. Further back it has Germanic roots, and is perhaps related to Dutch *droog*, 'dry', and so to English *dry* itself. The reference would be to the *dry* products or substances that form the basis of many drugs.

duck The bird is so named because it *ducks* or dives in the water to feed (although the verb came into English later than the noun).

duel The term for a combat between two people derives from Medieval Latin *duellum*, a poetic variant of *bellum*, 'war'. The word became popularly associated with Latin *duo*, 'two'.

> **FALSE**
>
> **duel** From Latin *dualis*, 'concerning two', as there are *two* contestants. Compare English *dual*.

dunce The word for a stupid person came from *Dunsmen*, a derisory nickname applied by 16th-century humanists to the followers of the Scottish theologian John *Duns* Scotus (died 1308).

dungeon The word for the castle keep ultimately goes back to Latin *dominus*, 'lord'. A dungeon was the chief or master tower of the castle.

dupe The word for a gullible person derives from Old French *duppe*, a contraction of *de huppe*, 'like a hoopoe', from the stupid appearance of this bird.

> **FALSE**
>
> **dupe** So called because of his *duplicity*.

dynamite The name of the explosive was devised by its inventor in 1866, the Swedish chemist Alfred Nobel (who also founded the Nobel prizes). He based it on Greek *dunamis*, 'force', adding the scientific suffix *-ite* (*-it* in the original Swedish).

dynasty The word for a line of kings or princes ultimately goes back, through Latin, to Greek *dunasthai*, 'to be powerful', from the same root word that much later gave ⟩dynamite.

dysentery The infection of the intestine has a name of Greek origin meaning literally 'bad bowels', from *dys-*, 'bad', 'wrong', and *entera*, 'bowels'.

E

ear The spike of corn that contains the grain is so called because it is pointed, from a Germanic word based on the Indo-European root element *ak-*, 'sharp', that also gave English *acute* and *edge*.

earwig The insect gets its name from Old English *ēare*, 'ear', and *wicga*, 'beetle'. It was so called because it was popularly believed to enter people's ears.

easel The support for a painting or blackboard derives its name from Dutch *ezel*, 'ass', 'donkey' (a beast of burden). Compare English *clothes-horse*.

> **FALSE**
>
> **earwig** From *ear*, in the sense 'cornbud', and *wick* in its old sense of 'settlement'. The insect lives in cornbuds.

Easter The Christian festival, celebrating the Resurrection or rising again of Jesus, has a pagan name, from the Germanic goddess of the spring *Eostre*. Her name relates to English *east*, as she personified the dawn and the sunrise (a daily 'resurrection').

eavesdropper A person who secretly listens to the conversations of others is so called because the original place where this was done was the *eavesdrop*, the space next to the wall of a house where rainwater *dropped* from the *eaves* (the edge of the roof).

eccentric The word literally means 'out of centre', ultimately from Greek *ekkentros*, comprising *ek-*, 'out', and *ketros*, 'centre'. Anyone or anything *eccentric* is thus 'far out'.

éclair The finger-shaped cake has a French name meaning 'lightning', apparently referring either to its *lightness* (in weight or colour) or to the 'streak' of cream that fills it.

eclipse The partial or total obscuring of the sun or moon takes its name from Greek *ekleipsis*, 'quitting', from *ek-*, 'away', and *leipein*, 'to leave'. During an eclipse, the sun or moon seems to leave the sky.

economy The word literally means 'home management'. Its origin is in Greek *oikonomia*, from *oikos*, 'house', and *nemein*, 'to manage'.

ecstasy The state of heightened pleasure takes its name from Greek *ekstasis*, literally 'displacement', from *ek-*. 'out', and *stasis*, 'standing'. If you are *ecstatic*, you are 'beside yourself'.

education The literal meaning of the word is 'drawing forth' or 'leading out', from Latin *educare*, 'to rear', comprising *e-*, 'out', and *ducere*, 'to lead'. This contrasts with *instruction*, which is literally 'building in'.

effigy The word for the portrait or representation of a person derives from Latin *effigies*, from *effingere*, 'to form', 'to portray', literally 'fashion out', from *ex*, 'out', and *fingere*, 'to fashion' (as also behind English *feign*, *figment*, and *figure*).

elastic The word comes from Greek *elastikos*, 'impulsive', literally 'driving', from the stem of *elaunein*, 'to drive'. Something elastic 'impulsively' returns to its original shape after stretching.

elbow The word arose as a combination of words that are now *ell*, originally meaning 'arm', and *bow*, 'bend'. The elbow is thus (obviously) the bend of the arm.

electric The word goes back through Latin *electrum* to Greek *elektron*, 'amber'. When rubbed, amber becomes charged with electricity.

elegant The origin of the word is in Latin *elegans*, 'tasteful', from a word related to *eligere*, 'to select', which itself gave English *elect*. Something that is *elegant* has thus been carefully *selected* or chosen.

elephant The name of the animal derives from Greek *elephas*, 'ivory', to which it (or part of it) may be indirectly related. Its ultimate origin is uncertain.

eleven The Old English word for the number was *endleofan*. This literally means 'one left', that is, one over ten. *Twelve* evolved as a similar formation, although meaning 'two left'.

elixir The word for a special tonic or restorative represents Arabic *al iksīr*, 'the elixir'. The second word of this probably derives from Greek *xērion*, a powder for drying wounds, from *xēros*, 'dry'.

elongate The original sense of the word was 'remove'. Its source is in Late Latin *elongare* 'to keep at a distance', from *e-*, 'away', and *longe*, 'far off'. This verb was later taken to represent *ex-*, 'out', and *longus*, 'long', so that the sense became 'lengthen out', as now.

embargo The term for an official ban or stoppage derives from the identical Spanish word, as a noun from the verb *embargar*, 'to arrest', 'to impede', from the conjectured Vulgar Latin word *imbarricare*, literally 'to bar in'.

emblem The source of the word is Latin *emblema*, from Greek *emblēma*, 'insertion', literally 'thing thrown in', from *en-*, 'in', and *ballein*, 'to throw'. The Latin word was used for inlaid work, or a raised ornament on a vessel, and this was the forerunner of the English *emblem*.

embryo The term for an animal in the first stages of development goes back to Greek *embruon* in the same sense. This literally means 'thing swelling in', from *en-*, 'in', and *bruein*, 'to swell'.

emery The mineral used as an abrasive and polishing agent derives its name, through French, from an ultimate source in Greek *smuris*, 'polishing powder' (English *smear*).

empathy The power of entering another person's feelings derives from Greek *empatheia*, 'affection', adopted to translate German *Einfühling*, literally 'feeling in'.

> **FALSE**
>
> **emery** From the name of Cape *Emeri* on the island of Naxos, Greece, where the mineral was originally obtained.

encore The call for a repeat performance represents the French word meaning 'again', 'once more', perhaps itself from Latin *in hanc horam*, 'until this hour'. The French actually call *bis*, 'twice', when they want a repeat.

encyclopedia The name comes from the identical Medieval Latin word meaning 'general education course'. This came from Greek *enkuklopaideia*, a mistranscription of *enkuklios paideia*, 'general education', from *enkuklious*, 'general' (literally 'circular') and *paideia*, 'education' (from *pais*, genitive *paidos*, 'child'). The Greeks had a 'circle' of arts and sciences that they regarded as an essential basic curriculum.

enemy As the word indicates, an enemy is the opposite of a friend, from Latin *inimicus*, 'hostile', comprising *in*-, 'not', and *amicus*, 'friend'.

energy The derivation is in Greek *energeia*, 'activity', literally 'working in'. from *en*-, 'in', and *ergon*, 'work'.

engine The basic concept of the word is 'skilled device'. The English word evolved, through French, from Latin *ingenium*, 'nature', 'talent' (the source also of English *ingenious*), from *in*-, 'in', and the root element *gen*-, 'born'.

enormous The word derives from Latin *enormis*, literally 'outside the norm', from *e*-, 'out' and *norma*, 'rule', 'pattern'. Something *enormous* is larger than expected or outside one's normal experience.

entertain The word evolved from Old French *entretenir*, literally 'hold among', from *entre*, 'among', and *tenir*, 'to hold'. Entertaining is a mutual activity.

enthusiastic The literal sense of the word is 'possessed by a god'. Its ultimate source is Greek *entheos*, 'inspired', from *en*-, 'in', and *theos*, 'god'. Compare ◊giddy.

ephemeral If something is ephemeral it doesn't last long. It literally lasts only a day, as the word specifies, from Greek *ephēmeros*, comprising *epi*-, 'on', and *hēmera*, 'day'. The English word was originally used as a medieval term for a fever lasting only 24 hours.

episode The source of the word is in Greek *epeisodion*, 'thing entering besides', from *epi*-, 'in addition to', and *eisodos*, 'entrance'. In Greek tragedy, an *episode* was a section of dialogue between two songs.

equator The great circle of the earth took its name from its equivalent in the celestial sphere, which was defined in Medieval Latin as '*circulus aequator diei et noctis*', 'circle equalizing day and night'.

equerry The title of an officer attending the sovereign was formerly that of an officer responsible for the royal horses. The word thus became associated with Latin *equus*, 'horse', but actually originated from Old French *escuirie*, 'stable', from a word that gave modern English *squire*.

era The word for an age or epoch derives from Latin *aera*, 'counters', the plural of *aes*, genitive *aeris*, literally 'brass'. The reference is to counters used for calculating (in this case the number of years from a starting point).

escape The word ultimately comes from a conjectured Latin verb *excappare*, literally meaning 'to get out of one's cloak', from *ex-*, 'out', and Late Latin *cappa*, 'cloak'. An escapee is the equivalent of a runaway dog that has slipped its collar.

> **FALSE**
>
> **era** From the abbreviation *A.ER.A.*, standing for Latin *Annis erat Augusti*, 'It was the year of Augustus', referring to the adoption of the Roman calendar during the reign of this emperor.

etiquette As used for a code of behaviour, the word came into English direct from French, in which it represents Old French *estiquette*, 'label', from *estiquier*, 'to stick'. The idea is presumably of a code of conduct that 'sticks' to a particular group or profession, in the sense of being visibly associated with it. The same source gave English ◊ticket.

eucalyptus The type of Australian tree has a Greek name devised to mean 'well covered', from *eu-*, 'well', and *kaluptos*, 'covered'. The reference is to the tree's flower, which before it opens is covered by a cap.

euphoria The feeling of great elation gets its name from Greek, in which it literally means 'enduring well', from *eu*, 'good', and *pherein*, 'to bear', 'to endure'.

event The word goes back to Latin *eventus*, 'happening', from the verb *evenire*, 'to come out', comprising *ex-*, 'out', and *venire*, 'to come'. Compare English *outcome*.

every The word evolved from the Old English phrase *æfre ælc*, literally 'ever each'. This emphasized that *all* individuals in a group were included. Today, *every* refers to a total number ('every child in the class'), while *each* refers to the individuals in that total ('each child in the class').

evil The word is of Germanic origin, and probably derives from an Indo-European root element *up-*, also giving English *up*. The concept is of something exceeding its proper limits.

exchequer The word came into English, through French, from Medieval Latin *scaccarium*, 'chessboard', with *ex-* added by association with a word such as *exchange*. The royal accounts were kept by means of counters on a table covered with a cloth divided into squares. This chequered cloth was thus the 'chessboard'.

exercise The word derives ultimately from Latin *exercitium*, with the same meaning. This came from the verb *exercere*, 'to drill', 'to train', literally 'keep active', from *ex-*, 'out of', and *arcere*, 'to enclose'.

exit The word derives from Latin *exitus*, 'departure', from the verb *exire*, 'to go out', comprising *ex-*, 'out', and *ire*, 'to go'. (As a direction to an actor to leave the stage, *exit* evolved from Latin *exeat*, 'let him/her go out'.)

exotic The literal sense is 'outside', from Latin *exoticus*, in turn from Greek *exoticos*, based on *exō*, 'outside'. *Exotic* things often come from abroad, ie, from *outside* one's own country.

expect The word has the literal sense 'look out', and comes from Latin *exspectare*, comprising *ex-*, 'out', and *spectare*, 'to look'.

experience Both this word and *experiment* are related and come from Latin *experiri*, 'to prove', from a root word that also gave English *peril*. *Experience* and an *experiment* involving a testing or proving of someone or something.

express The origin of the word is in Latin *expressus*, literally 'squeezed out', from the verb *exprimere*, comprising *ex-*, 'out', and *primere*, 'to press'. Something 'squeezed out' is explicitly shown or stated, or clearly used for a particular purpose. Hence *express train*, which was originally a special train, one having the *express* purpose of travelling fast.

extra This is a straight borrowing of Latin *extra*, meaning 'outside'. Something *extra* is outside what one normally has.

extravagant The word derives from Medieval Latin *extravagans*, a form of the verb *extravagari*, literally 'to wander outside', from *extra*, 'outside', and *vagari*, 'to wander'. An *extravagant* person exceeds or 'wanders outside' accepted limits.

> **FALSE**
>
> **exuberant** From Latin *ex*, 'out', and *uber*, 'breast', so literally 'full-bosomed', 'buxom'.

exuberant The word originally had the sense 'growing luxuriously'. Hence its origin in Latin *exuberare*, 'to be fruitful', from *ex-*, 'out', and *uber*, 'fertile' (related to English *udder*).

eyelet The term for a small hole that a lace or cord goes through (as in a lace-up shoe) derives from Old French *oillet*, literally 'little eye', from *oill* (modern French *oeuil*), 'eye', and the diminutive suffix *-et*. The English spelling evolved by association with *eye* and the diminutive suffix *-let* (as in *booklet*).

eyrie The word for an eagle's nest, also spelt *aerie*, derives from Medieval Latin *airea*, in turn from classical Latin *area*, 'open space' (English *area*). Eagles nest in open (but inaccessible) places.

fagged In its sense of 'tired', 'worn out', from the verb *fag*, the word is of uncertain origin. But the word's meaning suggests that there may be link with ◊*flag*.

fairy The word for the small supernatural being originally meant 'fairyland', so that the being itself was formerly known as a *fay*. (*Fairy* thus was literally *fay-ery*, with *-ery* meaning 'place', just as *piggery* means 'place of pigs' and *rookery* 'place of rooks'.) *Fay* is itself a word related to the *Fates*, the Greek goddesses who controlled human *fate*.

fake The word was originally thieves' slang for 'doing' someone, that is, tricking and robbing them. The word itself is probably related to German *fegen*, 'to sweep'. (Hence possibly *Fagin* as the name used by Dickens for the Jew who runs a gang of thieves in *Oliver Twist*.)

falcon The bird of prey has a name that may derive from Latin *falx*, 'sickle', referring to the bird's sickle-like claws.

fallacy The term for a delusive belief derives from Latin *fallere*, 'to deceive', a word that also gave English *false*.

fallow The reddish-yellow colour, as for *fallow* deer, comes from an Indo-European root word that also gave English *pale*.

famous The word has its origin in a root element found in Latin *fari*, 'to speak'. A *famous* person is thus one that people speak about. The same element lies behind English *fable* (a story that people say) and *fate* (what the gods say or predict).

fan In its sense of 'keen follower' the word is a short form of *fanatic*. This word itself derives from Latin *fanum*, 'temple', a place where worshippers were inspired by the gods.

fancy The word is a short form of *fantasy*, in the sense of something that one imagines or that one has a special liking for.

farce The term for a humorous play derives, through French, from Latin *farcire*, 'to stuff', 'to pad out'. In medieval times this word was used of phrases and passages inserted ('stuffed') into the text of a religious service. Later, the sense applied to similar passages inserted in religious plays, and so to the passages themselves, as plays in their own right.

fare The modern senses of 'get on' (how did you fare?) and of both 'food' (rich fare) and 'cost of a journey' (train fare) all derive from Old English *faran*, 'to go'. The 'food' sense relates to provisions for a journey. Hence also *farewell*, literally 'go well', formerly the equivalent of 'bon voyage'.

farm The word comes from Old French *ferme*, a term for rented land, from Latin *firmare*, 'to settle', which also gave English *firm* (meaning both 'secure' and 'commercial enterprise').

FALSE

farm From Old English *feorm*, 'food', 'provision'.

---

fascist The name was originally that of a member of the *Fascio nazionale di combattimento*, 'national fighting force', formed by Mussolini in Italy in 1919 to combat communism. Italian *fascio*, literally 'bundle', ie, 'grouping', derives from Latin *fascis*. The plural of this, *fasces*, was the term used in ancient Rome for a bundle of rods with an axe in the middle, representing a magistrate's power. The Italian fascists also had this as their symbol.

fast In the sense 'abstinence from food', the word relates to the other *fast* meaning 'firm', as in 'hold fast' or 'stand fast'. The idea was of holding to a strict observance. The sense 'quickly' developed from the 'firm' sense: someone who runs *fast* shows firmness of strength or intention.

fathom The word originally meant 'embrace', and from this came to denote the length of an adult's outstretched arms, which is about six feet. Hence the use of the word to denote a depth of equivalent measure. (A person's height is the same as the measure from fingertip to fingertip.)

fawn The word for a young deer derives, through French, from Latin *fetus*, 'offspring' (modern English *foetus*).

fax The word happens to suggest *facts* but is actually a short form of *facsimile*, referring to the exact copies that the machine transmits. The full word represents the Latin command *fac simile!*, 'make something like it!', from *facere*, 'to make', and *similis*, 'similar', 'like'.

February The second month of the year takes its name from Latin *februa*, the Roman festival of purification held on February 15. The Latin word is the plural of *februum*, 'purgation', (There is no relation to English *febrile* or *fever*, though there may be to *fume*.) The Old English name of February was *solmōnath*, 'mud month'.

feckless The word, describing a weak or feeble person, literally means 'lacking feck'. *Feck* is a shortening of *effeck*, a Scottish form of *effect*. The corresponding English meaning is thus 'ineffectual'.

feeble The word ultimately derives from Latin *flere*, 'to weep', since someone or something that is feeble is to be lamented, or wept over.

fellow The medieval meaning of the word was 'partner'. It derives from Old English *fēolaga*, literally 'fee layer', that is, someone who lays down money as an associate in a joint enterprise.

female The word goes back to Latin *femella*, a diminutive of *femina*, 'woman'. The word was regularly spelt *femal* until the 17th century, when its present spelling evolved by association with *male*.

fern The plant has a name that is related to Greek *pteron*, 'feather', referring to its feathery fronds.

ferret The name of the animal goes back through Old French to Latin *fur*, 'thief'. In its wild state, the ferret is a noted predator, as is the weasel, to which it is closely related.

ferry The word was originally used of the crossing-point of a boat on a river, that is, the place where people could *fare* over. As the word for a boat or ship, *ferry* is thus short for *ferry-boat*.

fetish The object believed to have magical powers is so called, via French *fétiche*, from Portuguese *feitiço*, 'sorcery', ultimately from Latin *facticius*, 'made by art' (English *factitious*).

fiasco The word for an utter failure derives from the identical Italian word meaning 'bottle', to which modern English *flask* corresponds. The association of ideas is uncertain, but perhaps it is something to do with breaking a bottle or falling into debt with regard to a consignment of wine.

fib The word for a trivial lie probably evolved as a shortening of *fibble-fabble*, 'unlikely story', itself based on *fable* (which can also have the sense 'lie').

field The word was originally used for a stretch of level, open land, like the related South African *veld*. The word thus comes from an Indo-European root element that also gave English *flat*.

> **FALSE**
> **field** So called as originally a place where trees had been *felled*.

filigree The term for delicate ornamental work of twisted gold or silver ultimately goes back to Latin *filum*, 'thread', and *granum*, 'seed' (English *grain*).

fillet The strip of boneless meat or fish derives its name, through French, from a diminutive of Latin *filum*, 'thread'.

filly The word for a young mare derives from an Old Norse word related to an Old High German word that gave modern English *foal*.

> **FALSE**
> **filly** From Latin *filia*, 'daughter', as a *filly* is a young female horse.

film The Old English meaning of this word was 'membrane'. It derives from a source word that also gave modern English *fell*, in the sense 'animal skin'.

filter The word is of Germanic origin and originally meant 'felt' (the cloth), as this was used for filtering liquids and freeing them of impurities.

finance The word is of French origin and is related to *final*. Its original English meaning was 'end', since when you have concluded a financial transaction or made a payment you have settled it, and it is at an end. English *fine*, as a penalty payment, has the same origin.

finger The word is Germanic in origin and is probably from a root word meaning 'five', to which it is thus itself related. Also related is *fist*.

flabbergasted The word may have arisen as a humorous blend of *flabby* and *aghast*. The picture is of someone open-mouthed with astonishment.

flag The word for the flying standard may be related to the other sense of *flag* as 'hang down', since this is often what a flag does, especially if suspended horizontally rather than vertically. The ultimate source of both words is uncertain. Compare ◊fagged.

flak The colloquial word for adverse criticism comes from the term for anti-aircraft fire. This itself arose in the Second World War from the German abbreviation of *Flugzeugabwehrkanone*, literally 'aircraft defence gun'. English *flak jacket* is of the same origin and has retained much of the physical 'firing' sense.

flamingo The bird is named for its bright pink and red plumage, from a Portuguese word that ultimately derives from Latin *flamma*, 'flame', and the Germanic suffix *-ing* that denotes the membership of a group (as in other bird and animal names such as *bunting* or *gelding*).

flannel The fabric and the facecloth are probably so called from a word that ultimately goes back to Welsh *gwlân*, 'wool'.

flatter The word is related to *flat* and is probably Germanic in origin. If you *flatter* someone, you verbally pat them on the head, so *flattening* their hair.

fleece The word for sheep's wool is of Germanic origin and probably ultimately goes back to Latin *pluma*, 'feather', so that modern English *plume* is a related word.

fleet The assembly of ships is so called as it *floats* or sails. *Fleet* in the sense of 'swift' is of the same origin. Both are to do with flowing water, as is the name of London's *Fleet* Street, from the River *Fleet* here (now underground).

flounder The verb for struggling or making mistakes probably evolved from a blend of *founder* (in the sense 'sink') and *blunder*, perhaps influenced by the other *flounder* that is the name of a fish.

flour The word for finely powdered grain is an altered spelling of *flower*, in the sense of something that is the best (as in the *flower* of youth). The spelling was *flower* for both meanings until the 18th century.

flu The word is a shortening of *influenza*, itself the Italian for *influence*. There was a severe flu epidemic in Italy in 1743 and this was reported in the English press: 'News from Rome of a contagious Distemper raging there, call'd the *Influenza*'.

The Italians regarded the epidemic as something that had 'flowed in' from elsewhere as a sort of visitation. See also ◊influence.

focus The origin of the word is in the identical Latin word meaning 'fireplace', 'hearth', as this was the central or *focal* point in a Roman house. In popular Latin *focus* later became the word for 'fire' itself. Hence French *feu*, Spanish *fuego*, Italian *fuoco*, as the standard word for 'fire'.

fogy Whether 'old' or 'young', the word itself is of disputed origin. It may be related to *fog* in some sense. It is first recorded in Scottish use in the 18th century.

fond The original meaning of the word was 'foolish', 'silly'. It probably derives from the obsolete dialect word *fon*, meaning 'fool', though the source of this word in turn is unknown. See also ◊fun.

foolscap The once popular size of paper, superseded by A4, was so called since originally it had a watermark in the form of a *fool's cap*.

> **FALSE**
>
> **foolscap** A corruption of *folio shape*.

forbid The *for-* here has a negating effect, so that the meaning is 'do the opposite of bid', in other words 'ban'. Other words with *for-* in this sense include *forget*, *forlorn* (but not ◊forlorn hope), *forsake,* and *forswear*.

foreign The word ultimately derives from Latin *foris*, 'outside', 'out of doors', itself from Latin *fores*, 'door'. Anywhere *foreign* is outside one's own country or territory. See also ◊forest.

forest The word derives, through French, from Medieval Latin *forestis silva*, literally 'outside wood', from Latin *foris*, 'outside'. (Compare ◊foreign.) A forest was originally woodland, especially a royal game preserve, outside an enclosed wood.

forlorn hope As a standard word, *forlorn* derives from Old English *forloren*, 'lost'. The expression *forlorn hope* has a different origin, however. It represents Dutch *verloren hoop*, 'lost troop' (literally 'lost heap'), a former military term for a detachment of soldiers sent to the front to begin an attack, and therefore likely to be 'lost'. Dutch *hoop* was later taken to be English *hope*.

fornication The term for sex outside marriage derives from Latin *fornix*, genitive *fornicis*, 'arch', 'vault'. The reference is to a vaulted room that was leased out to prostitutes in Roman times.

fossil Many fossils are dug up out of the soil or rock. Hence their name, which derives from Latin *fossilis*, 'dug up', from *fodere*, 'to dig'.

fox The name of the animal has been related to Russian *pukh*, 'down', 'fine woolly hair'. If so, its original sense may have been 'tailed one'. In hunting parlance a fox's bushy tail is known somewhat similarly as its *brush*.

> **FALSE**
>
> **foxglove** A corruption of *folk's glove*, alluding to the fairy *folk* said to live in the flower.

foxglove The elongated flower of the plant rather resembles a *glove*, or at any rate one of the 'fingers' of a glove. Hence its botanical name, *Digitalis*, from Latin **digitus**, 'finger'. The connection with the *fox* is obscure.

foyer The hall or lobby of a public building such as a theatre or hotel derives its name from the French word for 'hearth', itself related to French *feu*, 'fire', and therefore to ◊focus.

frangipane The word for a type of rich cake arose as a variant of *frangipani*, the perfume. This itself takes its name from the Marquis Muzio **Frangipani**, the 16th-century Roman nobleman who invented it.

fraught The original sense of the word was 'laden'. It is thus related to *freight*. If a person or thing is *fraught* with something, they are laden or filled with it.

free The prime sense of the word is actually 'beloved', and it originally applied to members of a household who were related to its head, as distinct from slaves, who were not. The word is of Indo-European origin and is linguistically related to modern *friend*.

friar The member of the religious order is so called as he is a *brother*. Related words are thus Latin *frater* and French *frère*, 'brother', as well as English *brother* itself.

Friday The sixth day of the week has a name of Old English origin meaning 'Freya's day'. Freya was the Norse goddess of love corresponding to the Roman Venus. Hence the French name of Friday, **vendredi**, 'Venus' day'.

fridge The word is obviously a colloquial short form of *refrigerator*. It may have been subconsciously thought of, however, as a blend of *freeze* (or *frigid*) and *ridge*, referring to the ledges and ribbed surfaces of its interior.

frieze The word now used for an ornamental band on a wall is properly the term in classical architecture for a similar band in a temple's entablature (the part above the columns). It is said to be so called because it originated in *Phrygia*.

frontispiece The term for the illustration facing the title page of a book derives from Late Latin *frontispicium*, literally 'inspection of the forehead', from Latin *frons*, genitive *frontis*, 'forehead', and **specere**, 'to look at'. The original reference was to the façade of a building. The spelling has been influenced by *piece*.

fruit The English word derives, through French, from Latin *fructus*, 'fruit', 'enjoyment', itself from the verb *frui*, 'to enjoy'.

frustrated The word ultimately goes back to Latin *frustra*, 'in error', a word related to *fraus*, English *fraud*.

fudge The type of soft sweet may take its name from the verb *fudge* meaning 'make clumsily'. Fudge could have originally been 'concocted' from various ingredients.

fuel The word came into English from the Old French word that gave modern French *feu*, 'fire'. It is thus related to ◊focus. There is no fire without fuel.

fulsome The original meaning of the word, recently revived in popular use, was 'abundant', 'plentiful', as with *fulsome* praise. It later came to mean 'offensive', perhaps by association with *foul*. Its source, however, is in *full* and *-some*, as in *loathsome*.

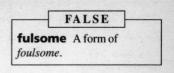

FALSE

fulsome A form of *foulsome*.

fumble The word is of Germanic origin and probably arose as an imitation of a faltering or clumsy movement or action. German *fummeln* has the same sense.

fun The origin of the word is uncertain. When it first emerged in the 17th century it was used of a hoax or a practical joke. It perhaps evolved as a dialect variant of *fon*, a verb meaning 'make a fool of', itself related to ▷fond.

fungus Although directly of Latin origin, the word is probably related to Greek *spongos*, 'sponge'. If so, English *sponge* is also related.

funky The word means 'authentic', 'earthy', as specifically applied to *funk*, black dance music, a name derived from it. The source of the word is probably in the slang term *funk* meaning 'smelly', related to a French dialect word that goes back to Latin *fumigare*, 'to smoke' (English *fumigate*). Early blues music was 'smelly' in the 'earthy' sense. The slang word *funk* for a state of nervousness is probably also related to the 'smelly' sense. People may sweat when they are nervous, and some animals emit an unpleasant smell when frightened or attacked.

funnel The word derives ultimately from Latin *infundibulum*, in the same sense, itself from the verb *infundere*, 'to pour in'.

FALSE

funnel From Welsh *ffynel* in the same sense.

furlong The old measurement for one eighth of a mile (220 yards) literally means 'furrow long'. A furrow in a field was usually a furlong in length, the field itself technically being a ten-acre square. (There are, or were, 4840 square yards in an acre.)

FALSE

furze A form of *firs*, as a general name for trees with needle-shaped leaves.

furze The prickly shrub, also known as gorse and whin, had the Old English name of *fyrs*. The origin of this is unknown.

fuss The word is of uncertain origin, though it has been popularly derived from *force*, as used in the former phrase *make no force*, meaning 'take no account (of)', 'attach no importance (to)'.

futile The origin of the word is in Latin *futtilis*, 'useless', literally 'pouring out easily', from *fundere*, 'to pour out'. If a vessel has had its contents poured out, it is *futile* to expect to get anything out of it.

fylfot The word is a rare term for a swastika, which was apparently so called because it was designed to *fill* the *foot* or lower part of a window as an ornamental device.

gaberdine The type of fabric gets its name from French *gauvardine*, a term for a pilgrim's cloak. This itself is probably from Middle High German *wallewart* (modern German *Wallfahrt*), 'pilgrimage'. Compare *pelerine*, a woman's narrow cape, which derives from French *pèlerin*, 'pilgrim'.

gadget The word is of uncertain origin, though some have associated it with French *gâchette*, a term for a locking device such as a trigger or spring catch. English *widget* is an altered form of *gadget*.

gaffer The colloquial word for an old man or a foreman arose as a shortened form of *godfather*. The female equivalent was *gammer*, from *godmother*.

gag The word originally meant 'choke', 'suffocate'. Hence its probable origin, in the sound of a choking person.

gainsay To *gainsay* someone is to contradict them. Hence the origin of the word, since by contradicting you *say* something a*gain*st what the other person says.

galatea The type of cotton fabric was formerly used for children's sailor suits. Hence its name, which comes from that of HMS *Galatea*, a ship commanded by the Duke of Edinburgh in 1867.

galaxy The word for a star system (and a name for one of them, better known as the Milky Way) derives ultimately, through Latin, from Greek *gala*, 'milk'.

gallery The word derives from Medieval Latin *galeria*. This was probably an alteration of *galilea*, 'galilee', the term for a porch or chapel at the entrance to a church (itself from the biblical *Galilee*). A *galilee* was probably so called as it was outside the church, just as Galilee was an outlying district of the Holy Land.

galoshes The waterproof overshoes get their name from Latin *gallica (solea)*, 'Gallic (shoe)', referring to the type of sandals worn by the Gauls. In English use, galoshes were originally wooden shoes.

gambit The word for an opening manoeuvre or comment is more narrowly used for the opening move in a game of chess, in which a pawn is sacrificed to gain an advantage. The origin is in Italian *gambetto*, 'tripping up', from *gamba*, 'leg'.

gamut The word for an entire range or scale derives from Medieval Latin, in which it represented *gamma ut*, from *gamma* (the Greek letter), the lowest note of the hexachord as established in the 11th century by Guido d'Arezzo, and *ut*, the first note (now *do*) of the scale *ut*, *re*, *mi*, *fa*, *sol*, *la*, *si*. These derive from a Latin hymn to St John: '*Ut* queant laxis *re*sonare fibris, *Mi*ra gestorum *fa*muli tuorum, *Sol*ve polluti *la*bii reatum, *S*ancte *I*ohannes'.

gang The word was originally used to mean 'journey'. It is ultimately related to *go*. A *gang* is thus literally a group of people who *go* together. Something of the 'going' sense still exists in *gangway*.

gaol See ◊jail.

garage The word is of French origin, and derives from the verb *garer*, 'to protect'. This itself is of Germanic origin and comes from a root element that also gave English *beware*.

garden The word came into English, through French, from a Germanic word related to Old High German *gart*, 'enclosure'. English ◊yard and ◊orchard are directly related words.

garter The word is probably of Celtic origin ultimately, and so is likely to be related to Welsh *gar*, 'thigh', 'ham'.

gas The word was invented by the Dutch chemist J B van Helmont (1577–1644), who based it on Greek *khaos*, 'chaos'. He explained (in Latin): 'halitum illum *Gas* vocavi, non longe a Chao veterum secretum' (I have called that spirit *gas*, as being not far removed from the *chaos* of the ancients). The original Dutch pronunciation of the word would have been something like 'hass', and so closer to Greek *khaos* than English *chaos* is.

gasket The word originally had a nautical sense as a term for a small rope lashing a furled sail. It probably comes from French *garcette*, literally 'little girl', as a feminine diminutive of Old French *garce*, 'boy' (modern *garçon*). Compare *euphroe* (a wooden block with holes through which ropes were passed), from Dutch *juffrouw*, 'young woman'.

gate The basic sense of the word is 'gap', 'opening'. It is distinct from the *gate* in some street-names, such as Brig*gate*, Leeds, where it means 'street', from an Old Norse word related to English *gait* (way of walking). See also ◊gauntlet.

gaunt The word, used of a bony and emaciated-looking person, is probably of Scandinavian origin. There is a Norwegian dialect word *gand* used for a tall thin person. The ultimate source of the word is unknown.

> **FALSE**
>
> **gaunt** A form of *want*, since a *gaunt* person is thin and in need of food.

gauntlet The type of glove derives its name from an Old French diminutive of *gant*, 'glove'. But the phrase *run the gauntlet* has a different word, from Swedish *gantlopp*, literally 'passageway', from *gata*, 'way' (the ◊gate in some English street-names), and *lop*, 'course' (English *leap*).

gawky A *gawky* person is awkward or ungainly, and can attract stares. Hence the basic sense of the word, which is probably related to *gawp*.

gazette The newspaper gets its name from the Venetian dialect word *gazeta*. This was a news-sheet costing one *gazet*, a small copper coin whose own name perhaps derived from *gaza*, 'magpie'.

geezer The colloquial word for a man, especially an old or eccentric one, is a corruption of *guiser*, as a term for someone wearing unusual clothes, that is, in dis*guise*.

generous The word derives from Latin *generosus*, 'nobly born', such a person being (traditionally) charitable and magnanimous. The root origin is in Latin *genus*, 'birth', 'race'.

genuine The word probably derives from Latin *genu*, 'knee', but was later associated with *genus*, 'birth', 'race' (see ◊generous). In a Roman family, a father placed a newborn child on his knee as a sign that he was the *genuine* father.

geology The literal sense of the word is 'earth study', from the Greek, just as *biology* means 'life study' and *zoology* 'animal study'. The original meaning was thus closer to *geography*. It later came to refer more specifically to the study of the earth's crust, and its flora and fauna.

geranium The flower is so called because its fruit is shaped like a crane's bill. Hence its origin, in Greek *geranos*, 'crane'. (The plant actually known as *cranesbill* is a member of the genus.)

geyser The once popular gas heater takes its name from that of a particular geyser in Iceland, as a spring that discharges steam and hot water. It is *Geysir*, in the southwest of the country, with its own name meaning 'gusher'.

ghost The original sense of the word was probably 'terrifying thing', from a root word related to Sanskrit *hēda*, 'fury', 'anger'. The word was spelt without *h* down to about the 16th century, as was the related word *ghastly*.

gibberish The word for incomprehensible talk probably derives from *gibber* (the meaningless chatter of monkeys) and *-ish* as in language names such as 'Span*ish*'.

> **FALSE**
>
> **gibberish** From the name of *Geber*, the 14th-century alchemist, famous for his abstruse formulae.

giddy The basic sense of the word is 'possessed by a god', and it is actually related to *god* itself. Compare ◊enthusiastic.

gillyflower The clove-scented flower derives its name from Old French *girofle*, ultimately from Greek *karuophullon*, 'clove tree', literally 'nut leaf', from *karuon*, 'nut', and *phullon*, 'leaf'. The present spelling has been influenced by *flower*.

gimlet The boring tool takes its name from Old French *guimbelet*, itself of Germanic origin, from a word that also gave English *wimble* (also used for boring).

gin The spirit derives its name as a shortened form of Dutch *genever*, 'juniper', ultimately from Latin *juniperus* in the same sense. The drink is thus named not for its base constituent (malted grain) but the *juniper* berries with which it is flavoured.

ginger The word goes back through Latin and Greek to a Sanskrit source literally meaning 'horn body', referring to the plant's root, which is antler-shaped.

gingerbread The cake or bread contains ginger, as its name suggests. The word derives from Old French *gingembras*, from Medieval Latin *gingibratum*, representing Latin *gingiber*, 'ginger', and the ending *-atum*. The final part of the word was altered in English by association with *bread*.

ginseng The plant with a medicinal root has a name of Chinese origin meaning literally 'man image', from *rën*, 'man', and *xiàng*, 'image. The root is forked, like human legs.

gipsy See ◊gypsy.

girl The ultimate origin of the word is uncertain, but it may be related to the North German colloquial words *Gör*, the equivalent of English 'kid' or 'brat', and *Göre*, 'cheeky little madam'. See also ◊lass.

> **FALSE**
>
> **girl** From Latin *garrula*, 'chattering' (English *garrulous*).

gist The word, now used for the essence or general import of a matter, derives from Old French *gist* (modern French *gît*), from the legal phrase *cest action gist*, 'this action lies'. English *gist* was earlier used for the grounds of a legal action.

> **FALSE**
>
> **gist** From Old French *giste* (modern *gîte*), 'lodging place'. The *gist* of something is where its general meaning lies.

git The slang term for a contemptible person arose as an altered form of *get*, from *beget*, referring to an ill-*begotten* person, otherwise a bastard.

glad The sense of the original Old English word was 'shining', 'bright'. Compare modern German *glatt*, 'smooth', and modern English *glade*, which was probably originally thought of as a bright and sunny place in an otherwise dark forest.

glamour The word evolved as an alteration of *grammar*. The sense link now seems unlikely, but *glamour* was originally used as the word for a magic spell, and occult practices were popularly associated with learning, which involved ◊grammar.

glass The word is of Germanic origin and is probably related to *glare*, perhaps with an ultimate sense 'shining'.

> **FALSE**
>
> **glass** From *glas*, a Celtic word meaning 'green'.

gloat The precise source of the word is uncertain. It is probably of Scandinavian origin and related to German *glotzen*, 'to stare', 'to gawp'.

glue The word ultimately derives from an Indo-European element that also gave English *clay*, *cleave* (in the sense 'adhere'), *clump*, and even *globe*, as being a round object formed from substances that are stuck together.

gnarled The word is probably a variant of *knurled*, as used of something ridged. It occurs once in Shakespeare ('gnarled oak', *Measure for Measure*), and was taken up by later writers from there.

god The basic sense of the word is probably 'one who is invoked', from an Indo-European source that also gave Irish *guth*, 'voice'. God exists not just to do things but to be called on to do things.

> **FALSE**
>
> **god** So called because a *good* being. See also the Bible: 'None is good, save one, that is, God' (Luke 18:19). Compare ♭devil.

gold The word derives from an Indo-European source element that also gave modern English *yellow*.

golf The origin of the word is uncertain, but it may derive from a Middle Dutch word *colf*, meaning 'club'. If so, the word is indirectly related to *club* itself.

golliwog The doll with the black face and shock of black hair takes its name from a doll in the children's books by the American writer Bertha Upton (1849–1912), illustrated by her daughter, Florence Upton (1873–1922). The name itself is probably an alteration of *polliwog*, an American name for a tadpole, with the first part suggesting *golly* or *by golly*, an exclamation common among black Americans.

goodbye The word evolved in the 16th century as a contraction of *God be with ye*. *God* became *good* by association with similar parting phrases, such as *good day* and *good night*.

goose The name of the bird is one of the few in English that are Indo-European in origin. (Others are *crane*, *sparrow*, and *thrush*.) Ultimately it is probably imitative of the bird's cackle. Its cry also gave *gaggle* as a group name for geese.

gooseberry The name of the fruit may well derive from a combination of *goose* and *berry* although it is not clear what the connection with the bird could be. There may also be a link with *groseille*, the French name of the fruit, itself of uncertain origin but possibly related to Dutch *kroes*, 'frizzy', 'fuzzy', referring to its hairy skin.

> **FALSE**
>
> **gooseberry** An adoption and corruption of German *Johannisbeere*, 'currant' (literally 'St John's berry').

gorgeous The word is related to French *gorge*, 'throat', and derives from some elegant garment that was worn round the head or neck.

gospel The word is of Old English origin and literally means 'good spell', *spell* here meaning 'message'. This translated Church Latin *bona annuntiatio*, itself translating Greek *evangelion*, English *evangel*. The 'good message' was the one proclaimed by Jesus Christ (that he had come to save the world).

gossamer The filmy cobweb spun by spiders in autumn is said to derive its name from *goose summer*, this being a term for a late summer spell (now usually called St Martin's summer) when goose was traditionally eaten.

gossip The word was originally a term for a godparent. Hence its literal sense of 'God sib', that is, someone who is related 'in God' to their godchild. The word was then extended to a woman's female friends at the birth of a child, and finally to anyone, especially a woman, who enjoys idle talk and 'chitchat' generally.

goulash The type of rich stew has a name of Hungarian origin meaning literally 'herdsman's meat', from *gulyás*, 'herdsman', and *hüs*, 'meat'.

graffiti The term now used for drawings or messages scrawled on the walls of public buildings is the plural of *graffito*, an archaeological term for an inscription or drawing scratched on a rock or on ancient pottery. The word itself is Italian for 'little scratches'.

grammar The term for the 'rules' of a language derives, through French and Latin, from Greek *grammatikē tekhnē*, 'grammatical art', itself ultimately from *gramma*, 'letter'. See also ▷glamour.

grampus The type of dolphin or killer whale gets its name, through Old French, from Latin *crassus piscis*, 'fat fish'. (A literal modern French equivalent would be *gras poisson*.)

granite The type of hard rock is so called as it is *granular*. Hence the immediate origin in Italian *granito*, 'grained'.

grape The fruit might well have come to be called 'wineberry', as this is the modern equivalent of its Old English name. Its actual name literally means 'bunch' (as modern French *grappe* does), but this later came to apply to a single fruit. The grapes in a bunch are hooked together, so that the word is akin to *grapple* and *cramp*.

grass The word comes from an Indo-European root element seen also in *green* and *grow*. *Grass* is thus something *green* that *grows*.

grateful The word was originally *grate*, from Latin *gratus* in the same sense. It then unusually added *-ful*, which is normally added to a noun, not an adjective. (Compare *thankful* and *beautiful*, meaning 'full of thanks' and 'full of beauty'. But *grateful* does not mean 'full of grate'.)

gravy The dressing for meat appears to have got its name by mistake, when Old French *grane* was misread as *grave*. The origin is thus probably in Old French *grain*, 'spice'.

greengage The type of *green* cultivated plum takes the latter part of its name from Sir William *Gage*, the English botanist who introduced it from France in the 18th century.

greyhound The Old English word for the breed of dog was *grīghund*, the first part of which is related to an Old Norse word meaning 'bitch'. It was later influenced by *grey*, although the dog's coat can be various colours.

> **FALSE**
>
> **greyhound** So called either because *grey* or because formerly used to hunt the *grey* or badger.

grocer A *grocer* originally dealt in *gross*, that is, as a wholesaler, as distinct from a retailer. Hence his name. The spelling with *c* instead of *s* arose by association with *spicer*.

grotesque The word was originally used in the 16th century to apply to a special kind of decorative painting or sculpture, with complicated and interweaving forms. It derives from Old Italian *pittura grotesca*, 'cave painting', with the second word the adjectival form of *grotta*, 'cave' (English *grotto*). The reference is said to be to mural paintings discovered in the chambers of old Roman buildings.

groundsel The plant, a weed with small yellow flowers, derives its name from Old English *grundeswelge*, an altered form (by association with *grund*, modern *ground*) of *gundeswilge*, literally 'pus swallower', from *gund*, 'pus', and *swelgan*, 'to swallow'. The plant was formerly used in poultices on abscesses.

grovel The literal sense of the word is 'lie face downwards'. It derives from Middle English *on grufe*, 'on the face', itself of Scandinavian origin. The word is indirectly related to *creep*.

grub As a colloquial word for food, the reference is to the *grubs* that are foods for birds.

gruesome The word has its origin in the northern and Scottish verb *grue*, meaning 'to feel horror', itself from a word related to modern German *Grauen*, 'horror'. The adjective was raised to literary status by Walter Scott: 'He's as grave and grewsome an auld Dutchman as e'er I saw' (*Old Mortality*, 1816).

guest The basic sense of the word is 'stranger', whether welcome or not. *Guest* thus links up with *hospitable* on the one hand and *hostile* on the other, the former implying the attitude of a friend and the latter that of an enemy. The word is also related to *host*, now its opposite. If a guest is a stranger to the host, then the host will also be to the guest.

guillotine The beheading instrument takes its name from Joseph Ignace *Guillotin* (1738–1814), the French doctor who advocated its use at the time of the Revolution (1789) on the grounds that it was speedy and humane.

gun The weapon takes its name from a short form of the Scandinavian female name *Gunnhildr*, both parts of which actually mean 'war'. Compare Mons *Meg*, the 15th-century cannon (made in Mons, Belgium) in Edinburgh Castle.

guru The word for a Hindu or Sikh religious teacher, or any special adviser, derives from Hindi *gurū*, 'teacher', itself from Sanskrit *guruh*, 'weighty' (in the sense 'grave', 'dignified').

guy As a colloquial term for a person (usually a male), the word has its origin in the name of *Guy* Fawkes (1570–1606), the conspirator involved in the Gunpowder Plot. The word first applied, as it still does, to effigies of him, then to a live person.

gymkhana The horse-riding contest evolved from sports in India in the time of the British Raj. These took place in a *gendkhana*, a Hindi word meaning literally 'ball house', from *gend*, 'ball', and *khānā*, 'house'. The present spelling came about by association with *gymnasium*.

gymnasium The modern sports hall evolved from the ancient Greek one, in which men and boys trained naked. Hence the origin of the word in Greek *gumnos*, 'naked'.

gypsy The nomadic people were originally thought to have come from *Egypt*, though it is now known that they actually came from India. Hence their name, from a shortened form of *Egyptian*.

H

haberdasher The word for a dealer in articles for sewing derives from Anglo-French *hapertas*, a term for small items of merchandise, itself of uncertain origin.

haggis The familiar Scottish dish may get its name from a word related to *hack*, referring to the chopped up ingredients it contains.

FALSE

haberdasher From the question the German haberdasher traditionally asked his customers, tempting them to buy: '*Habt ihr das?*', 'Do you have that?'

---

halleluja The exclamation of praise to God represents the Hebrew word meaning 'praise the Lord', literally 'praise Yah', that is, 'praise Jehovah'.

hallmark The word for a mark or sign of authenticity or excellence originally applied to the marks stamped on gold or silver articles by the London Guild of Goldsmiths. The word thus refers to the *mark* made in this way at Goldsmiths' *Hall*.

hallucination The word for an illusory perception of something derives from Latin *alucinari*, 'to wander in mind', from Greek *alussein*, 'to be uneasy'.

hamlet The word for a small village is of French origin, from *hamel* (modern *hameau*), a diminutive of *ham*, itself a word of Germanic origin related to English *home*.

hamper In the sense of 'basket', the word arose as an altered form of *hanaper*, the term for a small wickerwork basket for documents. Its own source is in Old French *hanap*, 'cup', from a word of Germanic origin related to modern German *Napf*, 'bowl'.

FALSE

hamper So called because originally a *hand panier*.

---

handicap The present word for a disadvantage or a specially weighted contest was originally used for a type of lottery. Hence its origin in the phrase *hand in cap*, referring to the drawing of forfeits from a cap or the depositing of money in one.

handkerchief The present object evolved as a *kerchief* held in the *hand*. A *kerchief* was originally a covering for the head, from Old French *covrir*, 'to cover', and *chef*, 'head' (English *chief*). The handy *hanky* has thus changed its use over the years, although it can still protect the head from rain or sun if required.

handsome The word was originally used of something that was easy to *handle*. A person who could handle things well was to be admired. Hence the present sense.

hanker The origin may lie in a dialect word related to *hang*. If you *hanker* after something, you are *hanging* on in the hope of getting it.

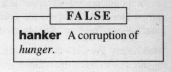

FALSE

hanker A corruption of *hunger*.

happy The word evolved as an adjectival form of the now old-fashioned noun *hap*, meaning 'chance', 'luck' (compare ◊perhaps), itself from Old Norse *happ*, 'good luck'. If you have had good luck, you will probably be *happy*!

hara-kiri The former method of ritual Japanese suicide involved disembowelling oneself with a sword. Hence its name, from *hara*, 'belly', and *kiri*, 'cut'. (Compare *kirigami*, the Japanese art of folding and cutting paper into decorative shapes.)

harbinger Although now used to mean 'forerunner' ('the evening star, love's harbinger'), the word was originally applied to a person who provided lodgings, especially for an army. The origin is in an Old Saxon word akin to Old High German *heriberga*, 'army shelter'.

harlequin This was originally the name of a stock character in Italian comedy and English pantomime. It came from *Herlequin*, the Old French name of the leader of a band of demon horsemen, who in turn was perhaps named after *Herle king*, 'King Herle', the Middle English name of a mythical being identified with the Anglo-Saxon god Woden.

harvest The word originally meant 'autumn' (as related modern German *Herbst* still does), then came to apply to the corn cut and stored in this season. Other related words are Latin *carpere*, 'to pluck', and Greek *karpos*, 'fruit'.

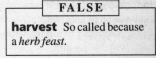

FALSE

harvest So called because a *herb feast*.

haughty The word derives from Old French *haut*, 'high', since a *haughty* person is 'lofty'. The spelling with *gh* probably came about by association with English *high* or *height*.

haunted The word is ultimately of Germanic origin, from a word related to modern English *home*. A *haunted* house is one where a ghost has made its *home*, and if you *haunt* a place you regularly go there, like someone going *home*.

haversack The literal meaning of the word is 'oat sack', from words related to modern German *Hafer*, 'oats', and *Sack*, 'sack'. The word was originally used for the bag in which cavalrymen carried the oats for their horses.

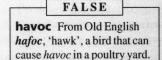

FALSE

havoc From Old English *hafoc*, 'hawk', a bird that can cause *havoc* in a poultry yard.

havoc The term for destruction or ruin derives from Old French *havot*, 'pillage'. The origin of this is unknown.

HEARSE

60

hearse Although now used for a funeral carriage, the word originally applied to the catafalque placed over a bier at a funeral. This was traditionally in the shape of a harrow. Hence the source of the word in the Old French word that gave modern French *herse*, 'harrow'. See also ▷rehearse.

heathen People who were not Christians, Jews, or Muslims were originally regarded as wild and uncivilized, like the inhabitants of open country, or *heath* dwellers. Hence their name.

heaven The word is of Germanic origin, and probably related to modern German *Himmel*. The ultimate source of the word is uncertain.

FALSE

heaven So called because it is raised or *heaved* up.

---

hectic The word was originally a medical term relating to the symptoms that usually accompany a fever. Hence its present sense to denote 'feverish' activity. The origin of the word is thus in Greek *hektikos*, 'habitual'.

helicopter The name of the aircraft was devised from Greek words meaning literally 'spiral wing', referring to the machine's rotors.

helium The gas gets its name from Greek *hēlios*, 'sun', since it was first detected (in 1868) in the solar spectrum.

hell The abode of the dead derives its name from an Indo-European root element meaning 'covered', found also in English words such as *conceal*, *cellar*, *hull*, and *occult*.

helpmate The term for a companion and helper, especially a wife, although a combination of *help* and *mate*, probably arose by association with the biblical phrase describing Eve as the wife of Adam: 'an help meet for him' (Genesis 2:18), that is, suitable for him.

henchman The word, originally the term for a page of honour, literally means 'stallion man', from Old English *hengest*, 'stallion', and *mann*, 'man'. (Hengist and Horsa, the Jutish brothers who are said to have conquered Kent in the 5th century, have names respectively meaning 'stallion' and 'mare'.)

hermaphrodite The biological term for a creature with both male and female sex organs derives from *Hermaphroditus*, in Greek mythology the son of *Hermes* and *Aphrodite* who merged with the nymph Salmacis while bathing in her fountain and so combined male and female characters.

hermit The religious recluse is so called because he traditionally lived a solitary life in the desert, from Greek *erēmia*, 'desert', itself from *erēmos*, 'lonely'.

heroin The drug is probably so called since a person taking it feels a *hero*.

herring The fish has a name of Germanic origin perhaps ultimately deriving from a root element seen also in *hoar*. If so, the word could relate to the colour of its silvery scales.

FALSE

herring From Old English *here*, 'army', because the fish swims in great numbers.

---

hiccup The word imitates the action. The alternative spelling *hiccough* arose under the influence of *cough*, although the pronunciation has always been as *hiccup*.

hick The colloquial (and mainly American) word for a 'country bumpkin' represents *Hick*, the pet form of the personal name *Richard*. British English formerly had *Hodge* in this sense, from *Roger*.

hidalgo The Spanish noble title literally means 'son of something', from Old Spanish *fijo dalgo*, itself representing Latin *filius de aliquo*. The title implies that its bearer's father is 'somebody', a man of some note or worth.

hierarchy The word originally had a religious sense, relating to a division of angels in three orders. Hence its origin from Greek *hierarkhēs*, 'high priest' (literally 'holy ruler').

hieroglyphics The ancient Egyptian picture symbols are literally 'holy carving', from Greek *hieros*, 'holy', and *gluphein*, 'to carve'.

higgledy-piggledy The word is simply a rhyming jingle based on *pig*. When things are *higgledy-piggledy* they are like pigs pushing and shoving together.

high-flown The term for something pretentious or over-ambitious literally means 'flowing fully'. The image is of a river about to flood its banks. The expression later came to be associated with *flying*, however, rather than *flowing*.

hippie A rejector of conventional values in the 1960s was so called through being *hip* or (earlier) *hep*, that is, up to date and trendy. The origin of *hep* itself is uncertain, but it may relate to the military command *hep* to marching soldiers. If you are *hep* you are thus 'in step'.

hippopotamus The name of the animal literally means 'river horse', from Greek *hippos*, 'horse', and *potamos*, 'river'. The original Greek phrase for the animal was *ho hippos ho potamios*, 'the riverine horse'.

hoax The word probably has its origin in the conjuror's magic spell that gave the phrase ◊hocus pocus. Its first appearance is later than the earliest record of the phrase.

hobby The word for a favourite pastime derives from a short form of *hobbyhorse*. If you indulge in a hobby you are like a child on a toy horse. The (real) horse itself got its name as a pet form of *Robin*. (The horse name *Dobbin* also came from this.) A *hobby* may also have come to be subconsciously thought of as something that keeps you *happy*.

hockey The name of the game is of uncertain origin. It was originally known as *hawkey*. A derivation from Old French *hoquet*, 'crook', is unlikely.

hocus pocus The phrase was used in the 17th century as a nickname for a juggler or conjurer, and derives from some kind of

---

FALSE

hocus-pocus From '*Hoc est corpus meum*' 'This is my body', words from the Latin mass, picked on to mock the Roman Catholic doctrine of transubstantiation.

meaningless magic spell, itself based on sham Latin words. *Hocus Pocus* was probably the name assumed by a famous early magician, and his use of the words would have helped to popularize them. See also ◊hoax.

hogmanay The Scottish New Year's Eve party probably gets its name from Old French *aguillaneuf*, 'watch at the new year', with the English word directly deriving from *hoguinané*, the Norman form of this.

hoity-toity The colloquial phrase meaning 'arrogant' probably derives from an obsolete verb *hoit*, meaning 'to romp', while also perhaps influenced by *haughty*. The expression also formerly existed as *highty-tighty*.

> **FALSE**
>
> **hoity-toity** A corruption of French *haut comme toit*, 'as high as the roof'.

holiday A holiday was originally a *holy day*, as it still is in many European countries, especially Catholic ones. Even in Protestant England, Good Friday, Easter Monday, and Christmas Day, all religious days, remain as bank holidays.

hollyhock The tall flowering plant has a name that literally means 'holy hock'. The second word represents Old English *hoc*, 'mallow'. It is not clear why the flower came to be regarded as holy.

holocaust The word for a mass destruction or great loss of life is Greek in origin, and literally means 'whole burning', from *holos*, 'whole', and *kaustos*, 'burnt'. The reference is to a burnt offering (in the religious sense) that was totally consumed by fire.

homage The word is now used for a public show of respect to someone or something. It was originally used for a formal statement of allegiance by one *man* to another. Hence its origin in Old French *homage* (modern French *hommage*), from *home*, 'man', ultimately from Latin *homo* in this sense.

homosexual The word relates to the same sex, whether male or female, and its first part represents Greek *homos*, 'same', not Latin *homo*, 'man'. The word itself is a 19th-century invention.

> **FALSE**
>
> **homosexual** From Latin *homo*, 'man'.

honeymoon The precise origin of the word is uncertain. It is said to allude to the feelings of newlyweds, which can become less 'honeyed' after the first month, and begin to wane, as the *moon* does.

hoodlum The word first appeared in San Francisco in the 1870s. Its origin is uncertain, but it may derive from the South German dialect word *Haderlump*, 'good-for-nothing'. The *hood* who is a gangster has a shortened form of the word.

hooligan The word is first recorded in 1898, and may derive from the Irish surname *Houlihan*. A music-hall song about a rowdy Irish family of this name was already current at that time.

hopscotch The children's game is so called because the players *hop* over lines *scotched* (scored or marked) on the ground.

horizon The word derives from the Greek phrase *horizōn kuklos*, 'limiting circle'. The horizon marks the visible limit of the circle of earth and sky.

horoscope The word for a star-sign forecast represents Greek *horoskopos*, 'ascendant birth sign', literally 'time observation', from *hōra*, 'time', 'hour', and *skopein*, 'to look at'.

hors d'œuvre The formal word for the 'starter' of a meal represents the French for what is literally 'outside the work'. The dish is so called as it is not part of the main course.

hospital In medieval times the word was used for a place where poor and sick people were cared for, and given *hospitality*. Only in the 16th century did the word take on its present, more specialized use. *Hospice* and *hostel* are related words. See also ♢hotel.

hostage The word originally applied not to a person but to a pledge to do something made by one side when handing a person over to another side. When the pledge was fulfilled, the person was handed back. The origin is either in Old French *hoste*, 'guest', 'host' (the person handed over is the guest, the recipient the host) or else in Late Latin *obsidatus*, 'hostage', literally 'sitting before'.

hotel The word derives from French *hôtel*, itself from Old French *hostel* (modern English *hostel*). The basic reference is to an establishment run by a *host* for the benefit of *guests*.

hubbub The word is of Irish origin and is intended to represent a confused shouting. A related word is Irish *abü*, 'for ever', a former battle cry.

huggermugger The word relating to confusion derives from some rhyming jingle that itself remains of uncertain origin. Middle English *hoder*, 'to huddle', has been suggested as a possible source.

human The word derives from Latin *humanus*, itself related to *homo*, 'man', and indirectly to English *humble* and Latin *humus*, 'earth'.

humbug The word first emerged in the 18th century, when it had the sense 'hoax', 'fraud'. Its origin is obscure. It may well have been a nonsense word, devised as a combination of *hum* and *bug*.

hurdle The word is of Germanic origin and ultimately goes back to an Indo-European root element denoting some kind of framework. Greek *kurtos*, 'basket', and Latin *cratis*, 'wickerwork', are related.

> **FALSE**
> **hurdle** So called because used to *herd* sheep in.

hurly-burly The word for a commotion evolved from the phrase *hurling and burling*, where *hurling* derives from *hurl* in its original sense of 'uproar' and *burling* is simply a rhyme.

> **FALSE**
> **hurly-burly** From the tumult of battle in former times, with agile men *hurling* spears and *burly* men wielding axes.

hurray The word used when cheering probably arose as an altered form of *huzzah*, itself possibly a sailors' cry used when hauling or *hoisting* a sail.

hurricane The word came into English from Spanish *huracán*, itself from Taino *hurakän*, based on *hura*, 'wind'. The present English spelling was probably influenced by *hurry* (in the now obsolete sense 'disturb').

> **FALSE**
>
> **hurricane** So called because it *hurries* the *canes*, or agitates the sugar plantations.

husband The original sense of the word is preserved to an extent in modern *husbandry*, relating to farming and the management of affairs. A *husband* was the master of a household, and the word represents a combination of Old Norse *hūs*, 'house', and *bōndi*, 'person who has a household', from *bōa*, 'to dwell'.

hussy The now derogatory term for a shameless or promiscuous woman represents an earlier colloquial pronunciation of *housewife*, its original sense in the 16th century.

hybrid The term for something that is a mixture of two others derives from Latin *hybrida* or *hibrida*, 'offspring', as originally applied to a cross between a tame sow and a wild boar, or to a person born of a Roman father and a foreign mother (or of a freeman and a slave). The Latin spelling *hybrida* may have been influenced by Greek *hubris*, 'excess', while in English the word has been associated with *half-breed*.

hydrogen The gas has a name of Greek origin literally meaning 'water producing', from *hudōr*, 'water', and *gennan*, 'to beget', 'to produce'. Water is produced by the combustion of hydrogen, ie, when it reacts with ⋈oxygen.

hysteria The basis of the word is Greek *hustera*, 'womb'. It was formerly believed that hysteria in women was produced by a disorder of the womb.

icicle The word looks like a diminutive of *ice* but is in fact a combination of *ice* and the obsolete word *ickle*, itself from Old English *gicel*, meaning 'icicle'. The literal sense is thus 'icicle of ice'.

iconoclast The word for someone who attacks the established or traditional order of things derives, through Latin. from Late Greek *eikonoklastēs*, literally 'image breaker', from Greek *eikōn*, 'icon', 'image', and *klastēs*, 'breaker'. The term literally and historically applies to members of a heretical movement within the Greek Orthodox Church who aimed to destroy icons and religious images in the 8th and 9th centuries.

idiosyncrasy The term for a person's special behaviour or mannerism derives from a Greek word literally meaning 'private mixture', from *idios*, 'private', and *sunkrasis*, 'mixture', 'temperament'.

ignoramus The word for an ignorant person derives from the legal Latin word meaning 'we do not know' (in the sense 'we take no notice of that'). The actual source of the word was the proper name *Ignoramus*, that of an incompetent lawyer in a play by the 17th-century dramatist George Ruggle.

ilk In the phrase 'of that *ilk*', loosely used to mean 'of that sort', the word derives from Old English *ilca*, 'same' (ultimately related to *like*). In Scottish use this refers to a person who is the proprietor or laird of the place of the same name, such as 'Guthrie of that *ilk*' (ie, Guthrie of Guthrie).

imbecile The word for a stupid or mentally weak person derives from Latin *imbecillus*. This literally means 'without a stick', from *in-*, 'not', and *bacillus*, a diminutive of *baculum*, 'walking stick'. An imbecile is thus a person 'without support' (mentally).

immaculate The literal sense of the word is 'without stain', from Latin *immaculatus*, representing *in-*, 'not', and *macula*, 'spot', 'blemish'.

immediate The word derives from Medieval Latin *immediatus*, representing the prefix *in-*, 'not' and *mediare*, 'to be in the middle'. Something *immediate* is direct, and does not need a mediator or a medium to have its effect.

imp The word was originally used for a young shoot or sapling, and only in medieval times for a young child. It represents Old English *impa*, 'bud', 'graft', referring to a shoot that is grafted onto an existing plant or tree. A young child is thus regarded as being 'grafted' into a particular family.

imply To *imply* something is to indicate it without spelling it out, in other words to 'involve' it in something larger. The literal sense is 'enfold', from Latin *implicare*, which also gave English *implicate*.

impression An *impression* is literally something 'pressed in', just as an *expression* is something 'pressed out'. If you make a good *impression*, you have given a good 'imprint' of yourself on the other person's mind.

impudent An *impudent* person is one who has no *pudency* or shame. The main part of the word represents Latin *pudens*, 'modest'.

inch The word for the twelfth part of a foot derives from Latin *uncia*, which also gave English *ounce* as the sixteenth part of a pound. The Latin word itself derives from *unus*, 'one', as it is a *unit*.

incongruous If something is *incongruous*, it does not accord with its surroundings or prevailing conditions. The ultimate source of the word is in Latin *congruere*, 'to agree', literally 'to fall together', from *com* (later *cum*), 'with', and the conjectured verb *gruere*, a form of *ruere*, 'to fall', 'to rush'.

individual The literal sense of the word is 'indivisible'. An *individual* thing or person is a single and complete one that cannot be divided into smaller units.

industry The word has its origin in Latin *industria*, 'diligence', literally 'building in', from *indu-*, 'in', and the root of *struere*, 'to arrange', 'to build'.

infant A young child or 'minor' is so called since he cannot speak or is legally not entitled to. The word derives from Latin *infans*, genitive *infantis*, 'not speaking', from *in-*, 'not', and a form of the verb *fari*, 'to speak'. See also ◊infantry.

infantry The term for soldiers who fight on foot, as distinct from cavalry, who are mounted, derives from Italian *infanteria*, from *infante*, 'boy', 'foot soldier'. The historical reference is to the noble youths who served on foot as pages to the mounted knights. See also ◊infant.

> **FALSE**
>
> **infantry** So called because first raised by an *infante* (king's son) of Spain or Portugal.

influence The source of the word is Medieval Latin *influentia*, a term literally meaning 'flowing in' that was used for a supposed emanation of power from the stars to human beings. See also ◊flu.

ink The word is all that remains from Late Latin *encaustum*, a term for a purplish-red ink that was itself adopted from Greek *enkauston*. This was a purple ink used by Greek and Roman emperors for their signatures. The word derives from Greek *enkaustos*, 'burnt in', from its corrosive effect.

inn The original basic meaning of the word was 'dwelling place', so that it was a place where people lived and that they were *in*.

innuendo The term for a suggestion (usually an unpleasant one) represents the Latin word meaning 'by hinting', literally 'by nodding in', from *in-*, 'in', and *nuere*, 'to nod'. The word was used in Medieval Latin to denote a parenthetical explanation in legal documents, as in the following: 'That knave your sonne—innuendo this deponentes sonne—made it'.

inoculate The verb was originally used for the grafting of a bud onto the trunk of a fruit tree. Hence its origin in Latin *inoculare*, from *in-*, 'in', and *oculus*, 'bud' (literally 'little eye'). When you are *inoculated* against a disease, you are 'grafted' or injected with its causative agent.

> **FALSE**
>
> **inoculate** From the fact that a disease is thus made *innocuous* or harmless.

insect The small creatures are so called because their bodies are divided into sections. The word thus represents Latin *insectum*, from *insecare*, 'to cut into', itself a translation of Greek *entomon*. (Hence *entomology* as the study of insects.)

inspiration The concept is of something that has been 'breathed into' you, from Latin *inspirare*, 'to breathe into'.

instigate The verb for bringing about an action by urging it derives from Latin *instigare*, literally 'to prick into', from *in-*, 'in', and *stigare*, 'to prick'.

instrument An *instrument*, whether musical or not, is a tool or implement for performing some action. It is thus something that has been constructed for this purpose. The origin is in Latin *instruere*, 'to equip', literally 'to build in'. This verb also gave *instruct*, in the sense of 'building in' a person's knowledge.

insulin The hormone injected by diabetics derives its name from New Latin *insula*, 'island'. It is so called as it is extracted from the *islands* of Langerhans in the pancreas of animals.

insult If you *insult* someone you offend or 'jump on' them. Hence the word's origin in Latin *insultare*, from *in-*, 'in', 'on', and *saltare*, 'to jump'.

intelligent The word derives from the Latin verb *intellegere*, 'to discern', literally 'choose between', from *inter-*, 'between', and *legere*, 'to choose'. An intelligent person can discriminate!

interest If you have an *interest* in something, it matters to you. Hence the origin of the word in Latin *interest*, 'it matters', from *interesse*, 'to differ', literally 'be between'.

> **FALSE**
>
> **interest** A corruption of *increase*. Money grows when earning *interest*.

interlude The word originally applied to a short light play inserted for relief between the acts of a long serious one. The literal sense is thus 'play between', from Medieval Latin *interludium*, representing *inter-*, 'between', and *ludus*, 'play'.

interval The word comes from Latin *intervallum*, which was the military term for a space between two ramparts, from *inter-*, 'between', and *vallum*, 'rampart'. The physical sense took on a temporal one in English in medieval times.

interview The origin is in Middle French *entrevue*, from the verb *s'entrevoir*, 'to see one another'. The English word came to be associated with words starting *inter-*, as if implying a difference *between* two *views*.

intestine Like many anatomical terms, the word came from Latin, with *intestinus*, 'internal', from *intus*, 'within'.

intimate The word derives from Latin *intimus*, 'very close friend', literally 'innermost', from *inter*, 'within'.

intransigent As applied to an obstinate person or attitude, the word derives from Spanish *los intransigentes*, 'the uncompromising ones', the nickname of an extreme left political party in the 19th century. The word itself literally means 'not carrying through', from *in-*, 'not', and a form of the Latin verb *transigere*, 'to carry across'.

intrigue The word is related to *intricate* and derives, through French and Italian, from the same Latin source, *intricare*, 'to entangle', literally 'put into tricks', from *in*, 'in', and *tricae*, 'tricks'. (The latter English and Latin words are related.)

invalid A sick or ill person is infirm and often physically weak. Hence the word's origin in Latin *invalidus*, from *in-*, 'not', and *validus*, 'strong'.

invest If you *invest* money, you give it a different status or 'form'. Hence the particular word, which derives from Medieval Latin *investire*, 'to clothe', literally 'put into clothing', from *in-*, 'in', and *vestis*, 'clothing' (English *vest* is related).

investigate If you *investigate* something, you track it down. The word derives from Latin *investigare*, 'to search after', literally 'to go on the track of', from *in-*, 'in', 'on', and *vestigare*, 'to track', 'to trace out'. (Compare English *vestige* in the sense 'trace'.)

invoice The document that accompanies goods and states terms of payment gets its name from the Old French plural word *envois*, 'messages', literally 'things sent'. (An English *envoy* is a diplomat *sent* to another country.)

iota The word for a very small amount derives from the name for the smallest letter in the Greek alphabet (equivalent to *i*). The particular meaning was adopted from the biblical phrase 'one jot or one tittle' (Matthew 5:18), in the original Greek *iōta hen ē mia keraia*. English *jot* is thus basically the same word.

island The word effectively repeats itself, since it represents Old English *īgland*, formed from a combination of *īg*, 'island', and *land*, 'land'. The *s* came in from *isle*, the other word for an island (usually a small one), from the identical Old French word that itself evolved from Latin *insula*.

ivory The hard white substance found in elephant tusks derives its name from Latin *ebur* in the same sense. The Latin word is related to Greek *elephas*, meaning both 'ivory' and 'elephant', so that the English word is itself indirectly related to the animal's name.

FALSE

island So called as it is an *eye* of land. Compare other natural features named from parts of the body, such as *head*land, *neck* of land, *tongue* of land, river *mouth*, *foot* of a hill, *arm* of the sea, etc.

jackdaw The bird was originally known as a *daw*, a word of uncertain origin. The name *Jack* was then added to this, as for *jackass*.

jacket The word evolved from Old French *jacquet*, itself from *jacque*, 'peasant', so called because nicknamed *Jacques*. The original jacket was like the short one that French peasants wore.

jade The semiprecious stone derives its name, via French and Italian, from obsolete Spanish *piedra de ijada*, literally 'stone of the flank', from *piedra*, 'stone', and *ijada*, 'flank' (Latin and English *ileum*). The stone was formerly believed to cure renal colic.

jail The word for a prison, formerly often spelt *gaol*, derives from Old French *jaiole*, 'cage', itself ultimately from Latin *cavea*, 'enclosure' (English *cage* and *cave*). The two spellings evolved from the two forms of the word in different parts of France, and *gaol* represents a former pronunciation with a hard *g* (ie, like *gale*).

jam The preserve probably takes its name from the other sense of *jam*, 'press tightly', referring to the squeezing of the fruit when it is being made. The basic word is probably imitative in origin, representing the sound made when squeezing or pressing something. A similar word is *champ*, used of food being munched noisily.

January The first month of the year is named after *Janus*, the Roman god of doorways, passages, and archways, traditionally depicted with two heads, one looking back and the other forward. January is the 'doorway' that leads out of the old year into the new.

jaunty The original meaning of the word was 'well-bred'. It evolved as a form of French *gentil*, 'noble', and is thus directly related to English *gentle*.

javelin The type of spear derives its name from a Celtic source, and may thus be related to Irish *gabhal* or Welsh *gafl*, both meaning 'fork'.

jaw The word is perhaps related to French *joue*, 'cheek', and derived from an earlier form of this. The present spelling may have been influenced by *chew*.

FALSE

javelin From Spanish *jabalina*, 'wild sow', related to *jabalí*, 'wild boar'. Javelins were used when hunting wild boar.

FALSE

jaw So called because it is used to *chew*.

jay The name of the bird is said to derive from the proper name *Gaius*. If so, it is similar to names such as ◊jackdaw, ◊magpie, and ◊robin.

jazz The origin of the word is obscure, but it probably evolved from black American slang and could have sexual connotations.

jealous The ultimate source of the word is in Greek *zēlos*, 'zeal'. The latter English word is thus related.

jeans The informal clothes are made from a cloth that developed from the cotton fabric known as *jean*. This was itself so called as it came from *Jene*, the Old French name of *Genoa*, Italy.

jeopardy To put something in *jeopardy* is to expose it to a risk. Hence the origin of the word in Old French *jeu parti*, literally 'divided game', implying an uncertain outcome. The *t* of the French phrase became *d* as it did in *card* from *carte* and *diamond* from *diamant*.

jersey The garment takes its name from *Jersey* in the Channel Islands, where the woollen sweaters worn by fishermen were knitted locally.

jet The hard black form of lignite takes its name, through French and Latin, from Greek *lithos gagatēs*, 'stone of Gagai', the latter being a town in Lycia, now in southwestern Turkey.

jewel The word for the gem or semiprecious stone derives from Old French *jourel*, itself probably from *jeu*, 'game', and ultimately from Latin *jocus*, 'jest', 'sport'. The implication is that jewels were regarded as playthings in Roman times.

jigsaw The puzzle is so called because the earliest types were made from a picture mounted on a sheet of wood that was cut into irregular pieces by a *jigsaw*, a saw with a fine blade that *jigs*, or moves rapidly up and down.

jimjams The colloqial expression for a state of nervous apprehension represents a whimsical reduplication of *jam*, in the sense 'stick', 'be unable to move'. The idea is of being petrified, or rooted to the spot.

jingo As occurring in the exclamation *by jingo*, the word was perhaps originally a euphemism for *Jesus*. The phrase was used in the patriotic chorus of a music-hall song of 1878: 'We don't want to fight, yet by Jingo! if we do, We've got the ships, we've got the men, and got the money too.' As a result, *jingoism* arose as a term for chauvinism, or belligerent patriotism.

jinx The word for someone or something that brings bad luck perhaps evolved from Greek *iunx*, 'wryneck'. The name of this bird was used in magic spells.

jockey The word for a professional horse rider comes from the proper name *Jock*, with the pet ending *-y* (as in *Jacky* from *Jack*). This was originally a general nickname for any young lad, much as *Mac* or *Jimmy* is today.

jodhpurs The riding breeches get their name from the town of *Jodhpur* in northwest India, where they were first worn in the days of the British Raj. The word happens to suggest *jumpers*, which is appropriate for a competitor in gymkhanas and other races and contests.

joss stick The phrase originally applied to a *stick* of incense burning before a *joss*, the idol of a Chinese god. A *joss* was so called, via pidgin English, from Portuguese *deos*, 'god'.

jot See ◊iota.

journal The word was originally used for a daily prayer book known as a *diurnal*. This related word means 'of the day', from Latin *diurnus*, the adjective of *dies*, 'day'. The word was later applied to a daily newspaper. Latin *dies* also lies behind English *diary*, which similarly has daily entries. (Modern French *journal* means both 'diary' and 'newspaper'.) See also ◊journey.

journey The word originally applied to a day's travel, but was later used for travel of any length. Its origin is thus in Old French *journee*, 'day'. Compare ◊journal.

jubilee The word for a 50th anniversary has its ultimate origin, through Latin and Greek, in Hebrew *yōbhēl*, 'ram's horn', referring to the horn blown in biblical times to proclaim the *jubilee* year. This was the 50th anniversary of the emancipation and restoration of the Jews, as decreed by God: 'A jubile (*sic*) shall that fiftieth year be unto you' (Leviticus 25:11). The word happens to suggest *jubilant*, but this is simply a coincidence.

judo The sport that developed from ◊jujitsu has a Japanese name of identical meaning, from *jū*, 'gentle', and *dō*, 'art'.

jug The word probably represents the proper name *Jug*, a former pet form of *Joan* or *Jenny*.

juggernaut The word now used for a huge lorry was adopted from the name of the idol of Krishna that is wheeled annually through the town of Puri, eastern India, on a chariot with gigantic wheels. (Worshippers are said to have thrown themselves under the wheels in the hope of going straight to paradise.) The idol's name itself means 'lord of the world', referring to Vishnu, chief of the Hindu gods.

jujitsu The Japanese system of unarmed self-defence has a name that literally means 'soft art', from *jū*, 'soft', 'yielding', and *jutsu*, 'art'. Compare ◊judo.

July The seventh month of the year was so named in honour of the Roman emperor *Julius* Caesar, who was born in this month. It is not clear how the name got its present pronunciation. It was formerly pronounced as the girl's name *Julie*.

jumbo The colloquial word for anything unusually large, such as a *jumbo* jet or *jumbo* crossword, derives from *Jumbo*, the large elephant exhibited by the American showman P T Barnum in the 1880s. Its own name is said to derive from Swahili *jumbe*, 'chief'.

jumper The knitted upper garment derives its name from obsolete *jump*, a type of man's jacket, itself coming from French *jupe*, in turn from Arabic *jubbah*, the word for a long cloth coat. (French *jupe* now means 'skirt'.)

June The sixth month of the year probably gets its name from the Roman goddess *Juno*, queen of the Olympian gods, to whom it was consecrated.

> **FALSE**
>
> **June** So named because dedicated to the Roman emperor *Junius*.

jungle The word represents Hindi *jangal*, itself from Sanskrit *jāngala*, 'desert'. The apparent contradiction (a desert has no vegetation, a jungle has plenty) is explained by the sense development: 'desert', 'scrubland', 'land overgrown with shrubs and bushes', 'dense forest'. Modern senses of the word, both literal and figurative, have probably become associated with *tangle*.

junket The word for the sweet dessert was originally used for a type of custard served on rushes. Hence its origin in a diminutive of Old French *jonc*, 'reed'.

junta The term for a group of people holding power after a *coup d'état* represents the Spanish word for 'council', itself from Latin *junctus*, 'joined'. In parts of Latin America the word is the regular one for an executive or legislative council.

K

kaleidoscope The name is that of an optical toy which reflects coloured pieces of paper in symmetrical shapes, so making attractive patterns. It was invented in 1817 by Sir David Brewster, who gave it a name based on *telescope* or *microscope*, the first part coming from Greek *kalos*, 'beautiful', and *eidos*, 'form'.

kaolin The type of fine white clay gets its name from the mountain in southeastern China where supplies for Europe were first obtained. The mountain's own name simply means 'high hill'.

karma The Buddhist term for fate or destiny represents the identical Sanskrit word meaning 'action', 'effect'.

kennel The word for the 'doghouse' evolved from Old French *chenil*, itself ultimately from Latin *canis*, 'dog'.

kestrel The type of small falcon gets its name from Old French *cressele*, 'rattle', a word itself from Latin *crepitare*, 'to crackle'. The reference is presumably to the bird's cry, rather than to the beating of its wings when hovering.

ketchup The piquant sauce has a Chinese name properly used for brine of pickled fish. Its origin is in *kōe*, 'seafood', and *tsiap*, 'sauce'.

kettle The word ultimately goes back to Latin *catillus*, a type of small pot, itself a diminutive of *catinus*, a deep pot for cooking food.

khaki The brownish-yellow colour used for army uniforms (since it matches the earth or land) derives, through Urdu, from Persian *khāk*, 'dust'. The word was imported into English from the uniforms worn by British troops in the Indian Mutiny (1857).

kibbutz The collective agricultural settlement in modern Israel derives its name from modern Hebrew *qibbūs*, 'gathering'.

kidnap The word originally applied to the stealing of children to be sent to America for work in the plantations. This meant that *kids* were *nabbed*. Hence the origin, with *nap* a form of *nab*.

kill The earliest meaning of the word was 'strike', 'beat'. It is Germanic in origin, and is related to *quell*.

kiss The word is of Germanic origin and is ultimately imitative of the sound made.

kit In the sense 'clothes', 'equipment', the word derives ultimately from Middle Dutch *kitte* 'tankard' (modern Dutch *kit*). The word was originally used in English for a wooden tub. The sense development then went: 'wooden tub for holding foodstuffs', 'box for holding foodstuffs', 'soldier's bag (*kir*bag) for his uniform and equipment', 'the clothes and equipment themselves'.

kitchen The word is (not surprisingly) related to *cook*, with both words ultimately going back to Latin *coquere*, 'to cook'.

kitten The word has its derivation in a North French form of Old French *chitoun* (modern French *chaton*), itself a diminutive of *chat*, 'cat'. The ending became English *-en* by association with other diminutive names, such as *chicken* and *maiden*.

knack The word for a 'dodge' or ingenious way of doing something probably evolved as an altered form of obsolete *knak*, a word of imitative origin meaning 'knock', 'rap'.

knickers The garment has a name that is a shortening of *knickerbockers*. These were originally loose-fitting breeches worn by Dutch immigrants to America. They take their name from Diedrich *Knickerbocker*, a fictitious Dutchman supposed to be the author of Washington Irving's *History of New York* (1809). The book had illustrations by George Cruikshank showing Knickerbocker wearing such breeches, and they were the direct inspiration for the name.

knit The word derives from Old English *cnyttan*, 'to tie in', from a root word related to *knot*. Both *knitting* and *knots* involve tying.

Koran The sacred book of Islam derives its name from Arabic *qur' ān*, 'reading', 'book'. Compare ◊Bible.

kosher The word properly applies to food prepared according to Jewish dietary laws. It is Yiddish in origin, from Hebrew *kāshēr*, 'right', 'proper'.

lackadaisical The word for a casual or lazy thing or person derives from *lackaday*, an expression of weariness, itself representing *alack the day*. *Alack* is based on *lack*, in the sense 'loss', and the implication is that something is missing.

laconic The term for something terse or concise derives from Greek *Lakōnikos*, 'Laconian', that is, Spartan. The Spartans were noted for the terseness of their speech (as well as the austerity of their way of life).

lacrosse The game originated in Canada. Hence its name, from Canadian French *le jeu de la crosse*, 'the game of the hooked stick'.

lady The present word is a 'smoothed' form of the original Old English *hlǣfdīge*, literally 'bread kneader', from words related to modern *loaf* and *dough*. The reference is to the occupation of the mistress of an Anglo-Saxon household. Compare ◊lord and see also ◊dairy.

lager The beer so called keeps well before being drunk. Hence its name, as a short form of German *Lagerbier*, 'beer for storing', from *Lager*, 'storehouse' (where it is *laid* up).

lair A *lair* is a place where an animal *lies*. The related words derive from an Indo-European source that also gave Latin *lectus*, 'bed', and (through German) English ◊lager.

lampoon The term for a satire in prose or verse ridiculing someone is said to derive from French *lampons*, 'let us drink', a word occurring as a refrain in songs and poems.

landscape The word originated as a term in painting among Dutch artists. It derives from Middle Dutch *lantscap*, 'region', the first part of this corresponding to English *land* and the second to the *-ship* in *township*.

language The word ultimately goes back, through Old French *langage*, to Latin *lingua*, 'tongue'. Language was speech long before it was writing!

lantern The word came into English as an alteration of Greek *lamptēr*, 'lamp'. This last English word is thus related. The word was formerly spelt *lanthorn* by association with *horn*, referring to the horn windows that lanterns once had.

lap The word was originally used for the lower edge of a garment. It is Old English in origin, and related to *lapel* ('little lap') and *lobe* (the lower part of the ear).

lapwing The bird is named for its erratic flight, from Old English words related to modern *leap* (fly up) and *wink* (fly sideways). The second part of the word was altered by association with *wing*.

> **FALSE**
>
> **lapwing** So called because it *flaps* its *wings*.

lariat The rope for lassoing or tethering animals represents Spanish *la reata*, 'the lasso', literally 'the retying rope', from *reatar*, 'to retie'.

larva The word for an insect in the grub state represents the identical Latin word meaning 'ghost'. The term was introduced by the 18th-century Swedish botanist Linnaeus, on the grounds that the future perfect insect is only dimly recognizable in this form.

laser The device amplifying an input of light to produce a concentrated beam derives its name as an acronym of '*l*ight *a*mplification by *s*timulated *e*mission of *r*adiation'. A similar device for amplifying microwaves is the *maser*, with the *m* representing '*m*icrowave'.

lass The word is of uncertain origin but is probably Germanic and may be related to German *lasch*, 'weak'. The reference could have been to a young woman who was 'weak' because unmarried.

> **FALSE**
>
> **lass** A shortening of *laddess*, the original feminine form of *lad*.

late The word goes back to an Indo-European root element that also gave English *let*, in the sense 'allow'. A person who is *late* has *let* the proper timing slip.

laugh The word goes back to an Indo-European root that is almost certainly imitative of a laugh. Other words for laughing are more obviously imitative in origin, such as *cackle*, *chuckle*, *giggle*, *guffaw*, *snicker*, *snigger*, and *titter*.

lavatory The word originally applied to a bowl or basin for washing the hands in. Hence its origin in Late Latin *lavatorium*, from Latin *lavare*, 'to wash'.

lawn The expanse of grass evolved from a glade or pasture known as a *laund*. This word came from Old French *lande*, a word related to English *land*. The French word was itself of Celtic origin, and was related to Old Welsh *lann*, 'enclosure' (from which modern *llan*, 'church', developed, as in Welsh place-names).

lay The word strictly speaking describes someone not in clerical orders. Its ultimate origin, through Old French and Church Latin, is in Greek *laos*, 'people'.

leap year The term for the year with one extra day (February 29) is so called since any fixed religious festival 'leaps' over the day following the one on which it fell the previous year. For example, Christmas Day in 1991 was on a Wednesday, but in 1992, a leap year, it was on Friday, having 'leapt' over Thursday.

lecher The word for a promiscuous or lewd man derives from Old French *lechier*, 'to lick', referring to the debauchery or gluttony associated with lechers.

left Old English *left* meant 'idle', 'weak'. Hence the use of the word for the hand that with most people is weaker than the right. The ultimate origin of the word is unknown.

legend In medieval times a *legend* was a story about the life of a saint. Such stories were recommended reading. Hence the origin of the word, in Medieval Latin *legenda*, 'things fit to be read', from Latin *legere*, 'to read'.

legion As now used of a large number of people, the word derives from the one used for a military unit of the Roman army that comprised thousands of *elected* infantry and supporting cavalry. Hence its origin in Latin *legere*, 'to choose', 'to levy'.

leisure The word comes from Old French *leisir*, ultimately from Latin *licere*, 'to be allowed', which also gave modern English *licence*. *Leisure* is the time when you can do as you wish.

lens The word is Latin for 'lentil', referring to the shape of most basic lenses.

Lent The period from Ash Wednesday to Easter Eve takes its name from Old English *lencten*, 'spring', itself so called since it is the time when the days *lengthen*.

leopard The animal is so called since it was originally believed to be a cross between a *lion* (Greek *leōn*) and a *pard* or panther (Greek *pardos*).

leper A sufferer from leprosy has, at the least, peeling skin. Hence the origin of the word in Greek *lepos*, 'scale'.

leprechaun The mischievous Irish elf gets his name from Irish *leipreachān*, itself ultimately from *lú*, 'small', and *corp* (Latin *corpus*), 'body'.

lesbian The term for a female homosexual derives from the name of the Greek island of *Lesbos*, where the lyric poetess Sappho was noted for her love poems to girls and women. (For this reason *Sapphic* is also sometimes used in the same sense.)

lettuce The salad plant probably gets its name from Old French *laitues*, the plural of *laitue*, itself ultimately from Latin *lac*, 'milk'. The reference is to the plant's milky juice.

lewd The original meaning of the word was 'lay', in the sense 'not clerical'. Such people were relatively uncouth and unlearned by comparison with the clergy. Hence the word's modern, stronger sense. It is likely that *lewd* and *lay* are related words.

libel In a legal sense, *libel* is the written or printed defamation of someone, as distinct from slander, which is verbal. Hence the origin of the term in Latin *libellus*, a diminutive of *liber*, 'book'. See also ◊library.

library   The word comes from Old French *librairie*, itself from Latin *librarius*, the adjective of *liber*, 'book'. (Modern French *librairie* means 'bookshop', while the word for 'library' is *bibliothèque*.)

lieutenant   Like most military ranks, the word is of Old French origin. It literally means 'holding the place', from *lieu*, 'place', and *tenant*, 'holding'. A lieutenant originally 'held the place' of a captain by acting for him.

limerick   The comic verse is said to take its name from a refrain, 'Will you come up to Limerick?', sung between extemporized nonsense verses at a party.

limousine   The luxurious car takes its name from an earlier type of car in which the roof over the rear seats projected over the driver's compartment, which was originally outside. The driver was thus obliged to wear a protective cloak, and this resembled the caped cloak worn by shepherds in the French province of *Limousin*. Hence the name.

liner   The passenger ship or aircraft is so called because it belongs to a particular shipping *line* or air*line*, itself running craft over a fixed *line* or route.

links   As applied to a golf course, the word derives from Old English *hlinc*, 'ridge', 'bank', referring to undulating sandy ground. (The word is also found in some place-names, such as Malvern *Link*, now a district of Great Malvern, Hereford and Worcester.)

linnet   The name of the bird goes back through French to Latin *linum*, 'flax'. The bird is so called because it feeds on flaxseeds.

liquorice   The confectionery is made from the dried root of the plant so called. Its name itself has evolved through French and Latin from Greek *glukurrhiza*, literally 'sweet root', from *glukus*, 'sweet' (English *glucose*) and *rhiza*, 'root' (English *rhizome*). The present form of the word has been influenced by *liquor*.

litany   Now often used for a long or tedious recital of things, the word properly refers to a type of prayer. Hence its ultimate origin, through French and Medieval Latin, in Late Greek *litaneia*, 'prayer', based on *litē*, 'entreaty'.

litter   Although now used for scattered waste paper and refuse, the word originally meant 'bed' (as it still does for animals and hence for their offspring). The source is ultimately in Latin *lectus*, 'bed', a word related to English *lie*. The present sense developed because the refuse is scattered like the straw in bedding.

livelong   In a phrase such as 'the whole livelong day', *livelong* was originally an emotional form of *long* meaning 'dear long', with the first part seen in old-fashioned *lief*. It was later taken to represent *live*, as if related to *lifelong*. Modern German has kept the original word, so that *den lieben langen Tag* is the equivalent of the English phrase above.

loaf   The original meaning of the word was simply 'bread', from a word ultimately akin to Latin *libum*, 'cake'. Other languages have related words still meaning 'bread', such as Russian *khleb* and Finnish *leipä*.

loft The original meaning of the word was 'air' or 'sky' (compare *aloft* and the German *Luftwaffe*, literally 'air weapon'). It was first used for an upper room in medieval times. The word *lift* is related.

lollipop The sweet on a stick is so called from the northern dialect word *lolly* meaning 'tongue' (which *lolls* from the mouth) and *pop*, since you 'pop' it into and out of your mouth.

loo The precise origin of the word meaning 'lavatory' remains uncertain, but it may derive from the (now old-fashioned) French phrase *lieux d'aisance*, literally 'places of ease'.

lord The present word is a 'smoothed' form of the Old English original, which was *hlāford*, itself a simplified form of *hlāfweard*, literally 'bread keeper', from *hlāf*, 'bread' (modern *loaf*) and *weard*, 'protector' (modern *ward*). The lord was the master of the Anglo-Saxon household and the forerunner of the modern 'breadwinner'. Compare ◊lady.

> **FALSE**
>
> **lord** From Old English *hlāford*, representing *hlāf*, 'bread' (English *loaf*), and *ord*, 'source'. The Anglo-Saxon lord was the source of bread in his household. Compare modern *breadwinner*.

lorry The origin of the vehicle's name is uncertain, but it may derive from a northern dialect word *lurry*, meaning 'to pull'. The word is first recorded in the north of England.

love In its sense of 'no score' in a game, the word derives from the phrase 'for love', meaning that the player has played 'for nothing'. Compare *labour of love*, as work done with no financial reward.

luck The word is Germanic in origin from a source that also gave modern German *Glück* in the same sense. The ultimate source is uncertain, but there may be a link with Greek *lugos*, 'pliant twig' or Latin *luxare*, 'to dislocate'. The idea is of something pliable or changeable.

luggage The word arose from *lug*, 'to carry' (especially something heavy), presumably as a whimsical alteration of *baggage*, which is the regular word in American English and has equivalents in other European languages (such as French *bagages*).

lunatic The former word for a mentally deranged person derives, through French, from Latin *lunaticus*, the adjective of *luna*, 'moon'. At one time it was believed that madness was caused by the changing phases of the moon (when someone was 'moonstruck'). See also ◊mad.

lunch The precise origin of the word is uncertain. It is probably a short form of *luncheon*, which was itself an altered form of *nuncheon*, a word meaning literally 'midday drink', from Middle English *noneschench*, representing *none*, 'midday' (modern *noon*), and *schench*, 'drink'.

lurk The word probably evolved as a form of *lour* (meaning 'be menacing'), with the final -*k* denoting a repeated or habitual action, as it does in *talk* (from *tale* or *tell*).

luscious The word was recorded in the 15th century as both *lucius* and *licius*. It is not certain where these came from, but they may be shortened forms of *delicious*.

FALSE

luscious A shortened form of *delicious*, influenced by *luxurious*.

---

lynch The verb used for giving a person a summary punishment has its origin in the surname *Lynch*, probably (though not conclusively) that of Charles *Lynch* (1736–1796), a Virginia justice of the peace who presided over a number of unofficial courts set up to punish lawlessness.

lynx The catlike animal is said to have very keen sight. Hence its name, from an Indo-European root element that gave Greek *leukos*, 'white', and English *light*. (Hence also *lynx-eyed* in the sense 'sharp-sighted'.)

macabre The word for something ghastly or grim derives from the French phrase *danse macabre*, 'dance of death'. This is probably an alteration of *Danse Macabë*, 'Maccabean Dance', translating Medieval Latin *Chorea Maccabaeorum*. The reference would perhaps be to a representation of the slaughter of the Maccabees (a Jewish family of patriots) in a miracle play.

macaroni The word is a dialect form of Italian *maccaroni*, itself probably from Greek *makaria*, a type of food made from barley. English *macaroon* has the same origin, although a quite different type of food.

macedoine The mixture of vegetables or fruits has a French name meaning 'Macedonian'. The reference is said to be to the mixed nationalities found in Macedonia.

machine The word goes back through French and Latin to Doric Greek *makhana*, 'pulley'. The ultimate source is in an Indo-European root element meaning 'power' that also gave English *may* and *might*. *Mechanical* is more directly related.

mad The ultimate origin of the word is in an Indo-European root element meaning 'change' that also gave English *mutate*. For the 'changing' aspect, see also ◊lunatic.

madrigal The term for a 16th-century amatory or pastoral song derives from Medieval Latin *matricalis*, the adjective of *matrix*, 'womb'. The implication is presumably that the song or poem comes 'straight from the heart'. Its pastoral aspect seems to have been suggested by an association with Greek *mandra*, 'sheepfold', 'stable'.

magazine The word goes back through French and Italian to Arabic *makhazīn*, the plural of *makhzan*, 'storehouse'. Magazines are 'storehouses' of information (and entertainment). The rifle *magazine* that contains cartridges is of the same origin.

magenta The purplish red colour is so called from the dye that produces it. This was discovered soon after the Battle of *Magenta* in Italy in 1859 (in which the Austrians were defeated by the French and the Sardinians). The allusion is to the colour of the blood spilt.

magnet The iron-attracting device takes its name from Greek *ho magnēs lithos*, 'the Magnesian stone', referring to *Magnesia*, the ancient coastal district in eastern Greece that is rich in mineral deposits.

magnificent The word literally means 'more splendid', from Latin *magnificentior*, a comparative form of *magnificus*, 'great in deeds', from *magnus*, 'great', and *facere*, 'to do'.

magpie The bird was originally simply *pie* (as it still is in French), said to be so called because it collects miscellaneous objects, like the mixed ingredients of a *pie*. The proper name *Mag*, a pet form of *Margaret*, was then added. Compare ◊jackdaw and ◊robin.

mail The word for the post (letters and parcels) derives from its container, Old French *male*, 'bag'. The word is not related to *mail* the armour or the *mail* of *blackmail*, which was a form of payment.

major The word for the military rank is short for *sergeant major*, which was formerly a much higher rank than it is now. The second word of this represents Latin *major*, 'greater'. For the first, see ◊sergeant.

malaria The disease is caused by the bite of an infected mosquito. It was previously thought, however, that it was caused by the gases given off from marshes. Hence the origin of the word in Italian *mal'aria*, a shortened form of *mala aria*, 'bad air'.

malinger The verb used of someone pretending to be ill derives from French *malingre*, 'sickly', itself perhaps from *mal*, 'bad', and Old French *haingre*, 'feeble'. The latter word is probably related to German *hager*, 'gaunt', 'thin'.

mammal The term for an animal that suckles its young derives from Latin *mamma*, 'breast', itself a word related to *mama* (the child's word for 'mother') and so to *mummy*.

mammoth The species of extinct elephant derives its name from Russian *mammot* (now *mamont*), a word of Siberian origin said to mean 'devourer', because it was supposed to burrow into the earth by eating it. Remains of mammoths have been discovered buried in the ice in Siberia.

mandarin The type of orange is probably so called since its colour is the same as that of the costumes worn by *mandarins*, the Chinese officials. Their own name comes from Sanskrit *mantra*, 'counsel'.

mandrake The plant formerly believed to have magic powers probably derives its name from Medieval Latin *mandragora*, a word ultimately of Greek origin that is its alternative English name today. The source of this is not known. It was altered to *mandrake* because its forked root, from which a narcotic was prepared, looked like a *man*, while *drake*, as an old form of *dragon*, suggested its magical powers.

manger The word for a feeding trough for cattle comes from Old French *mangier* (modern French *manger*), 'to eat'.

mania The word comes from Late Latin, from the identical Greek word meaning 'madness'. English *mind* and *mental* are indirectly related.

manna The word sometimes used for a windfall ('*manna* from heaven') strictly refers to the miraculous food that sustained the Israelites in the wilderness. It ultimately derives from Hebrew *mān*, the name of the exudation of the tree *Tamarix gallica* (a species of tamarisk). The word has been traditionally derived from Aramaic *mān hū*, 'what is it?', with reference to the Bible story: 'And when the children of Israel saw it, they said one to another, It is manna: for they wist not what it was' (Exodus 16:15).

manor The word comes from Old French *maneir*, 'to dwell', itself from Latin *manere*, 'to remain'. A *manor* is a dwelling-place. *Mansion* is a related word, as is modern French *maison*, 'house'.

manual The word for a book of instructions derives ultimately from Latin *manualis*, the adjective of *manus*, 'hand'. A *manual* is thus a *hand*book.

manure The word was originally a verb meaning 'to till', in the sense of preparing agricultural land to grow crops. The word then passed to animals' dung, which is used as a fertilizer when tilling. The word itself is actually a form of *manoeuvre*, a French word literally meaning 'work with the hand'.

map The word derives from Medieval Latin *mappa mundi*, literally 'sheet of the world', from *mappa*, 'cloth', a word that in classical Latin meant 'napkin'. (The *nap-* of this English word is related to the Latin word.)

march In the sense 'walk in step', the word has its origin in Old French *marchier*, 'to tread' (giving modern French *marcher*, 'to walk'), itself probably of Germanic origin and related to modern English *mark*. When soldiers *mark* time they move their feet as in *marching* but do not advance.

> **FALSE**
>
> **march** The verb derives from Welsh *march*, 'horse', so that the original sense was 'ride on horseback'.

March The third month of the year derives its name from Latin *Martius*, the adjective of *Mars*, genitive *Martis*, the name of the Roman god of war. In the Roman calendar, March was the first month, so a 'tough' start to the year was appropriate!

margarine The butter substitute takes its name from *margaric* acid, the glyceride of which was at one time thought to be present in animal fats (as constituents of margarine). The acid itself was so called from Greek *margaron*, 'pearl', for its pearly colour.

mark All senses of the word (including the German coin and the spot or stain) are probably ultimately related to the Germanic word meaning 'border' that gave all the meanings. English *margin*, directly from Latin *margo*, genitive *marginis*, is also related.

market The word derives from Latin *mercari*, 'to trade', with this also the source of English *merchant* and *mercenary*.

marmalade The preserve now usually made from oranges or lemons was originally made from quinces. Hence the origin of the word in Portuguese *marmelada*, the adjectival form of *marmelo*, 'quince', itself, via Latin, from Greek *melimēlon*, literally 'honey apple', from *meli*, 'honey', and *mēlon*, 'apple'.

FALSE

marmalade From the proverbial remark by a servant in a Scottish household, who seeing his mistress enjoy the new orange jam he brought to the table, daily asked 'Mair, ma lady?' ('More, my lady?').

---

maroon The word derives from American Spanish *cimarrón*, 'wild' (literally 'dwelling on peaks', from Spanish *cima*, 'peak'). As a noun, *cimarron* was the word for a runaway slave in the West Indies, who lived a wild and isolated life in the hills and forests. A person *marooned* on a desert island led a similar life.

marshal The name of the high military rank was originally a word for an official who was simply a groom. It comes, through French, from Old High German *marahscalc*, itself from *marah*, 'mare', and *scalc*, 'servant'. Compare ◊constable.

martinet The word for a strict disciplinarian derives from the name of General Jean *Martinet*, a French drillmaster of the 17th century.

martyr A *martyr* is literally a *witness* (ie, to Christ), with the word deriving from Late Greek *martus* in this sense. The Greek word itself comes from an Indo-European root that is also found in English *memory*.

mascot The word for a person or thing that is believed to bring good luck has its origin in Provençal *mascotto*, 'charm', itself from *masco*, 'witch'.

masochism The term for sexual pleasure derived from having pain or humiliation inflicted on one derives from the name of Leopold von Sacher *Masoch* (1836–1895), the Austrian novelist who described it. Compare ◊sadism, its opposite.

mass The name of the Roman Catholic service derives from Church Latin *missa*, ultimately from Latin *mittere*, 'to send'. The reference is said to be to the priest's words at the end of the service: '*Ite, missa est*', 'Go, it is the dismissal'.

mastiff The name of the large and powerful breed of dog derives, through French, from Latin *mansuetus*, 'tamed', literally 'accustomed to the hand', from *manus*, 'hand', and *suetus*, 'accustomed'.

matador The term for the principal bullfighter in a bullfight, deputed to kill the bull, is the Spanish for 'killer', from *matar*, 'to kill', a word related to the *mate* of ◊checkmate in chess.

mathematics The word represents Greek *mathēmatikos*, the adjective of *mathēma*, 'science', literally 'something learnt'.

mattress The word ultimately goes back to Arabic *al-maṭrah*, 'mat', 'cushion', literally 'the place where something is thrown', from *ṭaraḥa*, 'to throw'.

maudlin The word used to describe someone who is sentimentally tearful, usually when drunk, derives from the name of Mary *Magdalene*, who frequently appears in paintings as a tearful penitent.

Maundy money The money distributed by the sovereign on *Maundy* Thursday (the one before Easter) takes its name from the day, itself so called from the first word of a Latin prayer quoting the words of Christ after washing his disciples' feet: '*Mandatum novum do vobis*', 'A new commandment I give unto you' (John 13:34).

maverick Now used for an unorthodox member of a group, the word originally applied to a stray calf on a North American ranch, especially one that was unbranded. The word derives from the name of Samuel A. *Maverick* (1803–1870), a Texas rancher who did not brand his cattle.

May The fifth month of the year takes its name from the Roman goddess *Maia*, identified with the Greek goddess who was the mother of Hermes.

mayhem The word is Germanic in origin from a source that also gave *maim*.

FALSE

May So named because dedicated to the Roman senators, from Latin *maiores*, 'elders'.

---

maze The word derives from an identical but now obsolete verb meaning 'stupefy', 'daze'. This is itself closely related to *amaze*, which also formerly had this sense.

meadow The word represents Old English *mædwe*, itself from *mǣd*, the source of the now poetic *mead*. A directly related word is *mow*.

meal The original sense of the word was 'measure', hence the set ('measured') time when a meal is eaten and the meal itself. The 'measure' sense has survived in *piecemeal*, meaning 'bit by bit', literally 'measured in pieces'. See also ▷meat.

meander If you *meander*, you wander in different directions, like the winding course of the River *Maeander* (now the *Menderes* in southwestern Turkey). Hence the source of the word.

meat The original meaning of the word was 'food' in general (hence 'meat and drink'). The word is related to *mete*, in that food is *meted* or measured out at a meal. See also ▷meal itself, which similarly involves measuring.

medal The word is basically an alternative form of *metal*, since this is what medals are usually made of. The source of both words is ultimately Latin *metallum*, 'mine'.

mediocre The source of the word is Latin *mediocris*, 'moderate', literally 'halfway up the mountain', from *medius*, 'middle', and *ocris*, 'rugged mountain' (related to Welsh *ochr*, 'side').

melancholy The origin of the word is in Greek *melankholia*, literally 'black bile', from *melas*, 'black', and *kholē*, 'bile'. Melancholy was at one time thought to have resulted from too much 'black bile', *bile* being one of the bodily 'humours' or fluids. (Yellow bile caused anger.)

melodrama The term originally applied to a stage play with appropriate music. Hence its origin in a combination of Greek *melos*, 'song', and *drâma*, 'drama'.

mentor A counsellor or adviser is so called from the name of *Mentor*, the friend of Odysseus in classical mythology who was the adviser of the young Telemachus. His name can be loosely interpreted as *minder*, a word that *mentor* happens to resemble.

menu The origin of the 'bill of fare' is in the identical French word meaning 'small', from the phrase *menu de repas*, 'details of a meal'.

meretricious The word, now used to describe something showily or superficially attractive, has its origin in Latin *meretricius*, the adjective of *meretrix*, 'prostitute', itself based on *merere*, 'to earn money'.

mesmerize As a former synonym for 'hypnotize', the word derives from the name of Friedrich Anton *Mesmer* (1733–1815), the Austrian doctor who developed a theory of 'animal magnetism' and who was famous for his seances. (He did not actually practise hypnotism, however.)

message The literal sense of the word is 'something sent', from Latin *missus*, 'sent', a form of the verb *mittere*, 'to send'. Compare ⟩mass.

meteor The word derives from Greek *meteōron*, 'raised up', from the intensive prefix *meta-* and *aeirein*, 'to raise'. The word was originally used for any atmospheric phenomenon, not just 'shooting stars', and has preserved this sense in *meteorology* as the science of the atmosphere ('weather').

mettle The word arose as a spelling variant of *metal*, adopted in order to distinguish its non-literal senses (as in 'on one's *mettle*') from the literal ones of the more common word.

mews The name for a short and now sometimes fashionable street was adopted from *The Mews*, the royal stables at Charing Cross, London. These were so called as they had been built on the site of hawks' *mews*, a *mew* being a place of confinement for hawks when they were moulting. The word itself comes from Old French *muer*, 'to moult', related to English *mutate*.

midget The word for a small person arose in the 19th century as a development of *midge*, a small fly.

midriff The term for the middle part of a person's body evolved from Old English *midhrif*, from *midd*, 'mid'-, and *hrif*, 'belly'. It was originally the word for what is now more commonly known as the *diaphragm* (inside the body).

> **FALSE**
>
> **midriff** From *mid*, 'middle', and *rift*, 'split', since it divides the two halves of the body in the middle.

midwife The origin of the word is in Old English *mid*, 'with' (modern German *mit*), and *wif*, 'woman'. A midwife is a *woman* who is *with* the mother at the birth of her child. Compare ▷obstetrics.

mile The word ultimately comes from Latin *mille passuum*, 'a thousand paces', the Roman mile that was about 142 yards (130 m) shorter than the present standard mile of 1760 yards (1.609 km).

> **FALSE**
>
> **midwife** From Old English *mēd*, 'reward', 'price' (former English *meed*), and *wīf*, 'woman' (modern *wife*). The *midwife* was thus originally a woman of value.

milliner The now rather dated word for a seller of women's hats originally applied to a seller of fancy wares generally. The earlier form of the word was *Milaner*, since *Milan* was at one time famous for its fancy goods.

million The word literally means 'big thousand', as it arose from early Italian *millione*, from *mille*, 'thousand', with the augmentative ('big') suffix *-one* (as in modern Italian *ballone*, 'balloon', literally 'big ball').

mimosa The plant has a name of New Latin origin based on Latin *mimus*, 'mime'. It is so called as it is sensitive to touch, and so *mimes* the reaction of animals.

mincemeat *Mincemeat*, which is now usually sweet, was originally *minced meat*, which was savoury, and consisted of pieces of *meat* that had been *minced* or cut up small. The same development has occurred with *mince pies*, which now contain *mincemeat* (dried fruit and the like) but which earlier were pies with *minced meat*.

mine The explosive device is so called since it was originally laid underground in a *mine* (in the sense of an excavation). Mines are now as much submarine as subterranean, however.

miniature The word for something very small originally applied to an illumination in a manuscript. Hence the strict source of the word in *minium*, 'red lead', which was used in such illuminations. When the word was extended to apply to small portraits ('miniatures'), however, the sense was influenced by *mini-*, 'small' (as in modern *minimum*).

> **FALSE**
>
> **miniature** From the *min-* root denoting smallness, as in *minimal* and *minute*.

minister The government department head, the diplomat, and the clergyman now *minister* to others mostly at a lower level. Originally, however, a *minister* was a subordinate official appointed to serve those in higher authority. Hence the source of the word in Latin *minister*, 'servant', related to *minus*, 'less'.

mint As the place where coins are made the word has its origin in Latin *moneta*, meaning both *mint* and ▷money (which see for the rest of the story).

minute The sixtieth part of an hour is so called as it is a *minute* (small) division. More precisely the word comes from the Latin phrase *pars minuta prima*, 'first minute part'. The *second*, when it came later, was thus the *pars minuta secunda*, 'second minute part'. The divisions were originally those of a circle, rather than those of an hour.

miracle A *miracle* is an object of wonder, as its name implies, from Latin *mirari*, 'to wonder', 'to look at'. English *admire*, *mirage*, and *mirror* are related words.

miscellaneous The word simply means 'mixed', from Latin *miscellus* in this sense, itself from *miscere*, 'to mix'.

mischief The origin of the word is in Old French *meschief*, 'disaster', itself from *mes-*, corresponding to English *mis-* in the sense 'wrong', and a verbal form of *chef*, 'head'. *Mischief* is thus something that has 'come to a head' in the wrong way.

miser A *miser* is literally a *miserable* person. Hence the origin of the word, in the identical Latin word meaning 'wretched', 'unfortunate'.

miss As applied to a young woman, the word is a short form of *mistress*, which is itself a feminine form of *master* (as if 'master-ess'). (*Mrs* is an abbreviation of *mistress*, and *Mr* of *mister*, a form of *master*. *Ms* is an artificaly devised abbreviation of either *Miss* or *Mrs*.)

mistletoe The parasitic plant derives its name from Old English *mistel*, the original word for it (later *missel*, now obsolete), and *tān*, 'twig'. The original name is said to derive from a word meaning 'dung' (German *Mist*), referring to the sticky white berries, which resemble birds' droppings. (They were used for making birdlime, to 'glue' small birds to the branch.)

mitten The direct source of the word is in Old French *mitayne*. This is said to represent the Roman *medietana muffula*, a type of skin-lined glove cut off in the middle, with the first word from Latin *mediatas*, 'half'. If so, a *mitten* is essentially a 'half-glove'.

mob The word is a 17th-century shortening of *mobile*, itself representing Latin *mobile vulgus*, 'the fickle crowd', a phrase found in classical authors. The original sense of *mob* was 'the common people', 'the rabble', regarded in Roman times as capable of changing its allegiance at any time.

modest If you are *modest*, you show *moderation* in your opinion of yourself. The two words are related, and the actual source of the word is in Latin *modestus*, 'keeping due measure', 'restrained'.

mogul The word for an important or powerful person derives from *Mogul* as the title of one of the Muslim emperors of India (1526–1857), each of which was also known as the 'Great *Mogul*'. The title itself derives from the Persian form of *Mongol*.

moist The word goes back through French to a source ultimately related to Latin *mucidus*, 'musty', itself from *mucus*, 'mucus'. English *musty* and *mucus* are thus also related.

molecule The term for the simplest unit of a chemical compound derives from New Latin *molecula*, a diminutive of Latin *moles*, 'mass' (a word that gave English *mole* in the sense 'breakwater').

mollusc The ultimate source of the word is in Latin *mollis*, 'soft', since all molluscs (slugs, snails, mussels, octopuses, etc) have soft bodies. The scientific name *Mollusca* was devised for this group of invertebrates by Linnaeus in 1758.

moment A *moment* is literally a small *movement* of time, and both words ultimately derive from Latin *movere*, 'to move'.

monarch The word has its origin in Greek *monarkhos'*, literally 'ruling alone', from *monos*, 'alone', and *arkhein*, 'to rule'. The implication is that the ruler's power is absolute.

Monday The second day of the week has a name of Old English origin meaning 'moon day', translating the day's Latin name, *lunae dies*. Monday (a workday) thus follows Sunday (a holiday) as night (and the moon) follows day (and the sun).

mongrel The dog of mixed breed derives its name from a root word related to modern *mingle* and *among*. The *-rel* ending denotes a bad quality, as in *doggerel*, *scoundrel*, and *wastrel*.

monk Monks traditionally lead a solitary life. Hence the origin of the word in Greek *monos*, 'alone'. *Monastery* is a related word, as therefore is its derivative, *minster*.

monkey The name of the animal is of uncertain origin. However, in a 15th-century Low German version of the *Roman de Renart*, the medieval French verse tales with animals as characters, the son of Martin the ape is called *Moneke*, and this may be the source of the present word. (It is itself perhaps a Flemish diminutive of some personal name.)

> **FALSE**
>
> **monkey** A corruption of *manikin* in the sense 'little man'.

monopoly The term for the exclusive possession of a trading right derives, through Latin, from Greek *monopōlion*, literally 'selling alone', from *monos*, 'alone', and *pōlein*, 'to sell'.

monster The word derives from Latin *monstrum*, 'portent', since a *monster* is a *demonstration* of something bad or evil.

month The word is directly related to *moon*, since the duration of a month represents the time taken for the moon to circle the earth. In some languages the words for 'month' and 'moon' coincide exactly, as in Czech *měcíc*, Estonian *kuu*, and Turkish *ay*.

moose The North American deer has an Algonquian name related to Narraganset *moosu*, 'he strips', referring to the animal's habit of stripping bark from trees when feeding.

moratorium The term for an official postponement of something, or the suspension of an activity, represents the New Latin word formed as a noun from the Late Latin adjective *moratorius*, 'dilatory', itself from Latin *mora*, 'delay'.

morgue The word for a mortuary comes from *le Morgue*, a famous mortuary in Paris where people found dead were laid out for identification. The origin of its own name is uncertain, but French *morgue* means 'haughtiness', and the word could originally have applied to a room or building where prisoners were examined on entry. It then passed to the mortuary, where dead people were similarly examined.

mortgage The term derives from the identical French word literally meaning 'dead pledge', from *mort*, 'dead', and *gage*, 'pledge'. A mortgage was originally a pledge of land under which the creditor took the rents and profits for himself, so that it was 'dead' (profitless) to the debtor. It thus differed from a 'live pledge' (*vif gage*), under which the rents and profits gradually reduced the debt.

mosquito The word is Spanish in origin, and is a diminutive of *mosca*, 'fly'.

muffin The type of round flat cake may have a name of Germanic origin, deriving from Low German *muffen*, the plural of *muffe*, 'cake'.

mug The slang use of the word to mean 'face' probably evolved from the *mug* that is the drinking vessel, since such vessels were formerly often fashioned in the form of a grotesque face. The word for the vessel itself is probably Scandinavian in origin, but its ultimate source is uncertain.

> **FALSE**
>
> **mosquito** From the name of the *Mosquito* Coast, Nicaragua, where these insects are abundant.

> **FALSE**
>
> **muffin** A corruption of French *mou pain*, 'soft bread'.

mumps A *mump* was originally the word for a sulky grimace or 'face'. The disease is so called since the sufferer's swollen neck glands produce such an appearance.

murder The word ultimately derives from an Indoeuropean root element denoting death that is also found in *mortal* and *mortuary*.

muscat The strong sweet wine derives its name, through French, from Old Provençal *musc*, 'musk', referring to its *musky* flavour.

> **FALSE**
>
> **muscat** The grape that gives the wine of this name is so called from Latin *musca*, 'fly', since it attracts these insects.

muscle The word goes back, through French, to Latin *musculus*, a diminutive of *mus*, 'mouse'. Some muscles, such as the biceps, look like a little mouse under the skin, especially when moving. Compare ◊mussel.

museum In ancient Greece a *museum* was a building devoted to learning and the arts. As such, it was a 'home of the *Muses*'. Hence its name, which was first used in England in its modern sense for the Ashmolean Museum, Oxford, founded in 1683.

mushroom The word for the edible fungus derives from Old French (and modern) *mousseron*, itself from Late Latin *mussirio*, genitive *mussirionis*. The source of this is uncertain.

music The word goes back through French and Latin to Greek *mousikē tekhnē*, 'art of the *Muses*', that is, of the Greek goddesses of literature, music, and dance (and later of all intellectual pursuits).

> **FALSE**
>
> **mushroom** From French *mousseron*, in turn based on *mousse*, 'moss', where *mushrooms* grow. Compare French *champignon*, 'mushroom', from *champ*, 'field'.

mussel The bivalve derives its name from Latin *musculus*, a diminutive of *mus*, 'mouse'. The colour and shape of the shellfish resemble those of a mouse. Compare ◊muscle.

mustang The small breed of wild or half-wild horses, found in the southwestern USA, derives its name from Mexican Spanish *mestango*, from *mesta*, a term for a group of wild animals, itself from Latin *mixta*, 'mixed'.

mustard The word derives, through Old French (and modern) *moutarde*, from Latin *mustum*, 'must'. The reference is to the original condiment, which was made by making the ground seeds into a paste with *must* (the juice of newly pressed grapes).

> **FALSE**
>
> **mustard** From Spanish *mastuerzo*, 'cress', a plant with a hot taste, like that of *mustard* seeds.

nadir The word for the lowest point of something derives from an Arabic astronomical term: *nazīr as-samt*, 'opposite the zenith', that is, opposite the highest point. See also ⟰zenith.

naïve The word derives from Old French *naif*, 'native'. A *naïve* person is artless and unsophisticated, one who behaves in a way that is *natural*, who acts according to his *native* feelings, and who has an *innate* sense of what to do. All these words are related.

namby-pamby The word, used of a weakly sentimental thing or person, has its origin in a reduplicated form of the first syllable of the name of *Amb*rose Philips, an 18th-century poet ridiculed by other writers of his day. (He wrote pastoral poems and verses to babies.) The phrase itself was presumably based on *handy-dandy* or some similar jingle.

nanny In whatever sense the word is used, as for a children's nurse or a female goat, the ultimate origin is in the pet form of the name *Anne*. (Compare *billy*-goat for a male goat.)

napalm The incendiary liquid used in firebombs and the like takes its name from the first syllables of *naphthene* and *palmitate*, two of its chemical constituents.

nape The word for the back of the neck is of uncertain origin. It is not related to *nuque*, the French word for it. (This itself derives ultimately from Arabic *nuqa*, 'spinal marrow'.)

> **FALSE**
>
> **nape** So called from the *nap* or downy coating of fine hair growing on this part of the neck.

nasturtium The plant has a pungent smell. Hence its name, which literally means 'nose-twister', from Latin *nasus*, 'nose', and *tortus*, 'twisted'. (Latin *nasturtium* was originally the name of a type of cress.)

naughty The word originally meant 'poor', 'needy'. It thus represents the adjectival form of *naught*, 'nothing', itself from Old English *nāwiht*, literally 'no thing', from *nā*, 'no', and *wiht*, 'thing', 'person' (old-fashioned *wight*).

neck The word ultimately derives from an Indo-European root element meaning 'bump' which also gave Irish *cnoc*, 'hill' (found in Irish place-names beginning *Knock*-). It also gave Old English *hnecca*, 'neck', though a more common Old English word for this part of the body was *heals* (modern German *Hals*).

nectar The original literal sense of the word was probably 'triumphant over death', from elements found in Greek *nekros*, 'death', and Latin *trans*, 'across'. In classical mythology, nectar was the drink of the gods, who were immortal. (Their food was *ambrosia*, from Greek *ambrotos*, 'immortal'.)

neighbour The word has evolved from Old English *nēahbūr*, literally 'near dweller', from *neāh*, 'near' (modern *nigh*), and *būr*, 'farmer', 'dweller' (modern *boor*).

nerd The slang word for a feeble or stupid person, also spelt *nurd*, may perhaps have evolved as an altered form of *nut*, which can have a similar sense.

ness The word for a promontory or headland, found in such place-names as Shoebury*ness*, Foul*ness*, and Skeg*ness*, means 'nose'. The words are related, and have a common source in Indo-European *nas*.

nest The word is Old English in origin and has a basic sense 'place to settle down'. Words of related origin are *beneath* and *sit*.

neuralgia The word literally means 'nerve pain', from a combination of Greek *neuron*, 'nerve', and *algos*, 'pain'.

neutral The word has its origin in Latin *neuter*, 'neither one nor the other', itself from a blend of *ne*, 'not', and *uter*, 'either of two'. English *neuter* comes from the same source. In a linguistic sense, a *neuter* noun (as in Latin or German) is one that is neither masculine nor feminine.

newfangled The word now means 'unnecessarily modern', but originally meant 'liking new things'. Hence its origin in Middle English *newefangel*, from *new* and an element based on Old English *fang*, 'that which is seized' (modern *fang*).

news The reporting of current events is so called because (usually) what is reported is *new*. The word is plural because news invariably involves reports on several matters. Compare *tidings*.

> **FALSE**
>
> **news** From *N*, *E*, *W*, *S*, representing the four points of the compass. *News* comes from all directions.

newt The name of the small creature was originally *ewt*, which survived in dialect form as *eft*. The present form of the word is the result of the wrong division of *an ewt* as *a newt*. Compare ◊nickname.

next The word is the superlative ('most') form of *nigh*, as if *nigh-est*. Whatever is nearest is therefore *next*. *Near* itself is the comparative ('more') form of *nigh*, as if *nigh-er*.

nice The popular word originally meant 'foolish' or 'stupid'. Its ultimate origin is in Latin *nescius*, 'ignorant', from the verb *nescire*, 'to be ignorant', itself a blend of *ne*, 'not', and *scire*, 'to know'. Compare ◊science.

nickel The name of the mineral is a shortening of German *Kupfernickel*, literally 'copper demon'. It was so nicknamed by miners because it yielded no copper despite being copper-coloured in appearance.

nickname The word for an extra or substitute name derives from a wrong division of *an ekename* as *a nekename*, and hence as a *nickname*. The *eke* here means 'addition', from a Germanic source that also gave modern German *auch*, 'also'. For a similar development, compare ◊newt.

> **FALSE**
>
> **nickname** From French *faire la nique*, 'cock a snook', referring to the contempt with which many *nick*names are given.

nicotine The basic constituent of tobacco takes its name from Jacques *Nicot* (1530–1600), the French diplomat who introduced tobacco into France.

nightingale The bird is so called because it frequently sings at night. The origin of the word is thus in Old English *nihtegale*, from *niht*, 'night', and *galan*, 'to sing'. Modern *yell* is related to the latter word.

nightmare The second part of the word for a 'bad dream' is not the female horse but Old English *mare*, 'evil spirit'.

nightshade The name of the plant, familiar as deadly nightshade, apparently means what it says, with *night* and *shade* referring to the sleep-inducing or poisonous properties of its berries.

nincompoop The word for a stupid person is probably based on a personal name such as *Nicodemus*, with obsolete *poop* added in the sense 'cheat'. The first part of the word was probably influenced by ◊ninny. French *nicodème* formerly had the same meaning. The reference is to the biblical *Nicodemus*, who when told by Jesus that he must be born again to see the kingdom of God, naïvely asked: 'How can a man be born when he is old? Can he enter the second time into his mother's womb, and be born?' (John 3:4).

> **FALSE**
>
> **nincompoop** An alteration of Latin *non compos mentis*, 'of unsound mind'.

ninny The term for a foolish person apparently arose from the proper name *Ninny*, a pet form of *Innocent*, itself given as a meaningful nickname to such a person. Compare ◊nincompoop.

> **FALSE**
>
> **ninny** From Italian *nino* or Spanish *niño*, 'child'.

nitrogen The gas that is a chief constituent of the air (almost four fifths) is so called because it is also an essential constituent of *nitre*. The name was actually formed from Greek *nitron* (taken to mean 'nitre' but actually sodium carbonate) and the root of *gennaein*, 'to generate'.

nob The colloquial word for a wealthy or socially superior person was first recorded in the 18th century in the Scottish form *knabb* or *nab*. The origin is thus uncertain.

noble The word came into English, via French, from Latin *nobilis*, 'renowned', literally 'capable of being known'. This word itself was earlier *gnobilis*, from the root element that gave modern English *know* itself. English *knowable* is thus a modern development of *nobilis*, since English *-able* represents Latin *-bilis*.

> **FALSE**
>
> **nob** From the Latin abbreviation *fil. nob.*, standing for *filius nobilis*, 'noble son', entered against the names of sons of the *nobility* in college records. Compare ◊snob.

noise The word arose as a form of Latin *nausea*, itself specifically meaning 'seasickness' but more generally 'noisy confusion', and deriving ultimately from Greek *naus*, 'ship'.

nonchalant The word meaning 'casually unconcerned' derives from the identical French word which literally means 'having no warmth', from *nonchaloir*, 'to lack warmth', combining *non*, 'not' and *chaloir*, 'to care', itself from Latin *calere*', 'to be warm'. Compare modern English colloquial *cool*, which has a similar sense.

nonplussed The word, meaning 'confused', 'perplexed' (though often used as if meaning 'indifferent'), derives from the Latin phrase *non plus*, 'no further'. If you are *nonplussed* you are brought to a halt and can go no further.

noon The word derives from Latin *nona hora*, 'ninth hour', ie, 3 pm, as this is the ninth hour from sunrise (at 6 am), when the religious office of *nones* was held or said. The word came to mean 12 midday when the time of the office was brought forward three hours so as to follow straight after the morning mass.

nostalgia The word's basic meaning is 'homesickness'. It represents the identical New Latin word which combined Greek *nostos*, 'return home', and *algos*, 'pain'.

nostril The origin of the word is in Old English *nosthyrl*, a combination of *nosu*, 'nose', and *thyrel*, 'hole'. The latter word is also the source of modern *thrill* (literally, 'pierce a hole in').

nostrum The term for a patent or quack medicine derives from Latin *noster*, 'our', occurring in the form *nostrum*, 'our own make', on the label that was formerly attached to medicines.

nougat The name of the sweet refers to the *nuts* (a related word) that are one of its chief ingredients. The derivation is thus in Provençal *nogat*, from *noga*, 'nut', ultimately from Latin *nux* with the same meaning.

novel The word for a story or work of fiction ultimately derives from Latin *novella narratio*, 'new story'. Old stories can be favourites, but new ones are much more exciting!

November The eleventh month of the year has a name that actually means 'ninth', from Latin *novem*, 'nine'. The Roman calendar began in March, when this would have been accurate. Compare ◊September, ◊October, ◊December.

nuance The word, as a term for a subtle difference, was taken into English direct from French, in which it derives from *nuer*, 'to show light and shade', with an ultimate source in Latin *nubes*, 'cloud'.

nubile The literal meaning of the word is 'marrigeable', from Latin *nubilis*, the adjective of *nubere*, 'to marry' (English *nuptual*). Single Italian girls have *nubile* on official documents such as passports to indicate their marital status.

> **FALSE**
>
> **nubile** From Latin *nubes*, 'cloud', 'veil', because a bride, who is *nubile*, is *veiled* at her wedding.

nuisance The original sense of the word was 'injury', 'harm'. Its ultimate source, through the identical Old French word, is in Latin *nocere*, 'to harm', a word that also lies behind *innocent* ('not harmful') and *obnoxious*.

numb If you are *numb* you are in a sense paralysed or 'seized'. The source of the word is thus in Old English *niman*, 'to take' (modern German *nehmen*), with *b* added after *m* as happened elsewhere (for example in *thumb*).

nurse The original main duty of a *nurse*, as a woman who looked after young children, was to feed or *nourish* them. Hence the ultimate source of both words in Latin *nutrire*, 'to feed', 'to cherish'. English *nurture* and *nutriment* are related.

nutmeg The spice derives its name, via Old French *nois muguede*, from Old Provençal *noz muscada*, 'musk-scented nut', from words ultimately going back to Latin *nux*, 'nut', and *muscus*, 'musk'.

O

oaf The word for a stupid or loutish person evolved as a variant of the Old English word that also gave the small and mischievous *elf*.

oast The kiln for drying hops, in an *oast* house, derives its name from an Indo-European root element meaning 'heat' that also gave Latin *aedes*, 'hearth' and *aestes*, 'summer'. In the name of London's *Limehouse*, the 'house' is actually *oast*, so that the name means 'lime kilns'.

obese The word describing an excessively fat person literally means 'eating a lot'. It comes from Latin *obesus*, in which *ob-* is an intensive prefix and *-esus* derives from *edere*, 'eat'.

obey The word derives from Old French (and modern) *obéir*, itself from Latin *oboedire*, literally 'to hear to', from *ob*, 'towards', and *audire*, 'to hear' (English *audience*). Compare the servant's response familiar in eastern folktales: 'I hear and obey, O master'.

oblige If you are *obliged* to do something you have a 'binding' duty to do it. Hence the origin of the word in Latin *obligare*, literally 'to bind towards', from *ob-*, 'towards', and *ligare*, 'to bind' (the source of English *ligament* and *ligature*).

oblique The literal meaning of the word is 'slanting', implying 'not straight', 'out of the true'. The source is in Latin *obliquus* in this sense, from *ob-*, 'towards', and a word of obscure origin (perhaps related to Greek *loxos*, 'slanting').

oblivion The origin of the word, through French, is in Latin *oblivisci*, 'to forget', from *ob-*, 'towards', and an element of uncertain origin (perhaps related to Latin *livere*, 'to be black', the source of English *livid*).

oblong The literal sense of the word is 'very long', from Latin *oblongus*, in which *ob-* is an intensive prefix added to *longus*, 'long'.

oboe The woodwind instrument has evolved its English name, under Italian influence, as a form of French *haut bois*, literally 'high wood'. The reference is to its pitch.

obscene Latin *obscenus*, which gave the word, meant 'inauspicious', 'ill-omened', and was a term used in augury (divination by observing the habits of birds). The origin of the Latin word itself is perhaps in the intensive prefix *ob-* and *caenum*, 'filth'.

observe If you are *observing* a person or thing you watch them constantly. Hence the origin of the word in Latin *observare*, from *ob-*, 'towards', and *servare*, 'to watch', 'to attend to'.

obstacle An *obstacle* is literally something that stands in the way, from Latin *obstare*, representing *ob-*, 'against', and *stare*, 'to stand'. Compare ◊obstetrics.

obstetrics The branch of medicine concerned with childbirth derives its name from Latin *obstetrix*, 'midwife', literally 'woman who stands opposite', from *ob-*, 'against', and *stare*, 'to stand', with *-trix* denoting a female agent, corresponding to the male *-tor*. Compare ◊obstacle and ◊midwife itself.

obstreperous The word is now frequently used to mean little more than 'awkward', 'rebellious'. It literally means 'roaring against', from Latin *obstrepere*, in which *ob-* means 'against', and *strepere*, 'to roar', 'to make a noise'.

occasion The word came, via French, from Latin *occasio*, 'juncture', 'opportunity', literally 'falling towards', from *ob-*, 'towards', and *cadere*, 'to fall'. An *occasion* is the time when things happen, or 'fall towards' each other.

occult Something *occult* is secret or hidden to others. Hence the source of the word in Latin *occulere*, 'to cover over', from *ob-*, 'over', and the root of the verb that gave English *conceal*. See also ◊hell.

ocean The word has its origins in classical mythology, in the name of the Greek Titan *Oceanus*, who was god of the stream that was believed to flow round the earth. He was often called *Ōkeanos potamos*, 'swift-flowing river', with *Ōkeanos* itself deriving from *ōkus*, 'quick', and *naō*, 'I flow'.

October The tenth month of the year has a name actually meaning 'eighth', from Latin *octo*, 'eight', This is because the Roman calendar began in March. Compare ◊September, ◊November, ◊December.

odalisque The word for a female slave or concubine is a French alteration of Turkish *odalık*, representing *odah*, 'room', and the affix *-lık* expressing a function. She was thus a sort of 'mistress of the bedchamber'.

oesophagus The medical term for the gullet (between the throat and the stomach) derives from Greek *oisophagos*, representing *oisein*, the future infinitive of *pherein*, 'to carry', and a form of *phagein*, 'to eat'. It is thus the 'food carrier'.

ogre The word for a giant, especially one eating human flesh, perhaps derives from the name of *Orcus*, a Roman god of the underworld.

ohm The unit of electrical resistance was so named in honour of the the German physicist Georg Simon *Ohm* (1787–1854), who determined the law of the flow of electricity (Ohm's law). The name was suggested, along with *ohmad*, at a meeting of the British Association in 1861.

ointment The word evolved as a French form of Latin *unguentum*, from *unguere*, 'to anoint', which itself directly gave the exact synonym, *unguent*.

O.K. It is now generally agreed that the letters come from that of the *O.K.* Club, an American Democratic party club of the 1840s, itself so called after its president, Martin Van Buren, nicknamed *O*ld *K*inderhook from his birthplace, Kinderhook, New York. The letters were later popularly interpreted as standing for '*o*ll *k*orrect', a humorous alteration of '*a*ll *c*orrect'.

olive The name of the evergreen tree and its fruit is related to *oil*. Greek *elaion*, which has the latter meaning, is the source of the English word. Olive oil, used in both cooking and medicine, comes from ripe olives.

omega The name of the 24th and last letter of the Greek alphabet represents Greek *ō mega*, 'big o', as distinct from the 15th letter, *omicron*, from Greek *ō mikron*, 'little o'. An omega is pronounced 'long', as in 'coat', and the omicron short, as in 'cot'.

omelette The English word for the egg dish was adopted from the identical French word, which is an alternative form of *alumette*, from *alumelle*, 'blade'. This itself arose from a wrong division of *la lemelle*, 'the blade', in turn from Latin *lamella*, a diminutive of *lamina*, 'thin sheet of metal' (modern English *lamina*). The omelette presumably came to be so called because it is thin and flat, like the blade of a knife.

onion The edible bulb ultimately gets its name, through French, from the Latin word for it, *unio*, genitive *unionis*. This was probably related to *unus*, 'one', the source of English *union*, so that the Romans may have seen the bulb as a 'unity' of many layers.

opal The word for the whitish or bluish gemstone probably goes back ultimately, through Latin and Greek, to Sanskrit *upala*, 'precious stone'.

> **FALSE**
>
> **opal** From a Slavonic source with a basic sense 'burning', such as Polish *opał*, 'fuel', or Russian *opalit'*, 'to singe'. The reference is to the gemstone's 'burning' rays.

opera The word for the musical drama came into English from Italian, which took it from the identical Latin word meaning 'labour', 'product of labour', from a colloquial form (corresponding to the plural) of *opus*, 'work'.

opportunity The origin of the word is in Latin *opportunus*, literally 'driving towards the harbour', from *ob-*, 'towards', and *portus*, 'harbour' (English *port*). The picture is of a storm driving a ship towards a harbour, thus providing a welcome *opportunity* to take shelter.

opposite The origin of the word is in Latin *oppositus*, from *opponere*, literally 'to place against', from *ob-*, 'against', and *ponere*, 'to place'. Directly related English words are *oppose* and *opponent*.

optimism The word derives from Latin *optimus*, 'best'. It originally applied specifically to the doctrine proposed by the German philosopher Leibniz in *Théodicée* (1710) that our world is the 'best of all possible worlds', and was chosen as such by the Creator. In this work, Leibniz used Latin *optimum* as a technical term, basing it on *maximum* and *minimum*.

orange The word came into English, via French, from Old Provençal *auranja*, itself ultimately from Arabic *nāranj*, in turn of Persian origin, as the fruit itself is.

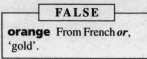

> **FALSE**
>
> **orange** From French *or*, 'gold'.

orang-utan The large long-armed manlike ape, of the forests of Sumatra, has a name deriving from Malay *orang hutan*, 'man of the forest', from *ōrang*, 'man', and *hūtan*, 'forest'. This was intended by the Malay as a name for tribes of forest dwellers, but was applied by Europeans to the ape.

oratorio The term for a dramatic but unstaged musical work on a religious theme represents the Italian word for *oratory*. It refers to the *Oratory* of St Philip Neri in Rome, where works of this type were first performed in the latter half of the 16th century.

orbit The origin of the word is in Latin *orbita*, 'course', from *orbis*, 'circle' (the source of English *orb*).

orchard The word goes back to Old English *ortgeard*. The first part of this derives from Latin *hortus*, ◊garden. The second is *geard*, ◊yard. Since these two English words are related (both to each other and to their sources), the word in a sense reduplicates itself. The overall meaning is that of an enclosed vegetable or fruit garden.

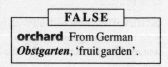

> **FALSE**
>
> **orchard** From German *Obstgarten*, 'fruit garden'.

orchestra The word was used in the ancient Greek theatre for the space in front of the stage where the chorus danced and sang. The word thus basically means 'dance floor' and derives from Greek *orkheisthai*, 'to dance'.

orchid The plant derives its name from Greek *orkhis*, 'testicle', referring to the shape of the tubers in most species. Compare ◊avocado.

ordeal The word represents Old English *ordāl*, related to Old High German *urteili* (modern German *Urteil*), meaning 'verdict', literally 'out-deal'. In olden times the *ordeal* was a method of judgement, in which the *verdict* (innocent or guilty) on an accused person was established by exposing him or her to physical danger, usually by fire or water. The outcome of this *ordeal* (in modern terms) was regarded as the judgement of God.

organ Whatever its present sense, the ultimate origin of the word is in Greek *organon*, 'tool', 'instrument', itself from *ergon*, 'work'. English *work* itself comes from the Indo-European root element that gave the Greek word. Compare ◊orgy.

orgy The word came into English, via French, from Greek *orgia*, a plural word used for the secret rites practised by the initiated at the worship of the goddess Demeter at Eleusis. The word itself derives from Greek *ergon*, 'work'. Compare ◊organ.

orient The word for the east derives from Latin *oriens*, genitive *orientis*, 'rising', referring to the rising sun. See also ▷orientate.

orientate The word is an alternative form of *orient*, in the sense 'find one's bearings'. It literally means 'find one's bearings with regard to the east' (see ▷orient), which can be done either by the rising sun or, lacking a compass, by the east–west *orientation* of a church.

orifice The word for an opening, especially one in the body, derives from Late Latin *orificium*, from *os*, genitive *oris*, 'mouth', and *facere*, 'to make'.

origin The source of the word is in Latin *origo*, genitive *originis*, 'beginning', itself from the verb *oriri*, 'to rise' (which also gave ▷orient).

orphan The word for a person deprived of his or her parents derives from Greek *orphanos*, related to Latin *orbus*, 'bereft'.

orthodox The word is Greek in origin and literally means 'right opinion', otherwise 'correct belief', from *orthos*, 'straight', and *doxa*, 'opinion', 'belief'.

oscillate The word derives from Latin *oscillare*, 'to swing', itself from *oscillum*, a diminutive of *os*, 'face'. This was the word in Roman times for a little mask of Bacchus, the god of wine, that was hung on trees in vineyards so that the wind could blow it to and fro and so bring a blessing on the grapes.

osprey The bird feeds on fish, and obtains its food by flying over the water, hovering over its prey, and then plunging feet first to seize it in its talons. Its name apparently derives from Latin *ossifraga*, literally 'bone breaker', from *os*, 'bone', and *frangere*, 'to break'. This is said to refer to the bird's habit of dropping its prey from a height to break its bones. But the osprey does not do this, so the reference must be to some other bird.

ostensible The word describing something that is probably not what it seems to be derives from Latin *ostendere*, 'to show', literally 'to extend towards', from *ob-*, 'towards', and *tendere*, 'to extend'.

ostracize The verb used for the banning or shunning of someone derives from the Greek verb *ostrakizein*. This was used for the act of selecting someone for banishment by voting with potsherds or tiles that bore the name of the person proposed for this fate. The ultimate origin is thus in Greek *ostrakon*, 'shell', 'potsherd', related to *osteon*, 'bone', and *ostreon*, ▷oyster.

ostrich The present form of the bird's name has evolved from a combination of Latin *avis*, 'bird', and Late Latin *struthio*, 'ostrich', itself from Greek *strouthion*, which could also mean 'sparrow' or 'eagle'.

otter The aquatic animal ultimately gets its name from an Indo-European root element meaning 'water' that also gave Greek *hudor*, 'water', and English ▷water itself.

oval Something that is *oval* is egg-shaped, as is implied by the origin of the word in Latin *ovum*, 'egg'.

overalls The protective work garment is so called as it is worn on top of what the person is already wearing, that is, it is worn *over all*. The word may have partly arisen as a translation of French *surtout*, which has the same literal sense and which was formerly the word for a type of overcoat.

overwhelm The original sense of the word was 'upset', 'overturn'. *Whelm* is now obsolete, but it had virtually the same meaning, from a Germanic source of uncertain origin. It may be indirectly related to Greek *kolpos*, 'bosom'.

oxygen The gas that is essential to life has a name that represents the Greek words for 'acid-producing', from *oxus*, 'sharp', 'acid', and *gennaein*, 'to generate', 'to produce'. Oxygen was at first believed to be the essential element in the formation of acids. The name was coined by the French chemist Lavoisier in 1777.

oyster The bivalve mollusc gets its name, through French and Latin, from Greek *ostreon*, a word related to Greek *osteon*, 'bone', and *ostrakon*, 'shell'. See also ◊ostracize.

ozone The gas, formed by an electric discharge in oxygen, is noted for its chlorine-like smell. Hence its name, from Greek *ozon*, the noun of *ozein*, 'to smell', a word that also ultimately gave English *odour*.

packet boat The now rather dated term for a boat that transports passengers, mail, and the like over a regular route derives from the fact that such boats originally transported 'the packet' of state papers. A document of 1598 referring to the service between Holyhead and Ireland mentions an 'allowance as well for serving the packets by land as for entertaining a barke to carie over and to returne the packet'.

paddock The enclosure for horses was originally known as a *parrock*, a dialect word of Germanic origin related to *park*. The town of *Paddock* Wood in Kent was thus recorded as *Parrocks* in a document of 1782.

> **FALSE**
>
> **paddock** From a blend of *pad*, an old word for a slow-paced horse, and *dock*, as for ships.

padlock The type of hanging lock perhaps derives the first part of its name from *pad*, a dialect word for a toad. The reference would be to the squat shape of early padlocks.

pagan The word for a person who does not belong to an established religion derives from Latin *paganus*, 'civilian', originally 'country dweller', from *pagus*, 'rural district', itself from *pangere*, 'to fix'. The sense of 'heathen' arose because someone who was not a soldier of Christ was thought of as a 'civilian'. Compare the origin of ◊heathen itself.

page As used for a boy attendant, the word came into English from Italian *paggio*, itself probably from Greek *paidion*, 'young slave', a diminutive of *pais*, 'boy', 'child'. Compare ◊pedagogue.

pageant The word for a colourful parade or display derives from Medieval Latin *pagina*, 'scene of a play', itself from the identical Latin word meaning 'page' (ie, sheet of writing).

> **FALSE**
>
> **pageant** From a Germanic word related to *wagon*, referring to the 'carriage' on which pageants were originally staged.

pagoda The Indian or Far Eastern temple derives its name, through Portuguese, from Sanskrit *bhagavatī*, 'divine', literally 'god-possessing', from *bhaga*, 'lord', and the suffix *-vat* meaning 'having', 'possessing'.

pal The word has its origin in English Gypsy *pal*, 'brother', 'mate', itself ultimately from Sanskrit *bhrātar*, 'brother'. This means that English *brother* is itself related.

palace　The word for a sovereign's residence derives from the *Palatine*, one of the seven hills of Rome. This was the site of the house of Augustus, the first emperor of Rome, and of the *palace* of the later Caesars.

palaver　The word for a conference or 'confab' derives from Portuguese *palavra*, 'talk', itself from Latin *parabola*, 'parable'. The word probably arose from the 'parleying' of Portuguese traders on the coast of Africa when negotiating with natives. See also ◊parable itself.

palette　The word for an artist's board represents a French diminutive of *pale*, 'shovel', itself from Latin *pala*, 'spade'.

palimpsest　The word is used for a manuscript on which two or more successive texts have been written, with each erased to make space for the next. The origin is in Greek *palimpsēstos*, 'rubbed smooth again', from *palin*, 'again', and *psēstos*, 'rubbed smooth', from *psēn*, 'to rub', 'to scrape'.

palindrome　The term for a word or phrase that reads the same backwards as forwards (such as EVE or MADAM, I'M ADAM) derives from Greek *palin*, 'again' (compare ◊palimpsest), and *dromos*, 'course'.

palm　The tropical tree derives its name from Latin *palma*, 'palm' (of the hand), referring to its leaves, which resemble a hand with the fingers outstretched.

pamphlet　The word for a booklet derives from *Pamphilus*, the short title of a popular 12th-century Latin love poem. The full title was *Pamphilus seu de Amore*, 'Pamphilus, or Concerning Love', with the name *Pamphilus* from Greek words meaning 'loving all'.

> **FALSE**
>
> **pamphlet**　From French *par un filet*, 'by a thread', referring to a small book with stitched pages.

panacea　The term for a universal remedy ('cure for all ills') derives, through Latin, from Greek *panakeia*, 'healing all', from *pan*, 'all', and *akos*, 'cure', 'remedy'.

pancreas　The body organ that secretes digestive juice has a name of Greek origin literally meaning 'all flesh', from *pan*, 'all', and *kreas*, 'flesh'. The reference is to its fleshy appearance and consistency. As edible animals' meat it is known as *sweetbread*. (The second half of this is probably Old English *brēd*, 'meat', rather than *brēad*, 'bread').

pandemonium　The word was coined by Milton as the name of the capital of Hell in *Paradise Lost* (1667): 'A solemn Councel forthwith to be held/At *Pandæmonium*, the high Capital/Of Satan and his Peers'. The word literally means 'all demons', from Greek *pan*, 'all', and *daimōn*, 'demon'.

pander　The verb now commonly meaning 'indulge' arose from *Pandarus*, the name used by the 14th-century Italian poet Boccaccio (and subsequently by Chaucer) for the man in medieval legend who procured Cressida on

> **FALSE**
>
> **pander**　From French *pendard*, 'rogue', 'scoundrel'.

behalf of Troilus. The word then came to mean 'procurer', 'pimp', and so came to have its present sense. The name *Pandarus* itself literally means 'all-flaying', from Greek *pan*, 'all', and *derein*, 'to flay' (English *tear*).

pane   The original sense of the word was 'piece of cloth'. Hence its origin in Latin *pannus* in that sense. English *panel* is directly related and is from a diminutive of the Latin word.

panic   The word was originally an adjective, as in the phrase *panic fear*. As such it derives from *Pan*, the Greek god of shepherds and flocks who was reputed to be the cause of sudden groundless fear. (His method of dealing with an enemy or unwelcome force was to shout at it and so scare it off.)

panorama   The word was originally used in the 18th century for a picture of a scene that unfolded to show the various parts in succession. It literally means 'viewing all', from Greek *pan*, 'all', and *horāma*, 'view'.

pansy   The flower derives its name from Old French *pensée*, 'thought', with apparent reference to its *pensive* appearance. ('There is pansies, that's for thoughts', says poor mad Ophelia in Shakespeare's *Hamlet*.)

pant   The word that means 'breathe quickly' ultimately goes back, via French, to Greek *phantasia*, 'fantasy'. The image is of someone experiencing an unpleasant vision, as in a nightmare.

FALSE

pansy   Evolved from *panacea*, since the plant was regarded by the Greeks as a cure for all diseases. Compare the English plant name *allheal*, and the pansy's own alternative name, *heartsease*.

---

panther   The word goes back to Greek *panthēr*, a name for various members of the cat family. It is probably ultimately Sanskrit in origin.

pantomime   The word was originally used for an actor in ancient Rome who performed in a dumb show. Hence its origin in a Greek word literally meaning 'miming all', from *pan*, genitive *pantos*, 'all', and *mīmos*, 'mime'.

pantry   The room in which provisions and cooking utensils are kept was originally a bread store. Hence the origin of the word in Old French *panetrie*, ultimately from Latin *panis*, 'bread'.

FALSE

pantry   So called because it is the room by the kitchen where the *pans* are kept.

---

pants   The word for the nether garment, whether now underwear or outerwear, is a shortened form of *pantaloons*. This comes from *Pantaloon*, the English form of Italian *Pantalone*, the name of a lecherous old man in 16th-century Italian comedy who wore slippers and tight trousers. He was said to have been so named, no doubt humorously, after *Pantaleone*, patron saint of Venice. (The saint's name literally means 'all lion', which Pantalone patently was not.)

paper　The word ultimately goes back to Latin *papyrus*, referring to the reedlike plant from which *paper* was made in ancient times.

parable　The word for the short story that illustrates a spiritual truth derives from Greek *parabolē*, 'analogy', literally 'thrown alongside', from *para*, 'beside', and *ballein*, 'to throw'.

parachute　The word came into English from French, and derives from the stem of Italian *parare*, 'to defend', 'to ward off', itself from Latin *parare*, 'to prepare', and French *chute*, 'fall'. A parachute is thus an 'antifall' device.

parade　The word is of French origin, and literally means 'preparation', ultimately from Latin *parare*, 'to prepare'. When troops are on *parade* they are *prepared* for duty or action.

paradise　The word ultimately goes back to Greek *paradeisos*, 'garden', 'orchard', from a Persian source related to Avestan *pairidaēza*, 'enclosure', literally 'walled-round place', from *pairi-*, 'around', and *daēza*, 'wall'.

paradox　The word originally applied to a statement or doctrine that was contrary to the established view. It thus literally means 'beside belief', from Greek *para*, 'beside', and *doxa*, 'opinion'. (Greek *para doxan* meant 'contrary to opinion'.)

paraffin　The name was originally that of *paraffin* wax, rather than the liquid fuel. It was formed from Latin *parum*, 'too little', and *affinis*, 'related', referring to its chemical inertia and lack of *affinity* to other substances. The name was coined in 1830 by Karl Reichenbach, the German industrialist who discovered paraffin in wood tar.

paragon　The word for a model of excellence derives, via French, from Italian *paragone*, 'touchstone', itself from Medieval Greek *parakonē*, 'whetstone', from Greek *para*, 'beside', and *akonân*, 'to sharpen'. (A touchstone is literally a stone used to test the quality of gold or silver.)

paragraph　The word for a new section in writing derives from Greek *paragraphos*, literally 'writing alongside', from *para*, 'beside', and *graphein*, 'to write'. The Greeks used this term for a short horizontal stroke below the beginning of a line in which a break of sense occurred. The term later applied to the passage itself that was marked in this way.

parallel　The origin of the word is in Greek *parallēlos*, 'alongside one another', from *para*, 'beside', and *allēlos*, 'one another', a reduplicated form of *allos*, 'other'.

paralysed　The word literally means 'loosened at the side', from Greek *para*, 'beside', and *lusis*, 'loosening'. If you are 'loosened' you are disabled.

paramedic　The word has two possible meanings. It is usually the word for a person who helps doctors or supplements medical work. In this case it derives from Greek *para*, 'beside' and English *medical*. It can also, however, be a *medic* who *para*chutes to an emergency situation, such as a skiing accident or plane crash.

paranoid The word derives from Greek *paranoia*, 'frenzy', literally 'state of being out of one's mind', from *para*, 'beside', 'beyond', and *noos*, 'mind'.

parapet The word for a low wall along a balcony derives from Italian *parapetto*, literally 'against the breast', from the root of *parare*, 'to defend', and *petto*, 'breast', 'chest'. A *parapet* is a breast-high protective wall.

paraphernalia Although now the word for miscellaneous articles or actions, the word originally had a specific sense. It comes from Late Latin *parapherna*, a term for the personal property of a married woman apart from her dowry, from Greek *para*, 'beside', and *phernē*, 'dowry' (from *pherein*, 'to carry').

paraplegic The term describing a partial paralysis literally means 'blow on one side', from Greek *para*, 'beside', and *plēssein*, 'to strike'. A *paraplegic* is paralysed in the lower half of the body.

parasite The literal sense of the word is 'eating at the table of another', from Greek *para*, 'beside', and *sitos*, 'food' (originally, 'grain'. In the biological sense, a *parasite* is a plant or animal that lives on or in another and feeds off it.

parchment The word for animal skin prepared for writing comes ultimately from *Pergamum*, the city in ancient Greece (now *Bergama*, Turkey), where it was first made. The form of the word has been influenced by Old French *parche*, 'leather' (a word that itself comes from *Parthia*, a country in ancient Asia).

pardon The word has evolved from Medieval Latin *perdonare*, 'to forgive freely', from Latin *per-*, an intensive prefix, and *donare*, 'to grant'.

pariah The term for a social outcast derives from Tamil *paraiyan*, the name of the largest of the lowest castes in southern India, literally meaning 'drummer'. Members of the caste were the drummers at festivals.

parish The ecclesiastical subdivision of a diocese ultimately gets its name from Greek *paroikos*, 'neighbour', literally 'living nearby', from *para*, 'beside', and *oikos*, 'house'. The implication is that such a person is a fellow Christian.

parlour The source of the word is in Old French *parleur*, as the name of the room in a convent that was set aside for receiving guests, from *parler*, 'to speak'. (Conversation in many religious houses was usually forbidden, except on special occasions.)

parlous The word evolved from Old French *perillous*, the source of the more common and synonymous *perilous*.

parody The term for a literary or artistic work imitating (and usually mocking) another derives from Greek *parōidia*, 'burlesque', literally 'beside the song', from *para*, 'beside', and *ōidē*, 'song' (English *ode*).

parsley The name of the plant ultimately derives, through Old French *persil*, from Latin *petroselinum*, 'rock parsley', from Greek *petra*, 'rock', and *selinon*, 'parsley'.

parson   The word for a clergyman derives, through French, from Latin *persona*, 'character', 'person'. The reference is to a parish priest, who was the *person* who legally represented his parish. See also ◊person itself.

passbook   The book for recording bank or building society transactions is so called because it *passes* to and fro between the holder and the bank or society.

passenger   The word was originally used of someone making a *passage* from one place to another. The letter *n* has been inserted as for *messenger* from *message* and *scavenger* from *scavage*, among others.

Passover   The Jewish festival commemorates the sparing of the Israelites in Egypt when God smote the firstborn of the Egyptians. The Israelites were to mark the doors of their houses with the blood of a sacrificed lamb: 'And when I see the blood, I will *pass over* you, and the plague shall not be upon you to destroy you' (Exodus 12:13). The words translate Hebrew *pesah*, from *pāsah*, 'to pass over'.

> **FALSE**
>
> **Passover**   From German *Paschopfer*, 'paschal sacrifice'.

passport   The document is one that allows its holder to *pass* from a *port*, that is, to leave a country. The word came into English from French *passeport*.

pastime   A *pastime* is a hobby or recreation which makes *time pass* pleasantly. The word is an English rendering of French *passe-temps*.

pasture   A *pasture* is a grazing or feeding ground, as its name implies, with an ultimate source in Latin *pascere*, 'to feed'.

pathetic   The word goes back through French and Latin to Greek *pathētikos*, the adjective of *pathos*, 'suffering' (modern English *pathos*). The Greek word is itself related to *penthos*, 'sorrow'.

patient   The literal meaning of the word is 'suffering', in the sense 'enduring'. The origin is in Latin *pati*, 'to suffer'. A doctor's *patients* are therefore his or her 'sufferers'.

patio   The paved area adjoining a house gets its name from the identical Spanish word for 'courtyard'.

patriot   As the name implies, a *patriot* is a person who loves and supports his country, from Greek *patris*, 'native land', a word itself based on *patēr*, 'father'.

patrol   Although now a professional and responsible business, *patrolling* was originally a much more basic and random action. The word derives from French *patrouiller*, a form of *patouiller*. 'to paddle about in mud', from *patte*, 'paw', 'foot', and the dialect word *gadrouille*, 'mud', 'dirty water'.

patronize   If you *patronize* someone, you treat them as if they were a child, that is, as if you were their *father*. This is the ultimate sense of the word, from Latin *patronus*, 'protector', itself from *pater*, 'father'.

patter The rapid talking associated with conjurors, market traders, and the like derives from the first word of Latin *Pater Noster*, 'Our Father', the opening words of the Lord's Prayer as gabbled by a medieval priest.

pattern The word for a decorative design or a model to be copied derives from French *patron*, 'model', 'pattern'. This is the same word that gave English *patron*, the link between the two words being that a pattern is a 'master' of which copies are made.

pavement A *pavement* has not only been *paved* but in a literal sense trodden down. The source of the word is ultimately in Latin *pavire*, 'to beat down', 'to ram'. Latin *pavimentum* was the word for a floor that had been beaten or pounded down thus.

pavilion The word was used in medieval times in English for a large peaked tent. The source is in Latin *papilio*, genitive *papilionis*, 'butterfly', since the roof of such a tent looked like a butterfly's wings.

pawn The name of the chessman with the lowest value derives, through French, from Medieval Latin *pedo*, genitive *pedonis*, 'foot soldier', from *pes*, 'foot'.

pay The word is ultimately related to *peace*. It came into English, through French, from Latin *pacare*, 'to appease', 'to pacify', in turn from *pax*, genitive *pacis*, 'peace'. The original concept was of *paying* a creditor to *pacify* him.

peach The fruit is so called since it originally came from *Persia*. The linguistic source of the word is ultimately in Latin *Persicum malum*, 'Persian apple'.

peal A *peal* of bells is intended to summon people, as to a church. Hence the origin of the word, which arose as a shortened form of what is now *appeal*, ultimately from Latin *appellare*, literally 'drive towards', from *ad*, 'towards', and *pellere*, 'to drive' (English *pulse*, *impulse*, etc).

peasant The word came into English from Old French *païsant* (modern French *paysan*), from *païs* (modern *pays*, 'country'), itself from Latin *pagus*, 'rural district'. Compare ◊pagan.

peculiar Something *peculiar* is characteristic of a particular person or thing, and belongs to them alone. Hence the origin of the word in Latin *peculiaris*, the adjective of *peculium*, 'private property', literally 'property in cattle', from *pecus*, 'cattle'. The same source gave English *pecuniary*, 'relating to money', since Latin *pecunia*, 'money', literally meant 'riches in cattle'.

pedagogue The term for a *pedantic* teacher represents Greek *paidagōgos*, literally 'boy leader', as the word for a slave that took a boy to school and brought him back again. The components of the word are Greek *pais*, genitive *paidos*, 'boy', 'child', and *agein*, 'to lead'. See also ◊pedant.

pedant The word was formerly applied to a schoolteacher. It probably developed from ◊pedagogue, but there may have been a later association with Latin *pes*, genitive *pedis*, 'foot', with reference to a 'plodding' person. (Compare *pedestrian* in this sense, as used of a dull or uninspiring person or action.)

pedigree The term for a line of descent, especially one from pure ancestry, derives from Old French *pie de grue*, 'crane's foot', alluding to the three-line claw-shaped mark formerly used to show succession in a genealogical chart.

> **FALSE**
>
> **pedigree** From a shortened form of French *pied de degrés*, 'stem of degrees'.

peer The word for a member of the nobility derives, through French, from Latin *par*, 'equal'. Peers are not equal to most people, of course, nor now even among themselves. But the medieval barons who held land direct from the king were equal in this respect, and the word originally related to them.

pelican The aquatic bird was known to the Greeks as *pelekan*, perhaps from *pelekus*, 'axe', referring to the shape or action of its long straight flattened bill.

pen The writing instrument was originally a quill. Hence the ultimate source of the name in Latin *penna*, 'feather'. Compare French *plume*, which was long the standard word for a pen.

penalty The word evolved from Medieval Latin *poenalitas*, itself a noun formed from Late Latin *poenalis*, in turn going back to Latin *poena*, 'punishment' (English *pain*).

pencil The ultimate origin of the word is in Latin *penicillus*, 'painter's brush', a diminutive of *peniculus*, 'brush', itself a diminutive of *penis*, 'tail', 'penis' (the source of the latter English word). See also ◊penicillin.

penguin According to some authorities, the distinctive black and white bird takes its name from Welsh *pen gwyn*, 'white head'. The true source of the name has not been established with any certainty.

penicillin The antibiotic drug takes its name from the *Penicillium* fungus from which it is derived. The fungus is itself so called from the tufted appearance of its sporangia (spore-producing organs), from Latin *penicillus*, 'painter's brush'. See also ◊pencil.

peninsula The piece of land partly surrounded by water is so called because it is 'almost an island', from Latin *paeninsula*, representing *paene*, 'almost', and *insula*, 'island'.

penknife The pocket knife is so called because it was originally used for making and mending quill *pens*.

pension The word came into English, through French, from Latin *pensio*, genitive *pensionis*, 'payment', from *pendere*, 'to pay', literally 'to weigh', referring to payment by weight of a particular metal in early times.

penthouse The word was originally used for a subsidiary structure attached to the wall of a main building, especially one with a sloping roof. Hence its source in Old French *apentis*, from Late Latin *appendicium*, 'appendage', itself from Latin *appendere*, 'to hang from'. The English word has been influenced by *house*.

peony The flower ultimately gets its name from Greek *paiōn*, 'physician'. The reference is to its former use in medicine.

peregrine falcon The first word of the falcon's name represents Latin *peregrinus*, 'foreign' (see ◊pilgrim). The bird was so called because its young were not taken from the nest, as were those of other species, but caught when on their way from it.

perfect The literal sense is 'done through', otherwise 'completed', from Latin *perficere*, representing *per*, 'through', and *facere*, 'to do'.

perfume The word literally means 'smoked through', from a French word ultimately representing Latin *per*, 'through', and *fumare*, 'to smoke'. The reference is to a scented vapour.

pergola The type of arbour for climbing plants usually consists of a horizontal trellis supported on posts. Hence the source of the word in Latin *pergula*, the term for a projection from a roof, from *pergere*, 'to go forward', literally 'to go through in a straight line', from *per*, 'through', and the root of *rectus*, 'right', 'straight'.

perhaps The word originated as a form of Medieval English *by hap*, 'by chance', based on an existing formation such as the one that gave modern *perchance*, where the first part is Old French *per*, from the identical Latin word meaning 'by'. The second half of the word is related to ◊happy.

peril The word ultimately goes back to Latin *periculum*, 'experiment', 'danger'. It replaced the native Old English word *fǣr*, related to modern German *Gefahr*, 'danger'.

period The word ultimately derives from Greek *periodos*, 'circuit', literally 'way round', from *peri*, 'around', and *hodos*, 'way'. The concept is not so much of a length of time as of a time that regularly reoccurs.

periscope The instrument is designed to give an all-round view, as its name implies. It was devised in the 19th century from Greek *peri*, 'around', and *skopein*, 'to look at'.

perks The word is a colloquial abbreviation of *perquisites*, as a term for customary or incidental benefits, from Medieval Latin *perquisitum*, 'acquired possession', in turn from Latin *perquirere*, 'to seek keenly for', formed on *per*, 'through', and *quaerere*, 'to seek' (English *quest*).

permanent The literal sense of the word is 'remaining to the end', from Latin *permanens*, 'continuing', formed from *per*, 'through', and *manere*, 'to remain'.

permission The word literally implies 'letting go through', from Latin *permittere*, 'to surrender', 'to allow', in turn from *per*, 'through', and *mittere*, 'to let go'.

perpetual The word derives, through French, from Latin *perpetualis*, 'universal', itself from *perpes*, 'continuous', formed on *per*, 'through', and *petere*, 'to go towards'.

perry The drink is a wine made from *pears*, as its name implies. The ultimate origin is in Latin *pirum*, 'pear'.

person The ultimate source of the word is in Latin *persona*, 'mask', referring to an actor who plays the part of a given character. The Latin phrase *dramatis personae*, 'characters of the play', is still sometimes used as the heading of a cast list. See also ◊parson.

perspire The verb comes from Latin *perspirare*, 'to blow' (of the wind), literally 'to breathe through', from *per*, 'through', and *spirare*, 'to breathe'. The reference is not to actual sweating (so-called sensible perspiration) but to vapour evaporating from the skin (insensible perspiration).

persuade The origin of the word is in Latin *persuadere*, literally 'recommend keenly', from *per-*, an intensive prefix, and *suadere*, 'to recommend', 'to urge'.

petrified If you are *petrified* you may be so scared that you cannot move, like someone turned into stone. Hence the ultimate origin of the word in Greek *petra*, 'stone'.

petrol The word evolved from Medieval Latin *petroleum*, literally 'rock oil', from Latin *petra*, 'stone', and *oleum*, 'oil'. Petrol is derived from petroleum, which itself occurs naturally as crude oil in sedimentary rocks.

petticoat As its name implies, the garment is (or was) literally a 'petty coat'. It was originally a small coat worn by men under a doublet. Both parts of the word are of French origin, although *coat* is ultimately Germanic.

pheasant The bird ultimately gets its name from the River *Phasis* in Colchis (now the Rioni, in Georgia, on the Black Sea east coast), from where it is said to have spread westwards.

phenomenon The word is pure Greek, literally meaning 'thing being shown', from what is grammatically a substantival (noun) use of the present participle passive of the verb *phainein*, 'to show' (the basis of English *fantasy*).

philately The official term for stamp collecting was devised in 1864 by a French stamp collector, M G Herpin, from Greek *philos*, 'loving', and *ateleia*, 'exemption from tax', itself from *a-*, 'not', and *telos*, 'tax'. The reasoning was that the stamp exempted the recipient from paying the postage ('tax').

philistine The word for a boorish or uncultured person derives from the *Philistines*, the warlike people of ancient *Palestine* (the names are related). The sense is said to come from the German biblical quotation '*Philister über dir, Samson!*', 'The Philistines be upon thee, Samson' (Judges 16:9), taken for the text of a sermon preached in 1683 at the funeral of a student killed by townspeople in a riot at Jena.

philosophy The literal meaning of the word is 'love of wisdom', from Greek *philosophos*, 'philosopher', from the root words *philos*, 'loving', and *sophos*, 'wise'.

photograph The word was adopted in 1839 from German *Photographie*, 'photography', itself coined earlier that year from Greek *phōs*, genitive *phōtos*, 'light', and *graphein*, 'to write'.

physical The ultimate origin of this word, and the related *physics* and *physician*, is in Latin *physica*, a translation of Greek *ta phusika*, 'natural things', from *phusis*, 'nature'. The term *physics* was originally used for natural science, that is, the sciences that together involve the study of the natural world (including biology, physics, chemistry, and geology).

piano The name of the instrument is short for *pianoforte*, itself adopted directly from the Italian phrase *gravecembalo di piano e forte*, 'harpsichord of soft and loud'. This described the forerunner of the modern piano, a harpsichord with variable tone, as distinct from the standard harpsichord of unvarying tone. The phrase itself dates from the early 18th century.

piccaninny The word for a small black or aboriginal child, originally meant kindly but now regarded as offensive, evolved either from Portuguese *pequenino*, 'tiny one', or from the word of which this is a diminutive, *pequeno* (Spanish *pequeño*), 'small'. It was no doubt associated in English minds with ◊ninny.

pickaxe The name of the implement ultimately derives from Old French *picois*, itself from *pic*, 'pick'. The latter part of the word became associated with *axe* to give the present spelling.

> **FALSE**
>
> **pickaxe** So called because it is a special type of *axe* for *picking* at the ground.

picnic The word is a borrowing of French *piquenique*, itself dating from the 17th century and of uncertain origin. It may derive from *piquer*, 'to bite' (now used of insects), influenced by *nique*, 'trinket' (possibly related to English *knicknack*).

picturesque The word came into English, via French, from Italian *pittoresco*, meaning 'in the style of a painter', from *pittore*, 'painter'. The present form of the word has been influenced by *picture*, so that its meaning is rather different.

pie See ◊magpie.

pier The word was originally used for the support of the span of a bridge, as it still is, rather than the seaside structure. It derives from Anglo-Latin *pera* in this sense. The ultimate origin of the word is unknown.

> **FALSE**
>
> **pie** A contracted form of *pastie*, a former spelling of *pasty*.

pigeon The word originally referred to a young dove. It derives, through French, from Late Latin *pipio*, 'young bird', itself from *pipire*, 'to peep' (in the sense 'chirp'). In the expression 'that's my pigeon', the word is a corruption of *business*.

> **FALSE**
>
> **pier** From French *pierre*, 'stone'.

piggyback The word is an alterated form of *pickaback*. An earlier form of this was *pickback* or *pickpack*, and it is not clear which came first. Either way, the word refers to someone or something that is carried as a *pack* on the *back*.

pilgrim the word originally meant 'wayfarer' before it gained its religious sense. Its ultimate source is in Latin *peregrinus*, 'foreign', literally 'through the land' (ie, on a journey), from *per*, 'through', and *ager*, 'field', 'land'. See also ◊peregrine falcon.

pill The medicinal tablet ultimately derives its name, through French, from Latin *pilula*, 'little ball', a diminutive of *pila*, 'ball'.

pilot The ultimate source of the word is in Greek *pēdon*, 'oar', itself a word related to *pous*, 'foot'.

pine In the sense 'long for', 'yearn for', the word ultimately goes back to Latin *poena*, 'penalty', 'punishment', the source of English *pain*.

pink The colour gets its name from the flower, the species of Dianthus. Its own name may originally have been *pink eye*, and so having the same sense as its French name, *oeillet*, 'little eye'. (English *pink-eyed* means literally 'having small eyes', from obsolete Dutch *pinck oogen*, 'little eyes'.)

pinny The word is a colloquial short form of *pinafore*, a type of apron, itself so called as it is (or was) *pinned afore*, or pinned over the front of the dress.

pint The liquid measure derives its name from Old French *pinte*. The source of this is uncertain. It may derive from Medieval Latin *pincta*, the plural word for the marks used in measuring liquids, itself from Latin *pingere*, 'to paint'.

> **FALSE**
>
> **pint** From a former spelling of the word that gave *pound*. The two measures thus have the same origin.

pirate The word goes back through Latin to Greek *peiratēs*, 'attacker', from the noun *peira*, 'attempt', 'attack'. (This word is itself related to the root of Latin *periculum*, the source of ◊peril.)

piss The word is imitative of the sound made when urinating. See also ◊dandelion.

> **FALSE**
>
> **pistol** From the name of *Pistoia*, Italy, the town from which the weapon was first brought to England in 1626.

pistol The word is said to have come into English, through French and German, from Czech *pišt'al*, 'pipe', related to Russian *pishchal*, 'shepherd's pipe' (also 'arquebus').

pittance The word was originally used for a donation made out of *pity*, as form of *piety* (the two words are related). Hence its ultimate origin in Latin *pietas*, 'dutifulness', 'pity'.

placard The word for a printed notice or poster came into English from Old French *plaquart*, itself from *plaquier*, 'to lay flat'.

placebo The term for a sham medicine or drug was originally used for any medicine given purely to *please* the patient. Hence its origin in the identical Latin word meaning 'I shall please'. This was already in use as a traditional name for the vespers for the dead, from its opening words: '*Placebo Domino in regione vivorum*', 'I shall please the Lord in the land of the living' (Psalm 114:9).

plague The word ultimately derives from Latin *plaga*, 'blow', related to Greek *plēgē*, 'stroke'.

planet The planets were originally regarded as special kinds of stars, in that they changed their position in the sky much more obviously and frequently than the regular stars did. Hence the source of their name in Greek *planētēs*, 'wanderer'.

plaster The word is Old English in origin, from Medieval Latin *plastrum*, itself from Latin *emplastrum*, adopted from Greek *emplastron*, 'curative dressing', from *en-*, 'in', and *plassein*, 'to form'.

platform The literal sense of the word is 'flat shape', from French *plateforme*, representing *plat*, 'flat', and *forme*, 'form', 'shape', 'layout'.

please The word goes back through Old French *plaisir* to Latin *placere*, 'to please', itself from the base of *placidus*, 'placid', and *placare*, 'to placate'. The use of *please* in 'yes please' and 'please hurry', for example, is short for the earlier phrase *please you*, meaning 'may it please you' (though it is now taken as short for 'if you please').

pliers The tool is so called since it is used for *plying* or bending objects.

plimsoll The type of light shoe, also known as *gymshoe*, derives its name from the resemblance of its rubber sole to a *Plimsoll* line, that is, the line painted on the side of a ship to indicate the level that the waterline should reach if the ship is properly loaded. The line itself, also known as a *loadline*, is named from Samuel *Plimsoll* (1824–1898), the MP who recommended its adoption. The name of the shoe is also spelt *plimsole* by association with *sole*. The adoption of this particular name doubtless arose because such shoes were worn on board ship as deck shoes.

plonk The colloquial word for 'wine' may derive from French *vin blanc*, 'white wine' (though 'plonk' is usually red wine, not white).

pluck In the sense 'courage', the word developed from its use for the heart, liver, and lungs of an animal, as being *plucked* out of a carcass for use as food. If you have 'heart', you have courage.

plumber The person who installs and repairs pipes, drains, and the like originally worked with lead piping. Hence his name, which derives, through French, from Latin *plumbum*, 'lead'.

plump It is not certain whether the senses of 'fall down heavily' and 'stout' derive from one and the same source. If they do, the word is almost certainly imitative in origin. A *plump* person *plumps* into or onto a chair when sitting down.

plus fours The baggy trousers formerly worn by golfers are so called because they were originally made with *four* extra inches of material for the overhang at the knee.

plutonium The metallic element produced in a nuclear reactor is named after the planet *Pluto* because Pluto lies beyond Neptune and plutonium occurs in the periodic table (of elements) after neptunium.

pneumonia The term for inflammation of the lungs ultimately derives from Greek *pneumōn*, 'lung'. (One might have expected *pneumonitis*, given that *-itis* denotes an inflammatory disease, such as *bronchitis*. The word does exist, but it has not replaced *pneumonia* as a general term.)

poach As used for cooking eggs, the word derives from Old French *poche*, 'bag' (modern English *pouch*). The reference is to the white of the egg, which is a 'bag' containing the yolk. (As now poached, eggs are usually cooked in 'cups' in a poacher. They were originally poached by being dropped into boiling water minus their shell.)

pocket The word derives from Anglo-Norman *poket*, a diminutive of *poke*, 'poke', 'bag'. French *poche*, 'pocket', is a related word. (English *poke* in this sense, now only in dialect use, is the origin of 'pig in a *poke*'.)

poem The word comes from Latin *poema*, from the identical Greek word that was a variant of *poiēma*, literally 'something created', from *poiein*, 'to make'. The original words did not thus denote the rhyme or metre that are now regarded as a poem's essential attributes.

poison Unexpectedly, the word literally means 'drink', and is directly related to *potion*. The origin is in Old French *puison*, from Latin *potio*, genitive *potionis*, 'drink'. This word came to be used for a specially prepared drink, hence for a drink prepared with poison. In modern languages the word then passed to the poisonous substance itself.

police The word goes back, through French, to Latin *politia*, 'administration', 'government', itself ultimately from Greek *polis*, 'city', the source of modern English *politics*.

policy As used of an insurance document, the word derives from Old French *police*, 'certificate', ultimately from Greek *apodeixis*, 'demonstration', 'proof'. The other sense of *policy*, referring to a plan of action, as of a government, derives from Latin *politia*, 'administration'. (See ◊police.)

polite A *polite* person has *polished* manners, and this is the literal meaning of the word, from Latin *politus*, the adjectival form of the verb *polire*, 'to polish'.

polo The name of the game, which is of ancient Oriental origin, derives from the identical word in Balti (a dialect of Kashmir, India) meaning 'ball'. The game was introduced to India in the 13th century, and was taken up there by the British in the heyday of the Raj.

poltroon The literary word for a coward derives, through French, from Italian *poltrone*, 'lazy good-for-nothing', itself probably from *poltro*, 'bed'. A poltroon was thus a 'lie-abed'.

FALSE

poltroon From Latin *pollice truncato*, 'having been deprived of the thumb'. Romans who wanted to avoid serving in the wars cut off a thumb so as to be unfit. They were thus cowards, or *poltroons*.

---

pompous The word goes back to Latin *pompa*, 'procession', in turn from Greek *pompē*, literally 'sending', from a word related to *pempein*, 'to send'. A *pompous* person puts on a 'show', like an important person in a procession.

pond The word has the same origin as *pound* (in the sense 'enclosure'), from the Old English word with that meaning (though originally found only in compound words, such as *pundfeald*, modern *pinfold*). A *pond* was originally an artificially formed pool of water, not a natural one, as now.

pontiff The former title of the pagan high priest at Rome, now used as a title of the pope, derives, through French, from Latin *pontifex*. This literally means 'bridge-maker', from Latin *pons*, genitive *pontis*, 'bridge', and the root of *facere*, 'to make'. However, this derived from some other word, perhaps of Etruscan origin, and was reformed to make it meaningful.

FALSE

pontiff From Latin *pontifex*, 'bridge-builder'. The first bridge over the Tiber was built by the chief priest.

---

pony The origin of the name of the small horse is uncertain. It may ultimately go back, through French, to a colloquial Latin word deriving from *pullus*, 'young animal' (the source of English *foal*).

pope The head of the Roman Catholic Church has a title that basically means 'father', from Church Latin *papa*, 'bishop' (referring to the Bishop of Rome), itself from Greek *pappas*, 'father'. The direct English equivalent of the title is thus *papa*.

porcelain The word for the fine type of earthenware or china came into English, via French, from Italian *porcellana*, 'cowrie shell', referring to the ware's shell-like finish. The word for the shell in turn is an adjectival form of *porcella*, a diminutive of *porca*, 'sow'. This came about because the shell was thought to resemble the vulva of a sow.

porcupine The animal with prickly spines derives its name from Old French *porc espin* (modern French *porc-épic*), 'pig with spines', from *porc*, 'pig' (English *pork*), and *espin*, 'spine' (the source of this English word).

pornography The origin of the word is in Greek *pornographos*, 'writing about prostitutes', from *pornē*, 'prostitute', and *graphein*, 'to write'. Although based on Greek, the word arose only in the 19th century.

porpoise The name of the small whalelike animal came into English, through French, from Medieval Latin *porcopiscus*, literally 'pig fish', from Latin *porcus*, 'pig', and *piscis*, 'fish'. This replaced its original Latin name, which was *porcus marinus*, 'sea pig'.

porridge   The word is an altered form of *pottage*, and originally applied to a thick meat or vegetable soup. It gained its present meaning in the 17th century. The alteration of *t* to *r* is as in Geordie *gerraway* for *get away*.

portcullis   The grating that can be raised and lowered at a castle entrance derives its name from Old French *porte coleïce*, 'sliding gate', from *porte*, 'door', 'entrance', and *couler*, 'to slide'.

portfolio   The word for a case for important documents, or for the documents themselves, derives from Italian *portafoglio*, literally 'papers' carrier', from *portare*, 'to carry', and *foglio*, 'leaf', 'paper'.

posse   The American word for a group of men that a sheriff can call on to help maintain order is short for *posse comitatus*, from a Medieval Latin phrase meaning 'strength of a county', ie, its manpower.

poster   A *poster* was originally a bill or placard *posted* on a *post* (as some are on telegraph *posts* and lamp*posts* still today). Hence its name.

posthumous   The word referring to something happening after a person's death derives from Latin *postumus*, 'last of all', as being the last thing connected with that person. The *h* in the word came in by association with Latin *humus*, 'earth', as if the meaning was 'after the burial' (from Latin *post*, 'after').

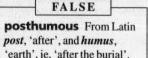

FALSE

posthumous   From Latin *post*, 'after', and *humus*, 'earth', ie, 'after the burial'.

posy   The word for a small bunch of flowers evolved from *poesy*, a former word for a poem or for poetry.

pot   The origin of the word is uncertain, but it may be from Latin *potus*, 'drink'.

potash   The popular name for potassium carbonate (used in making glass and soap) derives from *pot ashes*. This translated obsolete Dutch *potaschen*, and referred to the original method of obtaining potash, which was by evaporating the lye of wood *ashes* in *pots*. See also ◊potassium.

potassium   The name of the chemical derives from New Latin *potassa*, 'potash' (see ◊potash). It was coined in 1807 by the chemist Humphry Davy (basing it on *magnesium* and *sodium*) in order to designate the metallic element which is the basis of potash.

potpourri   The term for a miscellany of objects (originally a mixture of dried petals) represents French *pot pourri*, literally 'rotten pot', itself a translation of Spanish *olla podrida* in the same sense. This was a Spanish dish comprising a mixture of meat, vegetables, and the like. It was called 'rotten' because it was cooked slowly, so that the meat and vegetables gradually disintegrated, as if decomposing.

pounce The word was originally used for the claw of a bird of prey (which *pounced* on its object). It seems to have derived from some French word that was also the source of modern *punch* (a tool for piercing holes).

pound Whether the weight (lb) or the money (£), the word ultimately goes back to Latin *pondus*, 'weight'. Modern coinage evolved from amounts of weighed metal. Both *lb* and the pound sign £ (representing *L*) are short for Latin *libra*, 'scales'.

powder The word goes back through Old French *poldre* to Latin *pulvis*, 'dust' (the source of English *pulverize*).

prairie The word is French in origin, and ultimately derives from Latin *pratum*, 'meadow' (modern French *pré*).

pram The word for the baby carriage is short for *perambulator*, ultimately from Latin *perambulare*, 'to traverse', literally 'to walk through', from *per*, 'through', and *ambulare*, 'to walk'. Compare ◊ambulance.

prank The word for a trick or practical joke is related to *prance*, and is of Germanic origin. (Modern German *Prunk*, 'splendour', 'magnificence', is also related.)

precarious Although now applied to something liable to fail or collapse, the word was originally a legal term denoting something that depended on another person's favour or goodwill. Hence its origin in Latin *precarius*, 'obtained by begging', based on *prex*, genitive *precis*, 'entreaty' (English *prayer*).

precocious The word now commonly describing a bright young child ahead of his years literally means 'precooked', from Latin *praecox*, 'early ripening', representing *prae*, 'prematurely', and *coquere*, 'to cook', 'to ripen'. Compare ◊apricot.

predestination The term for the doctrine that our lives are planned in advance by God derives from Latin *praedestinare*, 'to determine beforehand'. This gained its special Christian meaning as early as the 3rd century, and the verb *predestinate* in the Bible (Romans 8:29, 30) is the English equivalent of the Latin word, which itself translated Greek *proorizein*, 'to predetermine'.

predicament The word for a difficult situation was originally used as a term in logic for the category of *predication* (relating to what is said about the subject of a proposition). It derives from Latin *praedicamentum*, which itself translated Greek *katēgoria*, 'accusation', 'charge', literally 'against the assembly', from *kata*, 'against', and *agora*, 'assembly'. This Greek word is the source of English *category*.

pregnant The word derives, through French, from Latin *praegnans*, genitive *praegnantis*, in the same sense. This literally means 'before being born', from *prae*, 'before', and the base of *nasci*, 'to be born'. English *prenatal* is thus directly related.

prestige The word is of French origin, and derives from Latin *praestigiae*, 'juggler's tricks', apparently from the verb *praestringere*, 'to bind tight' (in the sense of dazzling the eyes as if with a blindfold), from *prae*, 'before', and *stringere*, 'to bind', 'to draw tight' (English *stringent*). A person's *prestige* arises from a dazzling success or the like.

pretty The original sense of the word was 'cunning', 'crafty'. Its origin is in a Germanic word that gave modern Dutch *pret*, 'sport', 'fun'. Something of the original sense remains in the phrase 'sitting pretty', implying that one is exploiting an advantageous position.

priest The word apparently developed as a form of *presbyter*. This literally means 'elder' (in the sense of the head of a congregation), from Greek *presbuteros*, 'older man', ultimately from *presbus*, 'old man'.

print To *print* something was originally to *press* inked type onto paper. The words are related, so that *print* goes back through Old French *priente* to Latin *premere*, 'to press'. Hence also *press* as the term for the *printed* news media.

prison The word goes back through Old French to Latin *prensio*, 'capture', the act of *prehendere*, 'to lay hold of', from *prae*, 'before', and obsolete *hendere*, 'to grasp' (to which English *get* is ultimately related). The word thus originally related to the action of capturing a prisoner, rather than to the building.

privilege The word has its origin in the legal Latin term *privilegium*, denoting a law that related to the rights of an individual. The literal meaning is thus 'law of the individual', from *privus*, 'individual person' (English *private*), and *lex*, genitive *legis*, 'law'. A person enjoying a *privilege* thus has an individual right to it.

prize A *prize* is literally something taken or captured, from Old French *prise*, 'capture'. The word is directly related to *price*, since something captured has a value or worth, which is its *price*. Even a *prize* in the modern sense, as an award, has a particular value or *price*, and the association between prizes and money is a close one.

problem The word goes back through French and Latin to Greek *problēma*, the noun of *proballein*, 'to throw forward', from *pro*, 'forward', and *ballein*, 'to throw'.

prodigy The word for a talented child derives from Latin *prodigium*, 'portent', 'wonderful sign', from *pro-*, 'forward', and an element relating either to Latin *dicere*, 'to say', or *agere*, 'to drive'. English *prodigious* is of the same origin.

profane The original sense of the word was 'secular', as opposed to 'sacred'. As such, it has its origin in Latin *profanus*, literally 'outside the temple', from *pro*, 'before' (ie, outside), and *fanum*, 'temple'.

programme The ultimate source of the word is Greek *programma*, the word for a public written notice, from *pro*, 'before', and *graphein*, 'to write', that is, 'writing before the public'.

prominent The literal sense of the word is 'jutting out', from Latin *prominere*, 'to jut out', representing *pro*, 'forward', and *eminere*, 'to project' (English *eminent*).

prompt The word derives, through French, from Latin *promptus*, 'ready', 'evident', itself from *promere*, 'to produce', representing *pro*, 'forward', and *emere*, 'to take' (later 'to buy').

propaganda The earliest use of the word, in the 18th century, was for the committee of cardinals responsible for the foreign missions of the Roman Catholic Church. As such, it was short for the committee's Latin title: *Sacra Congregatio de Propaganda Fide*, 'Sacred Congregation for Propagating the Faith'. Hence the word's later sense to mean any deliberate spreading of information. The word is grammatically a feminine gerundive of *propagare*, 'to spread', 'to propagate'.

prophet The word comes ultimately, through French and Latin, from Greek *prophētēs*, 'interpreter', literally 'one speaking before', from *pro*, 'before', and *phanai*, 'to speak'. In the religious sense, this applied to someone who was the spokesman of a god and who could say what his or her will was.

prostate The clinical name of the gland at the junction of the neck of the bladder and the urethra derives from Greek *prostatēs*, 'thing standing in front', from *pro*, 'before', and *statos*, 'standing'. The reference is to the position of the gland in front of the bladder.

prostitute The origin of the word is in Latin *prostitutus*, from *prostituere*, 'to expose for sale', literally 'to set up in front', from *pro*, 'forward', 'in front', and *statuere*, 'to set up'. A prostitute advertises herself by putting herself before the public in the same way that a vendor sets out goods for sale (in some countries by sitting in or by a window, like goods displayed in a shop window).

prostrate The term for a position lying face down on the ground has its origin in Latin *prostratus*, from *prosternere*, 'to throw to the ground', from *pro*, 'forward', and *sternere*, 'to stretch (someone) out on the ground', 'to lay low'.

protein The organic compound found in all living organisms has a name that ultimately derives from Greek *prōteios*, 'primary', since *proteins* are *primary* to the body.

protest The word goes back, through French, to Latin *protestari*, 'to declare formally', from *pro*, 'forward', and *testari*, 'to assert', 'to be a witness'.

protocol The term for formal etiquette or a strict code of behaviour derives from Medieval Latin *protocollum*, a form of Greek *prōtokollon*. This was the word for a sheet glued to the front of a manuscript to describe the contents, from *prōtos*, 'first', and *kolla*, 'glue'.

proud The word goes back through Old English, Old French, and Late Latin to Latin *prodesse*, 'to be of value', from *prod*, a variant of *pro*, 'for', and *esse*, 'to be'.

proverb A *proverb* is literally 'words put forward', as its Latin origin implies, from *proverbium*, representing *pro*, 'forward', and *verbum*, 'word'. The word was first used in English for the title of the biblical Book of *Proverbs* in the 14th century.

proxy The term for an action by someone else, such as the casting of a vote on one's behalf, arose as a contraction of *procuracy*, from Latin *procuratio*, 'procuration', that is, the act of *procuring* or getting another person to do what is required.

prude The word for an excessively 'prim and proper' person derives as a shortening of French *prudefemme*, from Old French *prode femme*, 'respectful woman'. The word ultimately goes back to the same source as ◊proud. The origin implies that only women are prudes, although men may equally be.

prune The *prune* is a dried *plum*, and the words are related, with a common origin in Latin *prunum*, 'plum'. (Modern French *prune* is the standard word for 'plum'.)

psalm The word for the religious song or hymn ultimately goes back to Greek *psallein*, 'to pluck', 'to twang', that is, to play the harp or sing to it. The word may be indirectly related to Latin *palpare*, 'to stroke', 'to caress' (English *palpate* and *palpitate*).

psychological *Psychology* is literally the 'science of the soul', from a New Latin word formed from Greek *psukhē*, 'soul' (literally 'breath'), and *logos*, 'word'.

publish To *publish* a book or information is to bring it before the *public*. The origin is ultimately in Latin *publicus*, an altered form of *poplicus*, the adjective of *populus*, 'people'.

pudding The precise source of the word is uncertain. It was originally used for the equivalent of the modern haggis, that is, meat, seasonings, oatmeal, and the like prepared in a bag formed from an animal's stomach. The French equivalent for this, or for what is now called black *pudding*, is *boudin*. The words are similar, but there is no evidence that one derived from the other or that they have a common origin.

> **FALSE**
>
> **pulley** So called because used to *pull* up loads on a rope.

pulley The ultimate source of the word appears to be in an unrecorded Late Greek word *polidion*, 'little pole', from Greek *polos*, 'axis'. If so, the word is related to English *pole* (as in 'north *pole*'), which came from this Greek word.

pumpernickel The name of the German rye bread is of uncertain origin. One source derives it from New High German *Pumpern*, 'fart' (an imitative word), and *Nickel*, 'devil', referring to the fact that the bread is difficult to digest.

> **FALSE**
>
> **pumpernickel** From the derisory comment of a French cavalry officer, who said that the German bread was only *bon pour Nicolas*, 'good for Nicholas', meaning his horse.

pun The word apparently evolved as a shortened form of Italian *puntiglio*, 'point of detail', 'quibble' (the source of English *punctilious*. If so, it has a history similar to ◊mob.

punk The word emerged in the 16th century in the sense 'prostitute'. Its source is uncertain, but it may have derived from Spanish *puta* in the same sense. It is apparently unrelated to the *punk* that means 'touchwood' (dry decayed wood that smoulders when ignited).

puny The word, used of someone with a weak physique, derives from Old French *puisne*, literally 'born later', from *puis*, 'at a later date', itself from Latin *postea*, 'afterwards', and *né*, 'born', from Latin *nasci*, 'to be born'. A child born after the first was regarded as weaker. The spelling *puisne* was adopted for legal use to denote a subordinate judge.

pupil In its sense of 'student', the word goes back to Latin *pupillus*, 'orphan', a diminutive of *pupus*, 'boy', 'child'. When used for the centre of the eye, the word derives from Latin *pupilla*, a diminutive of *pupa*, 'girl', 'doll'. The latter sense refers to the tiny reflections of objects that can be seen in the pupil of the eye. The sources are thus effectively identical.

puppy The word came into English from Old French *popée* (modern French *poupée*), 'doll'. The word was used for a lap dog or toy dog in English before it was generally adopted for a young dog.

purple The colour name ultimately derives from Greek *porphura*, 'purple fish' (*Murex*), which yielded a purple dye. The word is related to the reddish-purple rock known as *porphyry*.

puzzle The word is itself a puzzle, and is of unknown origin. Attempts to derive it from *pose* have met with difficulties of chronology, and the word is first recorded only in the late 16th century.

pygmy The word for a small or unimportant person derives from the name of the *Pygmies*, the dwarf people of Equatorial Africa. They got it, through Latin, from Greek *pugmaios*, 'undersized', from *pugmē*, literally 'fist', but used as the term for a measure of length equal to the distance from the elbow to the knuckles, that is, about 13 inches (34 cm). The reference is to the people's small size (but hardly as small as this!).

pyjamas The word came into English, via Persian or Urdu, from Persian *pāē*, 'foot', 'leg', and *jāmah*, 'clothing'. The term thus originally applied to loose trousers tied round the waist, but was later extended to the sleeping suit with jacket.

quack In the colloquial (or derogatory) sense of 'doctor' the word is short for *quacksalver*. This is said to be of Dutch origin and to represent *quack*, 'to hawk', and *salf*, 'ointment' (English *salve*). The shortened word evolved in the same way as *rake* (dissolute person) from *rakehell*, *sap* (foolish person) from *sapskull*, and possibly *wag* (mischievous person) from *waghalter*.

FALSE

quack A *quack doctor* was originally a *quake doctor*, that is, one who treated the *quake* or ague.

---

quail In the sense 'cower', 'shrink back with fear', the word may have its origin in Old French *quailler* in this sense. Its own derivation is in Latin *coagulare*, 'to curdle' (English *coagulate*).

quaint The original meaning of the word was 'clever'. Hence its origin in Old French *cointe*, from Latin *cognitus*, 'known', a form of the verb *cognoscere*, 'to know' (English *cognisant*).

FALSE

quandary From the French phrase *Qu'en dirai-je?*, 'What shall I say about it?'

---

quandary The word for a problem or dilemma is of uncertain origin. It may have been formed from Latin *quando*, 'when', as if implying 'when shall I solve this?'

quarantine The term for a period of medical isolation derives from Italian *quarantina*, 'period of forty days', from *quaranta*, 'forty'. The word was originally a legal term for the period of forty days in which a widow had the right to remain in her husband's chief mansion house.

quarrel The original sense of the word was 'complaint'. This explains its derivation in Latin *querella* in this sense, itself from *queri*, 'to complain'.

quarry In its sense of 'hunted animal', the word goes back to Middle English *quirre*. This was the term for the entrails of a deer placed on its hide and given to the hounds. The ultimate source is in Old French *cuir*, 'hide', influenced by *coree*, 'entrails' (from *cor*, 'heart'). In the sense 'stone mine', the word goes back through Old French to Latin *quadrare*, 'to make square', referring to the cutting of square blocks of stone.

queasy The word originally meant 'troubled' or 'unsettled' generally. It is of uncertain origin, There is no support for a derivation from Old French *coisier*, 'hurt', 'wound'.

queen The word ultimately goes back to an Indo-European root element that also gave Greek *gunē*, Russian *zhena* (superseded by *zhenshchina*), and Irish *bean*, all meaning 'woman'. (The Greek word is the base of English 'gynaecology'.)

queer The word is probably related to or even derived from German *quer*, 'oblique', 'slanting', implying that something is 'not straight'. (Compare modern English 'bent'.)

> **FALSE**
>
> **queer** From Latin *quaere*, 'ask!' (English *query*), written by a trader against the names of customers whose ability to pay was uncertain.

queue The word came into English from French, in which it means 'tail'. It was first used for the tail of a beast in a heraldic shield, then for a pigtail, and finally for a line of people, which can curve like a tail.

quibble The word for a trivial objection perhaps ultimately derives from Latin *quibus*, 'by whom', 'by which', as occurring in legal documents, in which verbal niceties are still commonplace.

quick The original meaning of the English word was 'living', 'alive', as in the biblical 'the quick and the dead'. (Hence the modern sense, since a *quick* action is a 'lively' one.) The word goes back to an Indo-European root element that also gave Latin *vivus*, 'living', Greek *bios*, 'life', Russian *zhivoy*, 'alive', and so English *vital* and *vivid*.

quince The name of the fruit represents a plural word (compare *pence*) that goes back through Old French *coin* (modern French *coing*) and Latin *cotoneum* to Greek *kudōnion*, short for *mêlon kudōnion*, 'Cydonian apple'. Cydonia is an ancient city and port (now Canea, or Khaniá) in northwestern Crete.

quinine The bitter medicine is extracted from the bark of the cinchona tree, growing in South America. Hence the origin of the word in Quechua *kina*, 'bark'.

quinsy The term for inflammation of the tonsils goes back through French and Latin to Greek *kunankhē*, literally 'dog throttler', from *kuōn*, 'dog', and *ankhein*, 'to throttle', 'to strangle'. The condition is so called since it frequently occurs in dogs.

quintessence The word for an essential or basic representation of something derives from Medieval Latin *quinta essentia*, 'fifth essence', a translation of Greek *pemptē ousia*. In ancient philosophy there were five 'essences' or elements that were believed to be present in all things. The four basic ones were earth, fire, air, and water. The 'fifth essence', and the highest, was ether.

quip The word for a witty remark probably derives from Latin *quippe*, 'to be sure', 'indeed', as in the following exchange: '*Recte igitur diceres te restituisse?*

Quippe: quid enim facilius?', 'Would you therefore say that you have been correctly reinstated? Certainly: for what is easier?' (Cicero).

quite The word is an adverbial use of the identical adjective, itself an earlier form of *quit* meaning 'free', 'clear' (as in 'quit of all responsibility'). If you are *quit* of something, you are *quite* free of it.

quorum The term for a minimum number of people present (when transacting business) derives directly from the identical Latin word meaning 'of whom', occurring in Latin commissions designating such people, for example in the formula: '*quorum vos [...] duos esse volumus*', 'of whom we wish that you [...] be two' (the ellipsis naming them).

quota The word for a proportional amount derives from Latin *quota pars*, 'how big a share?'.

quote The word evolved from the Medieval Latin verb *quotare*, 'to number' (in the sense of giving numbered pages to passages), itself from *quot*, 'how many'.

R

rabbit The origin of the name is obscure. It was originally used for the young animal only, the adult being called a *cony*, itself ultimately from Latin *cuniculus*, 'rabbit'. (Hence New York's *Coney* Island, originally overrun by rabbits.)

> **FALSE**
>
> **rabbit** From Latin *rapidus*, 'rapid', referring to the animal's agility and speed in running.

racket As used in tennis, the word goes back through French *raquette* to Arabic *rāḥat*, 'palm of the hand'. In the sense 'noise', 'hubbub', the word probably arose as an imitation of a clattering sound.

radio The word arose as a short form of *radiotelegraphy*, in which it is a form of Latin *radius*, 'ray', referring to the transmissions, which *radiate* from the broadcasting station.

ragamuffin The origin of the word for a ragged or scruffy person is of uncertain origin. It is probably based on *rag*. In the late 14th-century poem *Piers Plowman*, one of the characters is a demon called *Ragamoffyn*.

raid The word for a military attack was originally used for a military expedition on horseback. It is an old Scottish form of ◊road, as revived by Sir Walter Scott in *The Lay of the Last Minstrel* (1805): 'In raids he spilt but seldom blood'.

raisin The fruit is a dried grape, and its name derives from the identical French word for 'grape'. (The French for 'raisin' is thus *raisin sec*, 'dry grape'.) The ultimate source of the word is in Latin *racemus*, 'cluster of grapes'.

rake The name of the gardening implement ultimately goes back to an Indo-European root element meaning 'straight', 'stretch', that also gave modern English *right*. The reference is to the straight pronged crossbar.

ramble The word is probably related to a Middle Dutch word that gave *roam* (as applied to animals, especially when seeking a mate). Its ultimate source is in the Germanic word that gave *ram* (male sheep).

> **FALSE**
>
> **ramble** From a shortened form of Latin *perambulare*, 'to wander about'.

rampage The word is of uncertain origin. It is first found in Scotland, and may be based on *ramp*.

ramshackle The word evolved as an adjectival form of ◊ransack, which see for the origin.

random The word came into English from Old French, in which a phrase such as **en un randon** meant 'at a gallop'. The ultimate source of the word is Germanic, from a word related to modern English *run*.

ransack The literal sense of the word is 'search a house', from Old Norse **rann**, 'house', and **saka**, 'to search'. The word originally applied not to plundering but to searching a house for stolen goods.

ransom The word evolved as a French form of the Latin word that itself gave English *redemption*. If you pay a *ransom* to get someone or something back, you have *redeemed* them.

rape The original sense of the word was 'take by force', from Latin **rapere**, 'to seize', 'to snatch'. The present sense evolved from the concept of seizing someone for a particular purpose. (English *ravish* is directly related.) Compare ◊rapture, ◊ravine.

rapture The literal meaning of the word is 'carrying off', from Medieval Latin **raptura**, 'seizure', from Latin **rapere**, 'to seize', 'to snatch'. (Compare ◊rape.) If you are in a state of *rapture* or ecstasy, you are *rapt*, and have been emotionally 'transported' to that heightened state.

rascal The word derives from Old French **rascaille**, 'rabble', its original sense in English. This itself may have evolved from Old Norman French **rasque**, 'mud', 'filth'.

raspberry The fruit was known in the 16th century as *rasp* or *raspis*. The source of this is uncertain. It does not appear to be related to *rasp* in any sense.

> **FALSE**
>
> **raspberry** So called because it is rough on the outside, like a *rasp*.

rather The word represents the comparative ('more') form of what is now the archaic or dialect word *rathe* or *rath*, which originally meant 'quick', 'eager'. The literal sense is thus 'more quickly', 'more eagerly'.

raven The big black bird has a name that ultimately imitates its raucous voice or *caw*. The same applies to its name in other languages, such as Latin *corvus* and Greek *korax*.

> **FALSE**
>
> **raven** So called because it is *ravenous*.

ravine The word derives from the identical Old French word meaning 'torrent', itself from Latin **rapina**, 'robbery', influenced by Latin **rapidus**, 'rapid'. Both these words are themselves related to Latin **rapere**, 'to seize' (see ◊rape).

raze In its sense of 'demolish', the word derives from Old French (and modern) **raser**, 'to shave', itself from Latin **radere**, 'to scrape'. English *erase* is related. See also ◊razor.

> **FALSE**
>
> **raze** From Spanish *raíz*, 'root'. To *raze* a building is to *root* it up.

razor The shaving implement is so called since it *razes* or removes hair from the skin by scraping it. The ultimate origin is thus in Latin *radere*, 'to scrape'. Compare ▷raze

reason The word goes back through Old French *reisun* to Latin *ratio*, genitive *rationis*, 'reckoning', 'account', from the verb *reri*, 'to think', 'to reckon'.

rebel The literal sense of the word is 'one who makes war again', from Latin, through French, *rebellis*, 'insurgent', formed from *re-*, 'again', and *bellum*, 'war'. The Latin word originally applied to conquered people who waged war again.

recalcitrant The word describing a stubborn or 'difficult' person literally means 'kicking again', from Latin *recalcitrare*, 'to kick back', formed from *re-*, 'again', and a word based on *calx*, genitive *calcis*, 'heel'.

recipe The word comes direct from Latin, in which it is the order 'take!', from the verb *recipere*, 'to receive'. It was originally used for the formula of a medical prescription, and passed to cookery only in the 18th century.

recollect The literal sense is 'collect again'. If you *recollect* something you call it to mind again.

recreation The word derives, through French, from Latin *recreare*, literally 'to create again'. The object of *recreation* is to 're-create' or restore yourself by some pleasant activity.

recruit The word comes from French dialect *recrute*, literally 'new growth', ultimately from Latin *recrescere*, 'to grow again'. The concept is of new troops brought in to reinforce a depleted army, and so enable it to 'grow again'.

redeem The literal meaning is 'buy back', from Latin *redimere* in this sense, formed from *red-*, a form of *re-* before vowels, 'again', 'back', and *emere*, 'to buy'. The figurative sense applies just as much as the literal: if you *redeem* yourself, you 'buy yourself back' from the action that had 'sold' you to a bad or evil influence.

redundant The word relating to someone or something that is superfluous derives from Latin *redundans*, 'overflowing' (the literal meaning of *superfluous*), from *redundare*, 'to run back', 'to stream over', from *red-*, a form of *re-* before a vowel, 'back', and *undare*, 'to be agitated' (of the sea), from *unda*, 'water', 'wave'.

refuse The verb comes from French *refuser*, itself from Latin *refundere*, 'to pour back', from *re-*, 'again', 'back', and *fundere*, 'to pour'. This same Latin verb also gave English *refund*, referring to money that is 'poured back'.

regatta The sporting contest for yachts or boats derives its name from an obsolete Italian dialect word *rigatta*, 'contest', used for a gondola race on the Grand Canal, Venice. Related Spanish *regatear* means both 'to race' and 'to haggle over'.

register The word ultimately comes from Latin *regerere*, 'to transcribe', literally 'to carry back', from *re-*, 'back', 'again', and *gerere*, 'to bear', 'to carry'. A *register* is a systematic record of something that already exists or has happened. Hence the sense of 'bearing back' written information about it.

regret   The word is ultimately, via French, of Germanic origin, based on a source word related to modern (Scottish) *greet*, in the sense 'weep', 'lament'.

rehearse   The word comes from Anglo-Norman *rehearser*, from Old French *rehercier*, literally 'to harrow again', from *re-*, 'again', and *herce*, 'harrow'. If you *rehearse* a part or a speech, you go over the ground again. See also ⟡hearse.

reindeer   The name of the animal comes from Old Norse *hreindȳri*, in which *hreinn* already means 'reindeer' and *dyr* means 'animal'. (See ⟡deer.)

> **FALSE**
>
> **reindeer**   From German *Rentier*, 'running animal'.

relay   The word for a person or team of people taking over from others, as in a shift or race, goes back through French to an ultimate source in French *re-*, 'again', and Latin *laxare*, 'to loosen' (the source of English *lax* and *laxative*). English *lease*, *relax*, and *release* are closely related words.

religion   The word ultimately derives from Latin *religio*, genitive *religionis*, 'superstition', 'obligation'. The Latin word itself probably comes from *religare*, 'to tie up', from *re-*, as an intensive prefix, and *ligare*, 'to tie'. The basic sense thus probably implies being bound or tied to a god.

> **FALSE**
>
> **religion**   From Latin *relegere*, 'to read again', referring to the word of God, which is recorded or *read again* in the Bible.

relish   The word ultimately goes back to Old French *relaisser*, 'to leave behind'. If you *relish* a food, you thus enjoy the taste that is left behind after you have eaten it.

remember   The word goes back, through French, to Late Latin *rememorari*, 'to recall to mind', from *re-*, 'again', 'back', and *memor*, 'mindful' (the source of English *memory*).

remorse   The word for a feeling of regret for a misdeed derives from Latin *remordere*, 'to bite again', implying that one's conscience has 'bitten back'.

render   The literal meaning of the word is not simply 'give' but 'give in return', 'give back', from a source that ultimately lies in Latin *reddere*, from *red-*, a form of *re-* before a vowel, 'again', 'back', and *dare*, 'to give', influenced by Latin *prendere*, 'to grasp'. The original sense is implicit in some biblical passages, such as 'See that none render evil for evil' (1 Thessalonians 5:15).

repeat   The word goes back to Latin *repetere*, 'to seek again', from *re-*, 'again', and *petere*, 'to seek'. If you *repeat* some words, you have to 'fetch' them from somewhere (such as your memory) in order to say or write them again.

repertoire   The term for the acts or items that a person can perform derives from the identical French word that itself comes from Late Latin *repertorium*, 'inventory'. 'storehouse'. The ultimate source is in Latin *reperire*, literally 'to bring forth again', from *re-*, 'again', and *parere*, 'to bring forth'.

reptile The creatures in this category are so called because they 'creep', or move with their body close to or actually on the ground. Hence the source of the word in Latin *repere*, 'to creep', 'to crawl'.

republic The term ultimately goes back to Latin *respublica*, literally 'public thing', from *res*, 'thing', and *publica*, 'public'. The Roman republic was one in the modern sense, in that the supreme power rested with the people.

repudiate The word meaning 'reject the authority of' derives from Latin *repudium*, 'separation', 'divorce'. If you *repudiate* something, you 'divorce' yourself from it.

rescue The origin of the word is in Old French *rescourre*, from conjectured Vulgar Latin *reexcutere*, 'to drive away', representing the Latin intensive prefix *re-* and *excutere*, 'to shake off', itself from *ex-*, 'out', 'off', and *quatere*, 'to shake'.

respect The word ultimately goes back to Latin *respicere*, literally 'to look back', from *re-*, 'again', 'back', and *specere*, 'to look'. The concept is of considering something carefully, and coming to a (favourable) conclusion about it.

restaurant The obviously French word literally means 'restoring'. A *restaurant* is thus a place where you *restore* your energy and well-being by eating. The same sort of idea lies behind *refreshment*, with which you *refresh* yourself.

retail The word goes back to Old French *retaillier*, 'to cut off', from *re-*, used as an intensive prefix, and *taillier*, 'to cut' (the source of English *tailor*). A *retailer* sells goods in small quantities, 'cut off' (in some cases literally) from wholesale stock.

reveal The ultimate source of the word is in Latin *revelare*, 'to unveil', from *re-*, denoting the opposite of the action, so meaning 'un-', and *velum*, 'veil'.

revolver The pistol is so called since it has chambers that *revolve*, so allowing several shots to be fired without reloading. The word was first applied to the revolver patented by its American inventor Samuel Colt in 1835.

reward The origin of the word is in Old Norman French *rewarder*, 'to regard', literally 'to take care of again', from *re-*, 'again', and *warder*, 'to guard', 'to take care of'. The ultimate source is Germanic. English *regard* is thus related.

rhapsody The term for a lyrical poem or piece of music derives, through Latin, from Greek *rhapsōidia*, literally 'stitched song', from *rhaptein*, 'to stitch', 'to sew together', and *ōidē*, 'song'. The concept is of a number of poems 'stitched' or strung together to make an epic. The individual books of the *Iliad* or the *Odyssey* were thus literally rhapsodies.

> **FALSE**
>
> **reward** From *rereward*, an older form of *rearward*, itself an obsolete word corresponding to modern *rearguard*. This was taken to mean 'reward' in the following biblical passage: 'The glory of the Lord shall be thy rereward' (Isaiah 58:8).

rhetorical   A *rhetorical* question is one to which no answer is required, and so asked for the sake of asking it. The word has its source in Greek *rhētor*, 'orator', related to *rhēma*, 'word'.

rhinoceros   The animal has a Greek name referring to its distinctive feature, the horn or horns on its nose, from *rhis*, genitive *rhinos*, 'nose', and *keras*, 'horn'. Some languages have the name in native words, such as German *Nashorn* (though *Rhinozeros* also exists) and Russian *nosorog*.

rhubarb   The name of the edible plant goes back through Old French *reubarbe* to Medieval Latin *reubarbum*, This was probably a form of *rha barbarum*, 'foreign 'rha'', from a Greek word said to derive from *Rha*, the ancient name of the river Volga, and *barbarus*, 'foreign'. In other words, the plant once grew on the banks of the Volga. The modern spelling has been influenced by Greek *rheuma*, 'flow', 'river' (the source of the river name).

rhyme   The word shares its origin with *rhythm*, and goes back ultimately to Greek *rhuthmos*, related to *rhein*, 'to flow'. The word was formerly written *rime*, a spelling revived in the 18th and 19th centuries (as for Coleridge's *The Rime of the Ancient Mariner*), but the influence of the closely associated *rhythm* prevailed.

ribbon   The word is apparently of Germanic origin, and probably evolved from a word that also gave *band*, with *o* replacing the expected *a* by association with *button* or *cotton*.

rich   The word derives from Old English *rīce*, when the meaning was 'great', 'mighty' (as applied to a person). The ultimate source is in a Celtic word related to modern Irish *rí*, 'king'.

rickshaw   The two-wheeled passenger vehicle, familiar in parts of Asia, derives its name as a shortening of *jinricksha*. This is Japanese in origin, and means literally 'manpower vehicle', from *jin*, 'man', *riki*, 'power', and *sha*, 'carriage'.

ricochet   The word for a rebounding bullet is French in origin, and comes from the phrase *fable du ricochet*, a term for an endless exchange of questions and answers. The origin of the word itself is obscure. It may go back to Latin *recalcare*, 'to retread', 'to trample again', but it has been popularly associated with some derivative of *coq* or *cochet*, 'cock', since the phrase quoted above has also been recorded as *fable du rouge coquelet*, 'story of the red cockerel'.

riddle   The word ultimately goes back to Old English *rǣd*, 'counsel', the source of modern *read*. Hence 'read a riddle' and similar phrases.

rifle   The firearm is so called from its *rifles*, the spiral grooves inside its barrel that spin the bullet for greater accuracy at long range. The word itself derives from Old French *rifler*, 'to scratch'.

righteous   The word has evolved from Old English *rihtwīs*, from *riht*, 'right', and *wīs*, 'manner'. This could have given *rightwise* (like other words in -*wise* such as *crosswise*), but the second element was influenced by words such as *beauteous* and *plenteous*. The literal sense is thus 'in the right way'.

rigmarole The word for a complicated procedure arose as an alteration of *ragman roll*. This was a *roll* with a list of characters in a medieval game, the first being *Ragemon le bon*, 'Ragman the good'.

rile To *rile* someone is to irritate them by 'stirring them up'. Hence the origin of the word, which is a form of *roil*, a dialect verb for the action of making a liquid cloudy or turbid by stirring its dregs or sediment. The source of this word itself is obscure.

rink The stretch of ice for skaters is so called from Old French *renc*, 'row', itself from a word of Germanic origin that also gave English *rank*.

riot The word derives from Old French *riote*, 'dispute', itself probably ultimately from Latin *rugire*, 'to roar'. Compare the 'Roaring Boys' as a name for the riotous young men who indulged in noisy pranks in London in the 16th and 17th centuries.

rissole The fried cake of meat has a name of French origin, itself probably deriving from Latin *russus*, 'red', referring to its colour.

rival The word literally means 'one who shares the same stream', from the adjectival form of Latin *rivus*, 'stream'. The reference is to two people living on opposite banks of a stream and sharing water rights.

river The word ultimately goes back to Latin *ripa*, 'bank'. This may seem strange, since the river itself as a source of water and power and a means of communication and transportation is what is important. But it is the bank that gives access to such facilities.

road The word is directly related to *ride*, since this is the action for which a *road* was originally used or constructed. See also ◊raid.

robin The bird was originally known as the *redbreast* (compare its French name, *rouge-gorge*, 'red throat'). This was then 'personalized' by the addition of the proper name *Robin*, which eventually took over as its general name. Compare ◊jackdaw and ◊magpie.

robust The source of the word is in Latin *robustus*, the adjectival form of *robus*, itself an altered form of *robur*, 'oak tree'. This tree is well known for its strength and hardiness.

rocket The word comes from Old French *roquette*, itself from Italian *rochetto*, a diminutive of *rocca*, 'distaff' (the rod on which wool or flax was wound). The reference is to the object's cylindrical shape.

rodeo The cowboy display has a name of Spanish origin, from *rodear*, 'to go round' (related to English *rotate*). The reference is to the *rounding* up of cattle.

rogue The precise origin of the word is uncertain. It may ultimately come from Latin *rogare*, 'to ask', 'to beg'.

rollick The word is of Scottish dialect origin and may have evolved as a blend of *romp* and *frolic*.

romance The word ultimately goes back to Medieval Latin *romanice*, 'Romanic', that is, in the language spoken by the *Romans* (the forerunner of *Romance* languages such as French, Italian, and Spanish). This gave Old French *romanz* (later *roman*) as a term for a medieval verse story of courtly love about King Arthur and his knights, Charlemagne and *his* knights, or classical heroes such as Alexander the Great. The English versions of these stories were known as *romances*.

rosary The word for a series of prayers counted on a string of beads originally meant, as it still can, 'rose garden', from Latin *rosarium*. The present meaning evolved from the adoption of the word as a fanciful title for a book of devotions. (One of 1533 was called *The mystik sweet Rosary of the faythful soule*.) (Compare ◊anthology.) The word then passed to the prayers themselves.

rosemary The evergreen aromatic shrub derives its name from Latin *ros*, 'dew', and *narinus*, 'marine', in other words it is really 'sea dew', referring to its common coastal location, especially by the Mediterranean. The present form of the name evolved by association with *rose* and *Mary*.

roster The word for a duty list or register derives from Dutch *rooster*, 'gridiron', 'list', with this word corresponding to English *roaster* (as a grill for cooking food). The present sense came from the resemblance of the lines on the paper to the bars of a gridiron.

rostrum The word for a platform or dais represents the singular form of *rostra*, the Latin word for a public speakers' platform in Roman times. This was traditionally decorated with the prows of captured ships. Hence the source of the word in Latin *rostrum*, 'prow' (literally 'beak'), from Latin *rodere*, 'to gnaw', which gave English *rodent*).

rota The term for a register of names for duties represents the Latin word meaning 'wheel'. This was originally adopted in 1659 for a political club that recommended the *rotation* of holders of government posts.

roué The word for a debauched or lecherous man represents the French word meaning 'one broken on a wheel', from *roue*, 'wheel'. The idea is that such a person deserves this punishment.

routine The word is of French origin, deriving from *route*, 'way', 'course', implying a regular or customary one.

rowlock The name is that of the swivelling device that holds the oar in a rowing boat. It was originally called an *oarlock*, for this reason, but the first part of the word was altered by association with *row*.

rubric The term for a set of rules was originally used for the directions in a prayer book. These were originally written or printed in *red*. Hence the source of the word in Latin *rubrica terra*, 'red earth', 'red ochre', from *ruber*, 'red'.

rucksack The word for the 'backpack' is German in origin, and means literally 'back sack', from *Rücken*, 'back' (related to English *ridge*), and *Sack*, 'sack'. The word came into English in the 19th century, when the German pastime of mountain and hill walking became popular with the British.

ruffian The word came into English, through French, from Italian *ruffiano*, 'procurer', 'pimp'. The ultimate source may be in a Germanic word *hruf*, 'scab', 'scurf'.

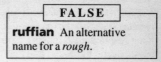

FALSE

ruffian An alternative name for a *rough*.

rum The name of the spirit is said to be a shortening of *rumbullion* or *rumbustion*, 'din', 'uproar', but the origin of these words themselves is uncertain.

rummage The word was originally in nautical use to mean 'stowage', referring to cargo packed in a ship's hold. Hence its origin in Old French *arrumage*, the noun of *arrumer*, 'to stow in a ship's hold', itself probably from a Germanic source.

rumour The word represents Latin *rumor*, 'common talk', itself probably related to Old Norse *rymja*, 'to roar'.

rune The word for the character of an early Germanic alphabet, with each character believed to have a magical significance, derives from Old Norse *rūn*, 'secret'.

ruse The word for a trick or dodge was originally used for the act of doubling in one's tracks to avoid capture, as a hunted animal does. Hence its source in Old French *ruser*, 'to retreat', probably from Latin *recusare*, 'to refuse'.

rusk The word for the hard crisp bread comes from Spanish or Portuguese *rosca*, 'screw', referring to bread shaped in a twist (something like a French loaf).

rust The word is Germanic in origin, from a source element that also gave *russet* and *red*, referring to the characteristic colour of *rust*.

rut The word for a groove or furrow in a soft road, as made by wheels, probably derives from French *route*, 'road'.

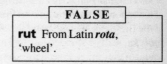

FALSE

rut From Latin *rota*, 'wheel'.

sabotage The word for a deliberately destructive or disruptive act is of French origin, from the verb *saboter*, literally 'to clatter in clogs', referring to the *sabots* or wooden shoes worn by French agricultural workers. The word is said to have arisen from a French strike of 1910 when railway workers destroyed the *sabots* (wooden shoes) that held the rails in place.

saccharin The white sweetening powder or tablet derives its name from Medieval Latin *saccharum*, 'sugar', in turn from Greek *sakkharon*, with the *-in* ending denoting a chemical substance.

sack The dry white wine was known in the 16th century as *wyne seck*. This represented French *vin sec*, 'dry wine'. The English word is no longer in general use, but occurs in trade names, as for the tautologically named sherry *Dry Sack*.

> **FALSE**
>
> **sack** So called as the wine was originally exported from the Canary Islands in goatskin bags or *sacks*.

sackbut The medieval musical instrument, a form of trombone, derives its name from French *saquebote*, literally 'pull/push', from Old French *saquer*, 'to pull', and *bouter*, 'to push' (English *butt*). This was earlier the name of a weapon for unseating a man from his horse. In the Bible, *sackbut* mistranslates Aramaic *sabb'ka*, really a stringed instrument: 'The sound of the cornet, flute, harp, sackbut, psaltery, dulcimer, and all kinds of musick' (Daniel 3:5).

> **FALSE**
>
> **sackbut** From Spanish *sacar del buche*, 'to draw from the belly', since the instrument has to be strongly blown when played.

sad The earliest sense of the word was 'weary'. It is Germanic in origin and ultimately derives from an Indo-European root element, meaning 'satisfy', that also gave Latin *satis*, 'enough' and English *sated* and *satisfy* itself.

> **FALSE**
>
> **sad** From German *Schatten*, 'shadow', 'shade', since a sad person likes to be alone, and withdraws into the shadows.

saddle The word is of Germanic origin and ultimately goes back to an Indo-European root element that also gave *sit* and *settle*.

sadism The term for the gaining of pleasure or sexual satisfaction from inflicting pain on others derives from the name of the French writer who described it, the (self-styled) Marquis de *Sade* (1740–1814).

safari The word for an overland journey or hunting expedition, as in Africa, represents the Swahili word for 'journey', itself from Arabic *safarīy*, an adjectival form of *safar* in the same sense.

saga Although now used in the sense 'never-ending story', the word properly applies to a medieval Norse narrative about the exploits of a hero. In the original Old Norse, the word thus means 'narrative', from a verb ultimately related to English *say*.

salad The cold dish of raw vegetables is so called from Old Provençal *salada*, literally 'salted dish', itself ultimately from Latin *sal*, 'sal'. Compare ◊sauce, as a preparation also adding flavour to a meal.

salary The word for a regular payment for work goes back to Latin *salarium*, the term for the allowance given to Roman soldiers to buy *salt* (Latin *sal*). Compare modern English 'He's not worth his salt', and the like.

saltcellar The container for salt has a name that effectively reduplicates itself. It has evolved from an earlier English form *salt saler*, in which *saler* derives from Old French *saliere*, 'saltcellar', ultimately from Latin *sal*, 'salt'. The second word subsequently became associated with *cellar*, also a type of container.

salvage The word was originally used for a payment made to someone who had *saved* a ship or its cargo. Hence its origin, through French, from Latin *salvare*, 'to save'. The meaning of the English word then passed to the saved ship or cargo itself.

> **FALSE**
>
> **salve** The ointment is so called from its ability to *save* or heal the skin.

salve The word for a soothing ointment or balm is Germanic in origin and related to Greek *elpos*, 'oil' and Sanskrit *sarpis*, 'lard'.

salver The word for a tray on which things are presented derives from Spanish *salva*, itself from *salvar*, 'to save', 'to make safe'. This was a tray from which the king's taster sampled food, so making sure that it was *safe* for him to eat.

samovar The Russian tea urn is so called since it is literally a 'self boiler', from Russian *samo-*, 'self' (related to English *same*), and *varit*, 'to boil'. The word implies that its water is boiled internally, as in an electric kettle, as distinct from water boiled separately, on a stove.

sample The word is simply an alternative form of *example*, from Latin *examplum* via Old French *essample*. A *sampler*, as a beginner's piece of embroidery, is similarly also an *exemplar*.

sandwich The article of food takes its name from that of John Montagu. 4th Earl of *Sandwich* (1718-1792), who ate sandwiches at the gaming table rather than break off for proper meals. His title came from *Sandwich*, in Kent.

sapphire The gemstone derives its name, through French and Latin, from Greek *sappheiros*, itself perhaps ultimately from Sanskrit *śanipriya*, literally meaning 'dear to the planet Saturn', from *śani*, 'Saturn', and *priya*, 'dear'.

Saracen The name of the Arab Muslim people who opposed the Christian Crusades in medieval times probably derives ultimately from Arabic *sharq*, 'sunrise', referring to their eastern origin.

> **FALSE**
>
> **Saracen** The nomadic people of northern Africa were the descendants of *Sarah*, Abraham's wife, and so were named after her.

sarcastic The word goes back through Latin to Greek *sarkasmos*, an adjectival form of *sarkazein*, 'to tear the flesh', itself from *sarx*, genitive *sarkos*, 'flesh'. A *sarcastic* person makes 'cutting' remarks or 'biting' comments.

sash A *sash* window is one that slides up and down (as distinct from a casement window, which opens on hinges). The *sash* is the window's frame. The word evolved as a singular form of *sashes*, itself a form of *shashes*, adopted from the French singular word *chassis*, 'frame' (now modern English *chassis*).

satellite The word was originally used in English for someone attending an important person. Only later was it adopted for a celestial body orbiting a planet or star. (The Moon is the Earth's only *satellite*.) The word thus derives from Latin *satelles*, 'attendant', in turn probably of Etruscan origin.

satin The silk fabric got its name, through Arabic, from that of *Tseutung* (now Quanzhou), the port in southeastern China from which the cloth was originally exported.

satire The word for a literary work ridiculing topical matters derives ultimately from Latin *satira*, 'mixture', itself from *satis*, 'enough'.

Saturday The seventh day of the week gets its name from *Saturn*, the Roman god of agriculture and vegetation. It is the only day of the week to be named after a classical god.

sauce The word came into English, via Old French, from Latin *salsus*, 'salted', ultimately from *sal*, 'salt'. Compare ◊salad, as a dish also adding flavour to a meal. See also ◊saucer.

saucer A *saucer* was originally a container for *sauce*. The word gained its present sense only in the 18th century.

saunter The original sense of the verb was 'to muse'. Hence its possible origin in a word that gave modern *saint*, referring to a person such as an actor who had a *saintly* expression, hence a musing one. A person who now *saunters* or strolls is often also deep in thought, so that something of the original sense remains.

sausage The meat food derives its name, through Old Norman French, from Late Latin *salsicia*, in turn from Latin *salsus*, 'salted', ultimately from *sal*, 'salt'. *Sausages* are still usually seasoned, and *salt* is still a regular ingredient.

savage The source of the word, through Old French *sauvage*, is in Latin *silvaticus*, 'belonging to the woods', from *silva*, 'wood'. The wildest creatures, whether animal or human, are those of the forest and jungle.

saveloy The type of sausage has a name that probably ultimately derives, through Italian and French, from Latin *cerebellum*, a diminutive of *cerebrum*, 'brain', this being one of the original ingredients.

saw The cutting implement has a name that is of Germanic origin, from a root element that also, via Latin and French, gave 'cutting' words such as *secateurs* and *section*.

saxophone The musical instrument takes its name from Adolphe *Saxe* (1814–1894), the Belgian instrument maker who invented it in 1846.

scaffold The word for a raised platform (not originally one for the execution of criminals) derives from Old French *echaffaut*, from a conjectured Vulgar Latin word *catafalicum* that also gave ◊catafalque.

scald The word came into English, through Old Norman French, as a 'smoothed' form of Late Latin *excaldare*, 'to wash in warm water', from Latin *ex-*, 'out', and *calida aqua*, 'warm water'.

scale In the senses 'horny body covering' and 'weighing instrument', the word is Germanic in origin, from a source that also gave *shell*. In the senses 'set of graded points' and 'to climb', the origin is in Latin *scala*, 'ladder'.

scamp The word for a rascal probably derives from Old French *escamper*, from a conjectured Vulgar Latin verb *excampare*, 'to decamp', 'to run away', from Latin *ex-*, 'out', and *campus*, 'field'. In the 18th century a *scamp* was a highwayman.

scan The word goes back to Late Latin *scandere*, 'to scan', in the sense of analysing verse according to its metre and versification. In classical Latin the same verb meant 'to climb', from a root element seen also in *ascend* and *descend*. See also ◊scandal.

scandal The word originally related to the discredit to religion caused by a religious person, for example by promoting some heresy or reason for doubting or not believing. Hence the source of the word in Late Latin *scandalum*, 'stumbling block', itself from Greek *skandalon*, 'trap'. This itself ultimately goes back to an Indo-European root element which also gave ◊scan. See also ◊slander.

scapegoat The word for a person made to bear the blame for others derives from the words used by William Tyndale when translating the Bible in 1530 to render Hebrew *azāzel*, probably really meaning 'goat for Azazel') (a desert demon): 'the goote on which the lotte fell to scape', in the Authorised Version: 'the goat, on which the lot fell to be the scapegoat' (Leviticus 16:10). A *scapegoat* is literally a 'goat that escapes', otherwise a goat symbolically laden with the sins of the Israelites and sent into the wilderness to die.

scarce The word goes back through Old Norman French to a conjectured Vulgar Latin word *excarpus*, 'plucked out', itself from Latin *excerpere*, 'to select' (English *excerpt*).

scarlet The word derives from Old French *escarlate* (modern *écarlate*), the name of a type of fine cloth. The precise origin of this is uncertain, but some authorities trace the word back to an ultimate source in Latin *sigillatus*, 'decorated with figures', referring to the small seals represented on the original rich cloth.

scatter The word probably evolved as a variant form of *shatter*, the root sense common to both words being 'disperse'. (If you *shatter* something, you usually *scatter* the broken pieces.)

scavenger A *scavenger* was originally a person who collected *scavage* (a toll formerly levied in London on visiting merchants) while also keeping the streets clean. The latter word came from a Germanic source that also gave modern *show*, since the official was a sort of inspector. The *n* came in as for *messenger* from *message* and *passenger* from *passage*.

scent The derivation is in Old French *sentir*, 'to sense', itself from Latin *sentire*, 'to feel' (the source of English *sense*. The *c* came in by association with some other word, though it is not certain what it was.

sceptical The word ultimately goes back to Greek *skeptikos*, from *skeptesthai*, 'to consider', itself containing the 'seeing' element found in *scope* and words ending in -*scope*. A *sceptic* thus 'looks about', or reflects on things.

schedule The term for a plan of procedure derives, via French, from Late Latin *schedula*, a diminutive of Latin *scheda*, 'paper', 'leaf of papyrus'.

scheme The term for a systematic plan of action derives, via Latin *schema*, from Greek *skhēma*, 'form'.

schizophrenia The name of the mental disorder (popularly thought of as a 'split personality') was devised in the mid-19th century from Greek *skhizein*, 'to split' (English *schism*), and *phrēn*, 'mind' (English *frenetic*, formerly *phrenetic*).

school The word goes back to Latin *schola* in the same sense, this in turn deriving from Greek *skholē*, 'leisure', that is, leisure in disputing and the pursuit of knowledge. This word replaced the native Old English one, which was *lārhūs*, literally 'lore house'.

schooner The word for the sailing vessel is of uncertain origin. Some authorities derive it from a New England word related to *skim*, as a vessel that *skims* over the water.

> **FALSE**
>
> **schooner** From Dutch *schoon*, 'beautiful', describing the ship's elegant lines and graceful motion through the water.

science The word derives, through French, from Latin *scientia*, 'knowledge', from the verb *scire*, 'to know'.

scissors The origin of the word for the cutting instrument is in Old French *cisoires*, itself from a conjectured Vulgar Latin word *cisoria*, in turn from Latin *caedere*, 'to cut'. The *c* came in by association with Latin *scindere*, 'to cut', the equivalent of Greek *skhizein* (see ◊schizophrenia.

scone The small round cake is of Scottish origin in both name and nature, and perhaps arose as a shortening of Middle Dutch *schoonbroot*, literally 'fine bread'.

scout The word has evolved from Old French *ascouter* (modern French *écouter*), 'to listen to', itself from Latin *auscultare* in the same sense (compare English *auscultation* as the medical term for listening to sounds in the body by means of a stethoscope). The base of the Latin word is probably *auris*, 'ear'.

scramble The word probably evolved as a blend of *scrabble* and *ramp*, thus combining the actions of clawing one's way and clambering over something, which is what *scrambling* is.

scrap The word derives from the same Germanic source that gave related *scrape*. *Scraps* of food are often the *scrapings* off plates and dishes.

scrawl The word may be a blend of *sprawl* and *crawl*, since *scrawled* writing both spreads out untidily and is done slowly.

screw The ultimate source of the word is in Latin *scrofa*, 'sow', presumably since this animal has a tail that coils in a spiral, like the thread on a screw.

script The word evolved through French from Latin *scriptum*, 'something written', from *scribere*, *to write*. Directly related words are *scribble*, *scribe*, and *scripture*.

scroll The word was originally *scrowe*, from Old French *escroe*, 'strip' (meaning one of parchment). It was influenced, however, by *roll*.

scrounge In the sense of obtaining something by cadging or begging, the verb evolved as an altered form of the dialect word *scrunge*, 'to steal'. The origin of this is uncertain. (Dickens may have based the name of the miserly *Scrooge* on this verb.)

scrumptious The word describing something very pleasant or delicious probably arose as an 'expressive' alteration of *sumptuous*.

scullery The word for the small room or part of a kitchen where washing up is done derives, through French, from Latin *scutella*, a diminutive of *scutra*, 'flat dish', 'pan' (for heating things in). (The same word gave English *scuttle*, as for the coal container.)

scullion The word for a person formerly carrying out menial tasks in a kitchen derives from Old French *escouillon*, 'cleaning cloth', from *escouve*, 'broom', itself from Latin *scopa* in this sense.

scythe The implement for cutting grass gets its name from a Germanic word that ultimately goes back to the root element which gave other 'cutting' words such as *secateurs* and *section* (see ◊saw). The Old English word for the implement was *sigthe*, and the *c* probably came in by association with ◊scissors.

seal The word for a device impressed on a piece of wax (for example) evolved, through French, as a 'smoothed' form of Latin *sigillum*, 'little figure', a diminutive of *signum*, 'sign'. English *sign* and *seal* are thus related.

search The word derives, via Old French *cerchier*, from Late Latin *circare*, 'to go round', in turn from Latin *circus*, 'circle'. If you *search* for something, you often go round in a *circle* looking for it.

season The word goes back, through Old French *seson*, to Latin *satio*, genitive *sationis*, 'sowing', from *serere*, 'to sow'. The basic sense for the Romans was 'time of sowing', which meant not only spring but also summer and winter.

second See ◊minute.

secretary A *secretary* was originally, as often even now, a confidant, a keeper of *secrets*. Hence the origin of the word in Medieval Latin *secretarius*, from Latin *secretum*, literally 'something hidden' (English *secrete*).

sect The term for a subdivision of a religious group derives from Latin *secta*, 'following', 'faction', itself from a form of the verb *sequi*, 'to follow' (English *sequence*). The basic idea is of a group of people *following* a leader or a certain set of principles.

secular The word relating to worldly things, as opposed to sacred things, derives, through French, from Late Latin *saecularis*, 'temporal', from Latin *saeculum*, 'generation', 'age'.

sedge The coarse rushlike plant has a name of Germanic origin ultimately going back to the Indo-European root element that gave *saw*, *secateurs*, *section*, and other 'cutting' words related to Latin *secare*, 'to cut'. The reference is to the plant's sharp stem.

seersucker The light fabric with a crinkled surface has a name deriving, through Hindi, from Persian *shīr o shakkar*, literally 'milk and sugar', alluding to its stripes.

seesaw The pivoted plank on which children play derives its name from a reduplication of *saw*. The up and down motion of a *seesaw* resembles the back and forth motion of a *saw*.

senate The legislative or governing body derives its name from Latin *senatus*, as the term for the Roman council of the kings, itself based on Latin *senex*, 'elder', literally 'old man'. Hence also *senator*. The same Latin word also gave English *senior*.

sentence In the sense 'sequence of words having unified meaning', the word goes back to Latin *sententia*, 'way of thinking', itself from *sentire*, 'to feel' (the origin of English *sense*). A *sentence* expresses a particular thought or opinion, even when it means 'judgement pronounced in court'.

sentry The word for a soldier who guards or prevents access perhaps evolved as a shortened form of *sentinel*, which itself ultimately derives from Italian *sentire*, 'to notice'.

September The name of the ninth month derives from Latin *septem*, 'seven'. The apparent disparity is explained by the fact that the Roman calendar began in March. Compare ◊October, ◊November, ◊December.

sepulchre The word for a tomb goes back, through French, to Latin *sepulcrum*, 'burying-place', from *sepelire*, 'to bury'.

serenade The term properly applies to music performed at night in the open air, as typically by a lover to a loved one. Its origin is ultimately in Latin *serenus*, 'calm' (English *serene*), but the meaning has been influenced by Italian *sera*, 'evening'.

sergeant The word for the military rank, like most others, is French in origin, and represents Old French *sergent*, itself from Latin *serviens*, literally 'serving', from *servire*, 'to serve'. The earliest meaning of *sergeant* in English actually was 'servant'. The notion of *serving* is still implicit in the role of the armed forces (armed *services*).

series The word comes direct from Latin, in which it meant 'row', 'chain', from *serere*, 'to link'. Compare ◊sermon.

sermon The source of the word is in Latin *serio*, genitive *serionis*, 'discourse', probably itself from *serere*, 'to link'. Compare ◊series.

serviette The alternative word for a table napkin is French in origin, from *servire*, 'to serve'. The napkin was originally used when *serving* dishes, rather than simply for wiping the hands or mouth.

settee The seat for two or more people derived its name as an alteration of *settle*, as which it is still sometimes known today, especially when one of the older sort. The basic origin is in the Germanic root element that gave *sit* and *set*, among other words.

several The word derives, through Anglo-French, from Medieval Latin *separalis*, itself from Latin *separare*, 'to separate'. If *several* people object, they do as a *separate* group, one *severed* from the others.

sewer As the word for the drain or pipe that carries away *sewage*, the word ultimately derives, through French, from a conjectured Vulgar Latin word *exaquare*, 'to drain', literally 'to let water out', from Latin *ex-*, 'out', and *aqua*, 'water'.

sex The word for the division into male and female derives from Latin *sexus*, itself from a root word related to *secare*, 'to cut', 'to divide'.

sextant The navigational instrument resembles a quadrant with a graduated arc equal to one *sixth* of a circle. Hence its name, from Latin *sextans*, genitive *sextantis*, 'one sixth', from *sex*, 'six'.

shabby The word is an adjectival form of obsolete *shab*, an altered form of *scab*, which in Old English was *sceabb*, pronounced 'shab'.

shaddock The grapefruit-like fruit, also known as the *pomelo*, is named after the man who introduced it to the West Indies in 1696. 'In Barbados the Shaddocks surpass those of Jamaica in goodness. The seed of this was first brought to Barbados by one Captain Shaddock, Commander of an East-India Ship, who touch'd at that Island in his Passage to England, and left the Seed there' (Sir Hans Sloane, *A Voyage to Jamaica*, 1707).

shallot The plant, with its edible bulb, derives its name from Old French *eschalotte*, an alteration of *eschaloigne*, itself from Latin *Ascalonia caepa*, 'Ascalonian onion', from its place of origin, the Palestinian town of *Ascalon* (biblical *Askelon*, modern *Ashqelon*), near Jerusalem.

sham The origin of the word is uncertain. It may have evolved as a northern dialect form of *shame*.

shambles The word was originally used for a meat market (hence the streets or buildings named *Shambles* in some older towns). Meat vendors used a table called a *shamble*, itself a word from Old English *sceamel*, 'stool', in turn from Latin *scamellum*, a diminutive of *scamnum*, 'bench'. The present meaning came about by association with the slaughtering of animals in the market.

shamefaced The word was originally *shamefast*, so that a *shamefaced* person was one held *fast* by *shame*, in other words restrained or subdued by it. The second part of the word was later altered by association with *face*, since such a person had an expression of *shame*.

shampoo The word was originally used of a massage (as in a Turkish bath), not a hair wash. Hence its derivation in Hindi *chāmpo*, from *chāmpnā*, 'to knead'.

shamrock The plant with leaves divided into three leaflets is Ireland's national emblem. Its name is thus Irish in origin, from *seamróg*, a diminutive of *seamair*, 'clover'.

shed The small building probably derives its name from an altered form of Old English *scead*, 'shelter'. It was an immediate form of this word that gave modern *shade*.

sheriff The administrative officer derives his name from Old English *scīrgerēfa*, literally 'shire reeve', from *scīr*, ᵱshire (in the sense 'county'), and *gerēfa*, 'reeve' (the historic term for the king's representative in a shire).

sherry The fortified wine is so called from its original place of manufacture, the *Jerez* region of southern Spain. The earlier form of this name was *Xeres*, pronounced 'shereez'. This gave an English spelling *sherris*, which was taken to be a plural. Hence the modern word as its supposed 'singular'.

shibboleth The term for the catchword of a group of people represents the test word in the Bible story (Judges 12:4–6) used by Jephthah to distinguish the Ephraimites, who could not pronounce *sh*, from his own people, the Gileadites. The word itself is Hebrew for 'ear of grain'.

shindy The colloquial word for a commotion arose as a variant of *shinty*, the Scottish game similar to hockey, itself said to be from the cry *shin ye* in the game. *Shindig*, as the word for a noisy party, is in turn a variant of *shindy*.

shingles The viral disease typically involves skin eruptions round the middle of the body. Hence the origin of its name in Medieval Latin *cingulum*, 'girdle', itself translating Greek *zōnē*, 'zone'.

ship The word is Germanic in origin but its ultimate source is unknown. A related word is *skiff*, as a type of small boat.

shire The word for a county, often occurring as the last part of a county name (as for *Yorkshire*), derives from Old English *scīr*, 'office', 'jurisdiction', referring to it as an administrative unit formerly ruled by an ◊alderman and a ◊sheriff.

shogun The title of the former Japanese military dictators is actually Chinese in origin, from *jiāngjūn*, 'general', literally 'army doer', from *jiāng*, 'to do', and *jūn*, 'army'. (For a word of similar origin, see ◊strategy.)

shoot The word is one of a number of Germanic origin that describe a sudden or rapid movement, especially one directed outwards. The ultimate source of all of them is probably imitative. Examples are *shoo*, *shout*, *shed* (in the sense 'cast off'), *shit*, and *shut*. (You *shut* a door to keep people out, not yourself in.)

FALSE

ship So called because the earliest boats were *shaped* from a hollowed-out tree trunk.

FALSE

shire So called because it is a territory that has been *sheared* off from a larger one. Most counties with names ending -*shire* were portioned out from Anglo-Saxon kingdoms. Where they were not, such as Essex, Sussex, and Surrey, their names have no -*shire*.

---

shrapnel The type of projectile that bursts a number of bullets derives its name from the British army officer who invented it in the Peninsular War, General Henry *Shrapnel* (1761–1842). (His German-sounding name is actually a form of *Carbonell*.)

shrewd The word meaning 'crafty', 'cunning', is literally *shrewed*, from the obsolete verb *shrew*, 'to curse', itself from *shrew* in the sense 'bad-tempered woman' (originally 'bad-tempered man').

shrift As occurring in the phrase 'short *shrift*', referring to brief and unsympathetic treatment, the word derives from a Germanic source that also gave *shrive*. This literally means 'to write', ultimately from Latin *scribere*, but the word came to apply to the prescribing of a penance after a person had made a confession, and so to a confession itself. Thus 'short *shrift*' was used of the brief time for a condemned prisoner to make a confession. The same word gave the name of *Shrove* Tuesday, when people made their confessions before Lent began.

shrimp The crustacean has a name of Germanic origin that is probably related to modern German *schrumpfen*, 'to shrink', and English *scrimp* and *crimp*, relating to its small size or wrinkled back.

shuttle The weaving device is so called since it *shoots* the thread backwards and forwards. Both words are thus of identical Germanic origin. See also ◊shoot itself.

shyster As used in its American sense to apply to a deceitful lawyer or politician, the word is said to derive from the name of one *Scheuster*, a disreputable 19th-century lawyer in New York.

sickle The word for the reaping hook derives, through Old English, from Latin *secula* in the same sense. This is a word related to *secare*, 'to cut', so that the *sickle* and the ◊scythe have names of ultimately identical origin.

sidesman The term for a churchwarden's assistant is an altered form of *sideman*, since he was a *man* who stood at the *side* of the churchwarden.

> **FALSE**
>
> **sidesman** The title of the church official evolved from *synodsman*.

siesta The word for an early afternoon rest in hot countries derives from the identical Spanish word meaning 'sixth'. A *siesta* was originally taken in the *sixth* hour of the day, that is, at noon, when the sun is overhead and at its hottest.

silhouette The outline drawing filled in with black, typically as a profile portrait, is said to be so called after the French politician Étienne de *Silhouette* (1709–1769), either because politicians were pictured in portraits of this type or because Silhouette's career as controller general was unusually brief and so in 'outline' only.

silk The name of the fabric goes back through Old English to Late Latin *sericum*, itself from Latin *seres*, representing the name of the *Seres*, an oriental people from whom *silk* was first obtained. Their own name is ultimately based on Chinese *sī*, 'silk'.

silly The word originally meant 'pitiable', and was itself a form of *seely*, which meant 'happy', 'blessed'. Hence the ultimate source of the word in Old English *sæl*, 'happiness', from a Germanic base that gave modern German *selig*, 'blessed'.

> **FALSE**
>
> **simple** A reduced form of the Latin phrase *sine plica*, 'without a fold'.

simple The source of the word is ultimately in Latin *simplex*, 'plain', from a root element also seen in Latin *semper*, 'always' and English *same*.

sinecure The word for a paid post involving little or no work derives from the Medieval Latin phrase *beneficium sine cura*, 'benefice without cure'. The reference is to an ecclesiastical benefice without any spiritual duties (*cure* of souls).

sinew The word, meaning 'tendon', is of Germanic origin from an ultimate source that presumably meant something like 'string', as it does for related German *Sehne*.

sinister Although the word came into English from French, it ultimately derives from the identical Latin word meaning 'left'. Roman augurers regarded the left side of someone or something as unlucky. Hence the word's modern sense of 'threatening evil'.

sir The title goes back in English through *sire* (from Old French) to Latin *senior*, 'elder', 'older'. Compare French *monsieur*, literally 'my lord', the equivalent of 'Mr'.

sirloin The prime cut of beef is from the animal's *loin*, especially the upper part. Hence the origin of the word in Old French *surlonge*, literally 'above the loin', from *sur*, 'above', and *longe*, 'loin'.

> **FALSE**
>
> **sirloin** So called from a famous occasion when James I 'knighted' a joint of beef as *Sir Loin*.

sisal The type of fibre for making ropes derives its name from that of its place of origin, the port of *Sisal*, eastern Mexico.

skedaddle The word now means 'run away', but its original sense was 'retreat'. Its origin is unknown. Perhaps it originated as a euphemistic form of *escape*, used by soldiers in battle.

skeleton The word goes back to the identical Greek word, as the noun form of *skeletos*, 'desiccated', implying a body that has dried up, leaving only bare bones.

sketch The word for a rapid drawing or brief piece of writing ultimately derives from Latin *schedius*, 'extempore', as applied to a poem composed 'off the cuff', itself from a Greek stem also found in English *scheme*.

skip As applied to the large container for building materials and the like, the word is a variant form of *skep*, now a word for a large basket. This is itself of Germanic origin.

skipper The word evolved from Middle Low German and Middle Dutch *schipper*, literally 'shipper', that is, the person in charge of a *ship*.

skirmish The word for a brief or minor military engagement derives from Old French *eskirmir*, the source of modern French *escrime*, 'fencing' (the sport). This itself derives from a Germanic root element meaning 'protection' that gave modern German *Schirm*, 'screen', 'shade'.

> **FALSE**
>
> **skirmish** From French *escarmouche* in the same sense, itself from *escarre*, 'scab', referring to the wounds inflicted, and *mouche*, 'fly', referring to their insignificance.

slack In its sense of 'not taut', 'idle', the word is of Germanic origin from a root word related to Latin *laxus*, 'loose' (English *lax*).

slander The term for defamation derives from Old French *escandle*, itself from Late Latin *scandalum*, 'cause of offence' (English ◊scandal).

slang The word is of uncertain origin and probably arose as a *slang* or cant term itself. It may be related in some way to *sling*, referring to a manner of speaking.

slave The word came into English, via Old French, from Medieval Latin *Sclavus*, 'Slav'. The *Slavonic* races were frequently held in bondage or *slavery* in medieval times.

slender The word is of uncertain origin. It is first recorded in a 14th-century text: 'He is fat, and thertoo tendre, / And my men are lene and slendre'. It may be related to *slim* and *slant*

slipper The footwear is presumably so called because it is simply *slipped* onto the feet. Compare similar garment names, such as *slip* itself and *drawers* (which are *drawn* on).

slogan The word for the catchphrase of a political party or commercial company (to advertise a particular product) was originally used for a war cry. Its origin is in Gaelic *sluagh-gairm*, from *sluagh*, 'army', and *gairm*, 'cry'. (The poets Chatterton and Browning took *slogan* in this sense to represent *slughorn*, as a type of trumpet, and used it as such in their poems.)

sloth The South American animal is so called because of its *sloth*, that is, because it is *slow*-moving. (English *sloth* is properly the noun of *slow*, just as *width* is of *wide*.) For a similar name, compare ◊slug.

slug The mollusc is so called because it is *sluggish*, or slow-moving. The word originally had the same sense as *sluggard* has now, and only became common for the shell-less snail in the 18th century. For a similar name, compare ◊sloth.

slush The word is imitative of the sound and consistency of the thing it names. Related words of similar nature are *sludge* and *slosh*, among others.

smear The word is of Germanic origin, from a root element also found in Greek *muron*, 'ointment'.

snapdragon The plant otherwise known as an antirrhinum is so called since its flowers look like the head of a *dragon*, with a 'mouth' which *snaps* shut if squeezed open and then released.

sneak The word probably derives from Old English *snīcan*, 'to creep', 'to crawl', and so is related to *snake*. Compare the similar uses of '*snake* in the grass' and *sneak* for a treacherous person.

snob The colloquial word for someone who likes to associate with 'superior' people was originally a term for a shoemaker or cobbler. Its origin is unknown. (Shoemakers were formerly known for their flattery, perhaps because they literally 'looked up to' their patrons.)

snuff As used for powdered tobacco, the word probably evolved as a shortened form of Dutch *snuftabake*, literally 'tobacco for snuffing', ie, for *sniffing* up.

FALSE

snob From the Latin abbreviation *s. nob.*, standing for *sine nobilitate*, 'without nobility', entered in college records against the names of students not of noble birth. Compare ◊nob.

sober The word goes back, through French, to Latin *sobrius*. This may itself be related to its opposite, *ebrius*, 'drunk' (modern English *ebriety* and *inebriated*).

sobriquet In its sense of 'nickname', the word came into English from French, in which it was earlier *soubriquet*. This originally meant 'tap under the chin', as if from *sous*, 'under', and a word related to modern *bec*, 'beak'. But the sense development is obscure.

soccer As used for football, the word is an abbreviation based on the second syllable of its formal name, Association Football, with -*er* as in *footer* or *rugger* (from *rug*by football).

sociable This word, together with others such as *social*, *society*, and *socialist*, all ultimately go back to Latin *socius*, 'associate', 'comrade'.

soil In its sense of 'earth', 'ground', the word probably derives ultimately from Latin *solium*, 'seat', 'throne' (the source of French *seuil*, 'threshold'). However, it was influenced by Latin *solum*, 'ground' (French *sol*).

sojourn Now rather a formal or mannered word meaning 'to stay temporarily', the word goes back through Old French *sojorner* to the conjectured Vulgar Latin verb *subdiurnare*, 'to spend a day', from Latin *sub*-, 'during', and Late Latin *diurnum*, 'day'.

solder The alloy for joining metal surfaces together is so called ultimately from Latin *solidare*, 'to strengthen', from *solidus*, 'solid'. The *solder* thus makes a *solid* bond between the surfaces.

soldier The word derives from Old French *soudier*, from *soude*, 'pay' (specifically army pay), in turn from Late Latin *solidus*, the name of a Roman gold coin (so called because it was *solid*). (It was this coin that gave the *s* of *£sd*, the abbreviation for currency in predecimal times.)

sole The word for the bottom of the foot or a shoe goes back to Latin *solea*, 'sandal', itself probably related to *solum*, 'ground'. The fish called *sole* gets its name from its flat elongated shape, which resembles that of such a sandal.

solecism The term for a grammatical mistake in speaking or writing has its ultimate origin, through French and Latin, in Greek *soloikos*. This meant 'speaking incorrectly', and itself derived from *Soloi*, the name of a colony in Cilicia where the inhabitants spoke a corrupt form of Greek.

solicit The original meaning of the verb was 'disturb', 'trouble'. Hence its origin in Latin *sollicitare*, 'to harass', itself from *sollicitus*, 'agitated', literally 'wholly excited', from *sollus*, 'whole', and *citus*, from the verb *ciere*, 'to excite'. A *solicitor* is thus literally so called because he or she 'stirs things up' and takes action.

sombrero The type of broad-brimmed hat derives its name from Spanish *sombrero de sol*, 'shade from the sun'.

somersault The term for a 'head-over-heels' jump or roll comes from Old French *soubresault*, probably from Old Provençal *sobresaut*, from *sobre*, 'over' (from Latin *super*), and *saut*, 'leap', 'jump' (from Latin *saltus*).

sonata The term for a piece of music for the piano or other instruments represents the identical Italian word literally meaning 'sounded'. This effectively meant 'played', as distinct from a *cantata*, which was 'sung'.

sonsy The word used to mean 'good-looking' or 'lucky' arose as a Scottish and Irish dialect word deriving from Gaelic *sonas*, 'good fortune', from *sona*, 'fortunate', 'happy'.

sophisticated In its sense of 'refined', 'cultured', the word ultimately derives, through Latin, from Greek *sophistēs*, 'wise man', itself from the verb *sophizesthai*, 'to act craftily', 'to devise', based on *sophos*, 'wise'.

sophomore The mainly American term for a second-year student is said to derive from a form of *sophism* (as if *sophismer*), meaning someone who indulged in 'wise' (Greek *sophos*) arguments.

sorry The word is ultimately related to *sore*, since someone who is *sorry* is pained or hurt at heart. However, the word has been associated with, and influenced in spelling by, the unrelated *sorrow*.

> **FALSE**
>
> **sorry** From *sorrow*, the associated emotion.

south The word is Germanic in origin, from an ultimate source that is perhaps also seen in *sun*. If so, the *south* is the *sun* quarter.

sovereign The term for a royal ruler came into English from Old French *soverain*, itself from a conjectured Vulgar Latin word *superanus*, based on Latin *super*, 'over', 'above'. The spelling of the word has been influenced by *reign*.

spaghetti The type of pasta in the form of long strings derives its name direct from the Italian word meaning 'little cords', as a plural diminutive of *spago*, 'cord'.

spaniel The breed of dog originally came from *Spain*. Hence its name, which came into English via Old French *espaigneul* (modern *épagneul*), from an ultimate source in Latin *Hispaniolus*, 'Spanish'. (All the main breeds of spaniel today, however, such as the Clumber, cocker, and springer, are English in origin.)

> **FALSE**
>
> **spaniel** From the name of *Hispaniola* in the West Indies, where the breed of dog originated.

spanner The tool for gripping and turning a nut gets its name from German *Spanner*, literally 'tightener', from *spannen*, 'to tighten', 'to stretch taut'. English *span* is directly related to this, since it represents a 'stretch' from one point to another.

spice The word for the aromatic vegetable substance goes back through Old French *espice* (modern French *épice*) to Late Latin *species*, 'spices', itself from Latin *species*, 'kind' (English *species*). A *spice* is a *specific* substance. However, the word also came to be associated with Latin *spica*, 'ear of corn' (English *spike*).

spider The *spider*, with a name of Germanic origin, is so called as it is a *spinner* Compare the related word *spindle* (the rod used to twist and wind thread in *spinning*).

spinach The name of the vegetable with its dark green leaves goes back ultimately, through Old Spanish *espinaca*, to Arabic *isfānākh*. It may have become associated with *spine* at some stage, with reference to the prickly seeds that some species have.

spinnaker The word for a three-cornered sail on a yacht probably evolved as a combination of *spin* and *moniker*, as the *moniker* (name) of the sail that makes the yacht *spin* (go fast). However, the word is traditionally derived from *Sphinx*, the name of the yacht that first adopted this type of sail.

spinster The formal word for an unmarried woman literally means *spinner*, as the traditional occupation of such a woman. The *-ster* is the feminine equivalent of *-er*, preserved in the surnames *Webster* (female *weaver*) and *Baxter* (female *baker*).

splendid The word ultimately goes back to Latin *splendere*, 'to shine'. Other forms of the English word formerly existed, such as *splendidious* and *splendidous*, but it was this one that prevailed.

splutter The word evolved as a blend of *sputter* (relating to the sound made) and *splash* (relating to the wetness involved).

spokesman A *spokesman* (*spokeswoman*, *spokesperson*) is someone who officially *speaks* on behalf of another person or an organization. It is not clear why this form of *speak* was adopted as the basis for the word.

sponsor The word was taken into English direct from Latin, where it means 'bondsman', 'surety', from the verb *spondere*, 'to promise solemnly'. The word was originally used in English for a godparent, who makes promises on behalf of the godchild. See also ◊spouse.

sporran The word for the pouch worn before a kilt by a Scotsman in Highland dress represents Scottish Gaelic *sporan*, 'purse'. English *purse* and Gaelic *sporran* are actually related words.

sport The word evolved as a shortened form of *disport*, itself from Anglo-French *desporter* (modern French *déporter*), literally 'deport', 'carry away'. The sense is of being 'carried away' by a diversion or enjoyable pastime.

spouse The word for a husband or wife derives, through French, from Latin *sonsus*, 'betrothed man' or *sponsa*, betrothed woman', in turn for *spondere*, 'to promise solemnly'. A *spouse* is thus literally someone who has made a promise with regard to another person, like a ◊sponsor.

spree The word for a boisterous session of self-indulgence is of uncertain origin. It may be an altered form of Scottish *spreath*, a term for plundered cattle, itself ultimately from Latin *praeda*, 'booty'.

spring The season is so called as it is the time of year when growth begins and plants *spring*. The word replaced the Old English name for the season, which was *lencten* (modern ◊Lent).

sprint The word now means 'run fast' but originally meant 'dart', 'spring'. Its source is uncertain, but it has links in Scandinavian words and possibly in English *spring* itself.

sprite The word for the elflike creature evolved in medieval times as a shortened form of *spirit*, itself from Latin *spiritus*, 'breathing', from *spirare*, 'to breathe'. English *sprite* in its turn gave the adjective *sprightly*, from the word's earlier spelling (now in rare use) as *spright*.

spud The colloquial word for a potato was originally used for a type of short knife. An implement of this kind was used as a sort of trowel for digging up weeds and, in due course, potatoes. Hence the evolution of the meaning, though the origin of the word itself is unknown.

squad The word for a group of soldiers or other people arose, through French, from Old Spanish *escuadra*, from *escuadrare*, 'to form a *square*'. The reference is to the shape of the formation. Compare ◊squadron.

squadron The word for a military division of some kind came into English from Italian *squadrone*, the term for a group of soldiers formed up in a *square* (Italian *squadro*). Compare ◊squad.

squib The word for a firework that hisses then gives a small explosion probably arose as an imitation of the sound it makes.

squiggle The word probably evolved as a blend of *squirm* and *wiggle* or *wriggle*.

squire The term for a country gentleman evolved as a short form of Old French *esquier*. This gave the full form *esquire* (the *Esq* still sometimes added after a man's name), which ultimately came from Late Latin *scutarius*, 'shield-bearer', from Latin *scutus*, 'shield'.

squirrel The small animal with the large bushy tail derives its name from Old French *esquireul* (modern French *écureuil*), in turn from Late Latin *sciurus*, itself from Greek *skiouros*, literally 'shadow-tail', from *skia*, 'shadow', and *oura*, 'tail'. The animal's tail is thus a 'shadow' of itself, being much the same length and always following behind.

stab The word is probably related to Middle English *stob*, 'stick', as well as modern English *stub*. If so, all three words probably have an ultimate origin in an imitative formation (suggesting the action and the agent that performs it).

stable In the sense 'home for horses', the word came into English from Old French *estable* (modern *étable*, 'cowshed'), in turn from Latin *stabulum*, 'shed', ultimately from *stare*, 'to stand'. A *stable* is thus literally a place where animals ◊stand, as is a ◊stall, from the same ultimate source. The adjective *stable* meaning 'steady' is also from this source (and even *steady* is related). See also ◊stud.

stadium The word for a sports arena comes from the identical Latin word, itself from Greek *stadion*, earlier *spadion*, 'racecourse', from *spân*, 'to pull'. The Greek word was itself probably influenced by *stadios*, 'steady'.

stalemate The chess position, not really a *mate* as such, is the one in which a move by either player would place his king in check. The origin of the term is in obsolete *stale* (modern ◊stall) and *mate* as in ◊checkmate.

stallion A *stallion* is so called as a male horse kept in a *stall* for breeding. The actual word derives from Old French *estalon*, itself of Germanic origin and ultimately going back to the root element found in other 'standing' words, including ◊stand itself. Compare ◊stable, and see also ◊stud.

stalwart The present word has evolved from Old English *stǽlwirthe*, 'serviceable', literally 'worthy of support', from *stǽl*, a shortened form of *stathol*, 'support', and *wierthe*, 'worth'.

> **FALSE**
>
> **stalwart** A Scottish form of *stalworth*, literally *stealworthy*, describing someone or something worth stealing.

stamina The word that now means 'enduring energy and strength' represents the identical Latin word that is the plural form of *stamen*, 'thread'. The concept is either of threads woven together to give added strength, or of the threads of life that were spun by the Fates in classical mythology.

stampede The word as used by Mexicans for the rushing of panic-stricken cattle was adopted from Spanish *estampida*, 'crash', 'uproar', itself from *estampar*, 'to stamp'. English *stamp* is itself of Germanic origin, and is perhaps related to *step*.

stand The word, directly of Germanic origin, goes back to Latin *stare*, 'to stand', and ultimately to an Indo-European root element found in many words to do with some aspect of 'standing', especially ones beginning *sta-* such as ◊stable, *state*, *station*, *static*, *statue*, *statute*, and *status*. Compare also ◊stall, ◊stallion, and ◊stud.

starboard The word for the righthand side of a ship derives from Old English *stēorbord*, literally 'steering side', from *stēor*, 'steering paddle' (modern *steer*), and *bord*, 'side' (modern *board*). Boats were formerly steered by a paddle over the righthand side.

starve The original meaning of the verb was 'die' (compare modern German *sterben* in this sense). It later meant more specifically 'die of hunger'. The ultimate origin is in a Germanic root element meaning 'rigid', seen also in *starch*, *stare*, *stark*, *stern* (in the sense 'severe'), and *stiff*.

stencil The word now applies to a type of plate with apertures used for transferring letters and the like to a surface. It was originally used, however, for a brightly coloured ornament. Hence its origin, through the Old French verb *estenceler*, in Latin *scintilla*, 'spark'.

stepson   The word for the son of a person's former spouse, together with all other *step-* relationships, is based on an element related to Old English *āstȳpan*, 'to bereave'. The relationship thus alludes to the bereavement of the widowed person. In like manner the Old English word for 'orphan' was *stēopbearn* ('stepbairn') or *stēopcild* ('stepchild').

stereo   As used of a radio, cassette player, TV, and the like, the word is short for *stereophonic*. In itself it represents Greek *stereos*, 'solid', in this instance referring to 'solid sound'.

sterling   The name for British money probably derives from a derivative of Old English *steorra*, 'star', referring to a small star stamped on early Norman pennies. The *-ling* has a diminutive sense, as in *duckling*.

> **FALSE**
>
> **sterling**   A corruption of *easterling*, referring to money from eastern Europe.

steward   In medieval times the word was used for the officer of a household, especially a royal one. Its origin is in Old English *stigweard*, from *stig*, 'house', 'hall' (modern lowly *sty*), and *weard*, 'ward'. It was this word that gave the surname *Stewart* (and its French-influenced form, *Stuart*).

stickler   The term for an insistent or demanding person derives from the rare verb *stickle*, itself an altered form of obsolete *stightle* which originally meant 'arbitrate'. Its own origin is in Old English *stihtan*, 'to arrange'.

stirrup   The *stirrup* that is now a metal loop with a flat footpiece for a horse rider was originally simply a looped rope. Hence the origin of the word in Old English *stigrāp*, from *stīg*, 'path', 'step' (related to modern English *stile* and *stair*), and *rāp*, 'rope'.

stomach   The word ultimately derives from Greek *stoma*, 'mouth', in this case referring to the opening to the stomach itself.

storey   The term for the floor or level of a building derives from Anglo-Latin *historia*, 'picture', itself from the identical Latin word meaning 'story', 'history'. The reference is probably to the pictures painted on medieval windows.

> **FALSE**
>
> **storey**   An altered form of *stagery*. Compare French *étage*, 'floor', 'storey'.

strain   In the sense 'ancestry', 'inherited character', the word is Germanic in origin, from a root element found also in Latin *struere*, 'to construct'. The present word should have been *streen*, evolving from the Old English form *strēon*. However, its spelling and pronunciation were influenced by the other *strain* meaning 'stretch tight'. This is French in origin, and goes back to Latin *stringere*, 'to bind tight' (English *stringent*).

strap   The word arose as a variant form of *strop*, itself ultimately, through some Germanic language and Latin, from Greek *strophos*, 'cord'.

strategy The word for a plan of action goes back, through French, to Greek *stratēgia*, referring to the function of a *stratēgos*, 'general', literally 'army leader', from *stratos*, 'army', and *agein*, 'to lead'. Compare ◊shogun.

strawberry The fruit may get its name from the *straw*like appearance of its runners. The precise source remains uncertain.

> **FALSE**
>
> **strawberry** An altered form of *strayberry*, from the runners that *stray* from the parent plant and take root independently.

street The ultimate origin of the word is in Latin *via strata*, 'paved way'. The Anglo-Saxons adopted this as a word for the Roman roads they found when they came to Britain in the 5th century. They had never seen roads of this type before, and had no native word for them. Hence the names of Roman roads such as Watling *Street*.

string The word derives from Old English *streng*, itself related to *strang*, the source of modern *strong*.

stripling The word for a youth derives from *strip* with the suffix *-ling*, not a diminutive, but denoting a person possessing the quality of the main word. A *stripling* is thus a lad who is as slender as a *strip*. Compare ◊darling.

> **FALSE**
>
> **stripling** From obsolete English *trippling*, 'tripping', 'dancing lightly', referring to the agility and energy of a young lad. Compare ◊tomboy.

stud As a word for a breeding establishment for horses, the origin is ultimately in a Germanic word that itself derives from the Indo-European root element meaning 'stand' found in both *steed* and *stand* itself, as well as many other words, including ◊stall and ◊stallion. Even now *stand* is used of a horse available as a *stud*. Compare related German *Stute*, 'mare'.

stun The word derives from Old French *estoner* (modern *étonner*), 'to daze', 'to stupefy', itself from a conjectured Vulgar Latin verb *extonare*, literally 'to thunder out', from *ex-*. 'out', and *tonare*, 'to thunder'. Two words of the same origin are *astonish* and *astound*.

sturdy Although now a term of approval, the original sense of the word was 'fierce', 'rough'. It derives from Old French *estordi*, 'dazed' (modern French *étourdi*, 'thoughtless'), from a verb that was perhaps ultimately related to Latin *turdus*, 'thrush', a bird popularly associated with drunkenness. (Compare the French saying *soûl comme une grive*, 'drunk as a thrush'. Even English 'drunk as an owl' is similar.)

> **FALSE**
>
> **sturdy** From Greek *stithros*, 'compact', 'solid', 'stout'.

stye The word for a swelling on the eyelid evolved from the obsolete dialect word for it, *styanye*, representing Old English *stīgend*, 'rising' and a form of *eye*.

However, the word was understood as *sty on eye*, and the first word of this alone was adopted for the condition.

suave The word meaning 'smoothly sophisticated' originally meant simply 'pleasing', 'agreeable'. Its origin is in the identical French word that itself came from Latin *suavis*, 'sweet'. Hence also related *persuade* (when you try to convince someone that something is pleasant) and *dissuade* (when you try to convince them that it is not). English ◊*sweet* is itself related.

subject The word has its origin in Latin *subjectus*, literally 'thrown under', from *sub*, 'under', and a form of the verb *jacere*, 'to throw'.

sublime The word relating to something noble or supreme derives from Latin *sublimis*, 'lofty', literally 'up to the threshold', from *sub*, 'under' (but extending up to), and *limen*, 'threshold'. If you *sublimate* a feeling or impulse, you raise it from a basic level to something more *sublime*.

subscribe The literal meaning is 'write under', since when you *subscribe* to something you add your signature at the bottom. When you *subscribe* to a view, you *underwrite* it or support it. the origin is thus in Latin *subscribere*, 'to write under'.

subsidy The term for financial support derives from Latin *subsidium*, 'assistance', literally 'sitting below' (as if to support or hold up), from *sub*, 'below', and a form of the verb *sedere*, 'to sit'. A directly related word is *subsidiary*.

subtle The term applied to something delicate or cunning derives from Old French *soutil*, itself from Latin *subtilis*, 'finely woven', in turn probably from *sub*, 'under', and *tela*, a form of *texla*, 'woven stuff', 'warp'.

succinct The word now means 'brief and concise', but originally meant 'girded', literally 'girded from below'. Hence its origin in Latin *succinctus*, from *sub*, 'below', and *cingere*, 'to gird'.

sue The verb meaning 'take legal proceedings against' evolved from Old French *sivre*, itself from Latin *sequi*, 'to follow'. Compare *prosecute* in its literal sense (from the Latin) of 'follow through'.

suede The type of leather, properly undressed kid, gets its name from what were originally known in English as '*suède* gloves', as a semi-translation of French *gants de Suède*, literally 'gloves from Sweden' (which were made of such leather).

suffer If you *suffer* you are in a sense 'borne under'. The word has its ultimate origin in Latin *sufferre*, from *sub*, 'under', and *ferre*, 'to bear', 'to carry'.

suicide The term for killing oneself derives from New Latin *suicidium*, from Latin *sui*, 'of oneself', and a noun form of the verb *caedere*, 'to kill'. The word was modelled on *homicide*, where the first element represents Latin *homo*, 'man'.

sullen The word may derive, through a conjectural Anglo-French word *solain*, from a source ultimately related to Latin *solus*, 'alone'. A *sullen* person is unsociable and unwilling to mix with others.

Sunday The first day of the week has a name that means what it says, 'day of the sun', to which it was dedicated. The name translated Latin *dies solis*, itself translating Greek *hēmera hēliou*.

supercilious The word meaning 'haughty' literally means 'of the eyebrows' (that is, raising them), from an adjectival form of Latin *supercilium*, 'eyebrow'.

supersede The word meaning 'take the place of' derives, through Old French, from Latin *supersedere*, 'to sit above', from *super*, 'above', and *sedere*, 'to sit'.

superstition The word comes from the noun of the Latin verb *superstare*, 'to stand on', from *super*, 'above', 'on', and *stare*, 'to stand'. The idea is of standing still in amazement or awe.

supper The evening meal takes its name from Old French *soper*, 'to sup', in the sense of taking a light meal based on a liquid food such as broth (which you *sup*). Directly related words are *sop* (bread that has been dipped in liquid) and *soup* (one early form of which was broth poured on slices of bread, which then became *sops*).

supple The word literally means 'bending under', from Latin *supplex*, 'bowed', representing *sub*, 'under', and the base of *plicare*, 'to bend', 'to fold'.

supply The word came into English, via French, from Latin *supplere*, 'to complete' (the source of English *supplement*), literally 'fill up', from *sub*, 'under' (so up to), and *plere*, 'to fill'.

suppose If you *suppose* something, you effectively substitute a possibility for a reality. Hence the origin of the word in Latin *supponere*, 'to substitute', literally 'to place under', from *sub*, 'under' (here in the sense 'from below'), and *ponere'*, *'to place'*.

surf The word for waves breaking on the shore may have evolved as a blend of *sough* and *surge*, referring to their repeated 'sighing' sound and rushing or sweeping action.

surface The word came into English from the identical French word, itself literally meaning 'on face', from *sur*, 'on', and *face*, 'face'. The French word may have been modelled on Latin *superficies*, 'upper side', from *super*, 'above', and *facies*, 'face'.

surgery As the art (or science) of the *surgeon*, the word has its origin, via Old French, in Latin *chirurgia*, itself from Greek *kheirurgia*, literally 'handiwork', from *kheir*, 'hand', and *ergon*, 'work'.

surname The word literally means 'name above', from Old French *surnom*, itself translating Medieval Latin *supranomen*, representing *supra*, 'above', and *nomen*, 'name'. The reference is to an additional name, one 'over and above' the original name. Surnames evolved in order to distinguish people of identical personal name.

surplice The long white vestment worn over a cassock by clergy and choir in a church service is so called because it was originally worn over a furred garment.

The word evolved, through Old French, from Latin *superpellicium*, from *super*, 'over', and *pellicium*, 'fur coat', itself from *pellis*, 'skin'. (Compare *pelisse* as the name of a type of fur-trimmed cloak.)

surrender If you *surrender* you give yourself up. Hence the origin of the word in Old French *surrendre*, 'to yield', literally 'to give up', from *sur*, 'above', and *rendre*, 'to render', 'to give back'.

> **FALSE**
>
> **surrender** A corruption of French *se rendre*, 'to give oneself up'.

surreptitious The word relating to something done secretly or improperly derives from Latin *surripere*, 'to steal', literally 'to snatch underneath', from *sub*, 'under' (implying 'secretly'), and *rapere*, 'to snatch'), 'to seize' (English ◊rape).

surrogate In its sense of 'substitute' (as in a *surrogate* mother, who bears a child for another woman), the word has its origin in Latin *surrogare*, 'to substitute', literally 'to ask in place of', from *sub*, 'under' (in the sense of replacing), and *rogare*, 'to ask', 'to propose the appointment of'.

surround The ultimate source of the word, through Old French, is in Late Latin *superundare*, literally 'to rise in waves above', from *super*, 'above', and *undare*, 'to flood', from *unda*, 'wave'. The original meaning of the word was thus 'to overflow'. It gained its present sense by association with *round*.

suspect The word has its origin in Latin *suspicere*, 'to mistrust', literally 'to look up to', from *sub*, 'under' (therefore from below up to), and *specere*, 'to look'. The idea is of looking askance (*suspiciously*) at something.

svelte The word used of an attractively slender person was adopted directly from the French. It was originally an artist's term for a person who had been imaginatively 'picked out' in a portrait. Hence its ultimate origin, via Italian *svelto*, in Latin *evellere*, literally 'to pluck out', from *ex*, 'out', and *vellere*, 'to pluck'.

swagger The word is presumably based on *swag*, which was originally a dialect term for a swaying movement.

swastika The type of cross with its arms bent at right angles, adopted as the emblem of Nazi Germany, was originally a primitive religious symbol. Hence the origin of its name in Sanskrit *svastika*, from *svasti*, 'prosperity', from the belief that it brought good luck.

sweet The word is Germanic in origin, and goes back to an Indo-European root element meaning 'pleasant', seen also in related Greek *hēdonē*, 'pleasure' (English *hedonism*) and Latin *suavis* (English ◊suave).

swindle The word came into English in the 18th century as a verb derived from the German noun *Schwindler*, 'cheat', literally 'giddy person', from *schwindeln*, 'to feel dizzy', 'to tell lies'.

switchback The roller coaster or big dipper is so called since originally its carriages were *switched back* from one end to the other at the end of a run. Today the route is usually circuitous.

swop The word at first meant 'strike', 'hit', and is imitative in origin. It then gained the specialized sense of two people *striking* hands on *striking* a bargain. Finally it acquired its present sense of simply 'exchange'. It is also spelt *swap*.

swot The verb meaning 'study hard' evolved as a dialect form of *sweat*. The word is also spelt *swat*. (Compare ◊swop.)

sybarite The word for a person who indulges in luxury or pleasure derives from the name of the *Sybarites*, the inhabitants of *Sybaris*, an ancient Greek colony in southern Italy, who were notorious for their luxurious way of living.

sycamore The name is that of both a species of fig tree and a species of maple. The word goes back to Greek *sukomoros*, literally 'fig-mulberry', from a combination of *sukon*, 'fig', and *moron*, 'mulberry'.

syllable The term for a unit of sound in a word (*syllable* has three) derives ultimately, through French and Latin, from the Greek verb *sullambanein*, 'to bring together', from *sun* 'together' (English *syn-*), and *lambanein*, 'to take'.

syllabus The word for an educational course of study goes back ultimately, through Latin *sittybus*, to Greek *sittuba*, the term for a parchment strip giving the name of title and author of a written work (the classical equivalent of a record card or library slip). The present spelling came about because some time in the 15th century the *tt* of the Latin word was miscopied as *ll*.

sylph The word for an imaginary being at one time believed to inhabit the air probably arose as a (perhaps intentional) combination of Latin *silva*, 'wood', and Greek *numphē*, 'nymph'.

sympathy The literal meaning of the word is 'suffering with', from Greek *sumpatheia*, representing *sun*, 'together' (English *syn-*), and *pathos*, 'suffering' (English *pathos*). Latin-derived *compassion* is the exact equivalent, from the verb *compati*, representing *cum*, 'with', and *pati*, 'to suffer'.

symptom The medical term for the bodily sensation that a function has changed derives from Greek *sumptōma*, 'chance', literally 'falling together', from *sun*, 'together' (English *syn-*), and *piptein*, 'to fall'.

syndicate The word derives from Old French *syndicat*, referring to the office of a *syndic*, a magistrate. His title goes back, through Latin, to Greek *sundikos*, the term for a defendant's advocate, literally 'justice together', from *sun*, 'together' (English *syn-*), and *dikē*, 'justice'.

syndrome The medical term for a combination of symptoms derives from Greek *sundromē*, literally 'running together', from *sun*, 'together' (English *syn-*), and *dramein*, 'to run'.

syphilis The venereal disease has a name of literary origin. It derives from *Syphilis, sive Morbus Gallicus*, 'Syphilus, or the French Disease', the title of a Latin poem of 1530 by the Italian physician and poet Girolamo Fracastoro. In this, the shepherd *Syphilis* is portrayed as the first victim of the disease. The shepherd's name itself is of uncertain origin. (It may be an altered form of *Sipylus*, the name of a son of Niobe in classical mythology.)

syrup The thick sweet liquid derives its name, through Latin, from Arabic *sharāb*, 'drink', the noun form of the verb *shariba*, 'to drink'.

system The word is of Greek origin, from *sustēma*, literally 'made to stand together', from *sun*, 'together' (English *syn-*), and *histanai*, 'to cause to stand'.

tabby The striped cat probably gets its name from the pet form of the personal name *Tabitha*. However, it was also influenced by *tabby* as the word for a type of fabric that originally had a striped pattern. Its own name comes, through French, from Arabic *al- 'attabiya*, literally 'the quarter of *'Attab*' (a famous prince), the district of Baghdad where the fabric was first made.

tabloid The term for a popular newspaper was adopted from the word devised in 1884 as a trade name (*Tabloid*) for a type of medicinal *tablet*. The popular papers are so called since they print the news in condensed form, like the ingredients compressed into a tablet.

tactics The art and science of conducting forces in battle derives its name, through New Latin, from Greek *ta taktika*, 'the matters of arrangement', from the plural form of *taktikos*, the noun of *taktos*, 'arranged', ultimately from *tassein*, 'to arrange'.

tadpole The young of a frog or toad is so named from its appearance, from a combination of *tadde*, an early form of *toad*, and *pol*, 'head' (modern *poll*). The creature appears to be all head and no body.

taffeta The thin silk fabric ultimately gets its name, through Latin, from Persian *tāftah*, 'spun', in turn from *tāftan*, 'to spin'.

> **FALSE**
>
> **tadpole** A combination of Old English *tāde*, 'toad', and *fola*, 'foal', in other words *toad foal*, or a young frog or toad.

tailor The person who makes clothes is basically a 'cutter', and the word derives from Old French *taillier* (modern French *tailler*), 'to cut'.

talent The word for a natural 'gift' for something derives from Latin *talenta*, the plural of *talentum*, 'sum of money', itself from Greek *talanton*, 'balance', 'weight'. The meaning comes from the biblical parable of the *talents* (Matthew 25:14–30), in which they are actual money.

talisman The word for an object believed to have magical powers derives, through French and Arabic, from Greek *telesma*, 'consecration', literally 'completion', from the verb *telein*, 'to complete', itself from *telos*, 'end'.

tally-ho The hunting cry perhaps evolved from a similar French 'view halloo', *taïaut*, itself a meaningless call used to spur on hounds.

> **FALSE**
>
> **tally-ho** From the French hunting cry *au taillis*, 'to the woods', which if repeated sounds like *tally ho*.

tamper The word, meaning 'meddle', 'interfere', evolved as an altered form of *temper*, in the sense of 'adjust', 'alter'. The verb *tamper* originally had the literal sense of working in clay by mixing or blending it.

tandem The word for a 'bicycle made for two' arose as a humorous adoption of Latin *tandem*, 'at length' (properly meaning in time). The word was originally applied to a vehicle drawn by two horses one behind the other.

tangerine The type of orange-like fruit is so called since originally it came from *Tangier*, the Moroccan port. (The fruit was at first known as a *Tangerine orange*.)

tank The military tracked vehicle made its first appearance as a 'secret weapon' in the First World War. It was officially code named thus for reasons of security, from its general resemblance to a benzene *tank*.

> **FALSE**
>
> **tankard** From *tank*, describing the original sense of the word, as applied to a large tub-like vessel, or one in which water was carried.

tankard The origin of the word is unknown. It was originally the term for a large tub before it was adopted for a drinking vessel.

tansy The yellow-flowered plant has a name that ultimately derives, through French and Latin, from Greek *athanasia*, 'immortality'. It was presumably believed to prolong life.

tantalize The word used for teasing or frustrating someone (by offering something they can't have) derives from the name of *Tantalus*, the king in Greek mythology who was punished by having to stand in water that went down when he tried to drink it and under fruit that moved away when he tried to pick it.

tapioca The type of starch from the cassava root has a name of Tupi origin meaning literally 'squeezed-out dregs', from *tipi*, 'residue', and *ok*, 'to squeeze out'.

tarantula The big hairy spider is named after *Taranto*, the town in southeastern Italy, where it was once common. Its bite was formerly believed to cause *tarantism*, a nervous disorder that made the sufferer weep and dance about. The rapid whirling dance known as the *tarantella* was said to be a cure for this, and to take its name from it. It actually comes from the same Italian town, however.

target The word derives from Old French *targette*, a diminutive of *targe*, 'shield', itself a word of Germanic origin. Shields were at one time marked with concentric circles to serve as a butt (or *target*) for archers when practising.

tarpaulin The heavy waterproof fabric is made of canvas coated with *tar*. Its name is thus probably based on this word, with the middle part representing *pall* in the sense 'covering'.

tart The colloquial word for a prostitute or promiscuous woman arose as a shortening of *sweetheart*.

tartan The cloth with a distinctive Scottish design or pattern is said to derive its name from Old French *tertaine*, 'linsey-woolsey' (cloth that is a mixture of linen and wool), itself from Old Spanish *tiritaña*, a type of fine silk fabric.

tattoo The military display or pageant, such as the Edinburgh *Tattoo*, evolved as an elaborate staging of the *tattoo* that was originally a signal by drum or bugle ordering soldiers to return to their quarters at night. The word comes from Dutch *taptoe*, from the command *tap toe!*, literally 'tap to', in other words 'turn off the tap', referring to the taps on a barrel.

tawdry The word applied to something shoddy or cheap was originally used of *tawdry lace*, a shortened form of *Seint Audries lace*, referring to the necklaces sold at the fair of *St Audrey* (Etheldrida), the 7th-century queen of Northumbria and patron saint of Ely, Cambridgeshire, who died of a tumour of the throat that she regarded as divine punishment for wearing gorgeous necklaces when she was young.

tax The word goes back through Old French *taxer* to Latin *taxare*, 'to appraise', itself a form of *tangere*, 'to touch'.

taxi The word is short for *taximeter cab*, this being a cab with a *taximeter*, a meter fitted to register the distance travelled and the fare due. This word itself represents French *taximètre*, literally 'tariff measurer', from French *taxe* in its sense of 'tariff', 'rate of charges' rather than 'tax'.

teddy The name of the toy bear represents the pet form of the personal name *Theodore*, in this case that of the American president Theodore Roosevelt (1858–1919), who was well known as a hunter of bears.

teetotal The word describing a person who does not drink alcohol is said to have been coined in 1833 by Richard Turner, a Lancashire advocate of *total* abstinence. The origin of the initial *tee-* is uncertain. It may simply have been for emphasis. But see also ◊teetotum.

> **FALSE**
>
> **teetotal** From a faltering English pronunciation of Irish *díotáil*, 'indictment', referring to a prohibition law.

teetotum The name is properly that of a spinning top that had letters of the alphabet on its four sides. One of the letters was *T*, standing for Latin *totum* 'whole'. Hence the name of the toy, *T-totum*. (The other letters were *A* for *aufer*, *D* for *depone* and *N* for *nihil*, making the Latin sentence *Totum aufer, depone nihil*, 'Take away everything, put down nothing'.) The word ◊teetotal may have been based on this word.

television The word is a blend of Greek *tēle*, 'far', and Latin *visio*, genitive *visionis*, 'sight', 'seeing'. Most words for scientific apparatus of this kind have Greek origins for both elements, such as *telegraph* ('far writing'), *telephone* ('far sounding') and *telescope* ('far seeing'). *Television* is thus a hybrid.

tempest The word goes back, through French, to Latin *tempestas*, 'storm', *stormy season*, itself based on *tempus*, 'time'.

temple   As applied to a religious building, the word derives ultimately from Latin *templum* in this sense. The Latin word itself may be related to *tempus*, 'time', or to Greek *temenos*, 'sacred enclosure', literally 'cut-off place', from *temnein*, 'to cut'.

tennis   The game is believed to derive its name from Anglo-French *tenetz* (modern French *tenez*), 'hold!', 'take!', as the server's call to his opponent. (The original form of the game was the one that gave modern real tennis, played in a walled court.)

tenor   The male singer is so called from Italian *tenore*, literally 'holding'. It was this voice that formerly 'held' or continuously sang the melody, while other voices sang 'against' it. (Hence *countertenor* for the chief of these.).

tent   The word derives, through French, from Latin *tentorium*, itself based on the verb *tendere*, 'to stretch'. When Roman armies pitched camp, they stretched out skins over their huts for protection against the weather and to conserve heat.

termagant   The word for a shrewish woman derives, through French, from Italian *Trivigante*. This was the name of an arrogant character in medieval mystery plays who was supposed to be a Muslim god. The name itself has been explained as representing Latin *tri-*, 'three', and *vagans*, 'wandering', from *vagari*, 'to wander' (English *vague*), referring to the Moon wandering under the names of the three Greek goddesses Selene, Artemis, and Persephone (or the three corresponding Roman goddesses Luna, Diana, and Proserpina), in heaven, earth, and hell respectively.

> **FALSE**
>
> **termagant**   From Old English *triewe*, 'true', and *magan*, 'to be able', 'to be strong', that is, 'truly strong'.

terrace   The raised level area derives its name from Latin *terra*, 'earth', from the mound or bank of earth that originally formed it.

terrier   The breed of dog is so called since it was originally used to pursue animals that lived underground into their burrow or earth and flush them out. The name thus comes from French *chien terrier*, literally 'earth dog', ultimately from Latin *terra*, 'earth'.

tetanus   The infectious disease, also known as lockjaw, involves sustained spasms and rigidity of the muscles. Hence its name, from Greek *tetanos*, 'taut', from the verb *teinein*, 'to stretch'.

textile   The word is used for any fabric or cloth, especially a woven one. Hence its origin in Latin *textilis*, 'woven', from *texere*, 'to weave'. *Text* and *texture* are related words.

theatre   The word goes back, via Latin *theatrum*, to Greek *theātron*, literally 'place for viewing', from *theāsthai*, 'to look at'.

theory The word literally means 'sight', 'view', and ultimately derives from Greek *theōrein*, 'to look at', as of a spectator at public games. A *theory* is a mental 'picture' or conception of something, otherwise a 'view' about it. (Greek *theōros*, 'spectator', is literally 'one who regards a god', that is, consults an oracle, from *theos*, 'god', and *ōra*, 'care', 'regard'.)

therapeutic The word used of something curative or healing derives from Greek *therapeutikos*, from *therapeuein*, 'to minister to', ultimately from *theraps*, 'attendant', 'servant'.

thesaurus The term for a dictionary of selected words, usually synonyms or near-synonyms, derives from the identical Latin word meaning 'treasure'. (English *treasure* is also from this source.)

thimble The word was originally used for a fingerstall for the *thumb*, as its name implies.

threshold The present word for the entrance to a building evolved from Old English *therscold*. The first part of this represents *therscan*, 'to thrash', in its basic sense of 'tread', 'trample'. The source of the second part is uncertain. An expected meaning would be 'ground'. (The French word for 'threshold', *seuil*, derives from Latin *solum*, 'ground'.)

FALSE

threshold An altered form of *threshwood*, 'threshing floor', the part of a barn where the horses entered when drawing cartloads of corn.

---

thug As *Thug* (with a capital letter), the word originally applied to a professional robber and murderer in India. Hence its derivation in Hindi *thag*, 'thief', from Sanskrit *sthaga*, 'scoundrel', ultimately from *sthagati*, 'to conceal'.

thumb The word is Germanic in origin, and ultimately derives from an Indo-European root element meaning 'swelling', so that a related word is Latin *tumere*, 'to swell'. Related English words are *tumour* and *tumult* (a 'swelling' noise).

Thursday The fourth day of the week is named after *Thor*, the Norse god of *thunder*. The name arose as an equivalent to Late Latin *Jovis dies*, 'Jupiter's day' (the source of French *jeudi*).

thyme The aromatic herb derives its name, through French and Latin, from Greek *thuein*, 'to burn a sacrifice', from its use for incense at this ceremony.

ticket The word came into English from Old French *estiquet* or *estiquette*, 'label', from *estiquier*, 'to stick'. A *ticket* is thus literally a label or notice that is *stuck* on. (Compare modern *sticker*, which can also serve as a *ticket* of some kind.) The word ▷*etiquette* is from the same French source.

tiddlywinks The game with counters probably derives its name from a combination of *tiddly* (referring to the small moves of the counters) and a dialect form of *winch* (referring to the way in which they are raised into the cup).

tidy The word is related to *tide* in the sense 'time'. Something *tidy* was thus originally timely or seasonal. The sense then passed from 'well ordered in time' to 'well ordered in habits' or 'well ordered in position'.

timber The word is Germanic in origin and at first had the sense 'building', meaning one made of wood. Compare related modern German **Zimmer**, 'room'.

tingle The word may be an altered form of *tinkle*, perhaps by association with *ring*.

tinker The word for a (former) travelling mender of pots and pans probably came from *tink*, referring to the tinkling and clinking sound as he made his way or did his job.

FALSE

tinker From his occupation of making or repairing *tin* articles.

---

tinsel The origin of the word is in Old French *estincele*, 'spark', in turn from Latin *scintilla* with this meaning. The word originally applied to clothing embellished with gold or silver thread.

tint The word for a light or pale colour evolved as a form of the now rare word *tinct*, itself from Latin *tinctus*, 'dyed' (English *tincture*), from *tingere*, 'to dye', 'to colour' (English *tinge*).

tissue The word originally applied to a type of rich cloth, especially one interwoven with gold or silver. It then came to apply to any woven fabric. Hence its derivation in Old French *tissu*, 'woven cloth', from *tistre*, 'to weave', itself from Latin *texere* (English *texture*) in the same sense.

titbit The word for a delicate or tasty morsel derives from the former dialect word *tid*, 'delicate', 'nice', and standard *bit*. The origin of *tid* is not known.

titivate The word meaning 'make oneself smart' perhaps evolved as a blend of *tidy* and *cultivate*. It is not recorded earlier than the 19th century.

toast As now used of a proposal of health, the word originally applied to a lady to whom the gathered company was asked to drink. The idea was that the name of the lady would flavour the drink like a piece of spiced *toast*.

tocsin The word for an alarm or warning signal, especially one sounded on a bell, evolved from Old French *toquassen*, itself from Old Provençal *tocasenh*, representing *tocar*, 'to touch', and *senh*, 'bell' (related to English *signal*).

toff The colloquial word for a rich or upper-class person is said to derive from *tuft*, referring to a titled student at Oxford University who wore a cap with a gold tassel.

toffee The name of the chewy sweet apparently arose as an alteration of *taffy*, a similar sweet now mainly found in America. Its own name may have come from *tafia*, a type of rum, from its colour.

together The meaning of the original Old English word was '*into* one place', not '*in* one place'. Hence the derivation in what amounts to a combination of modern 'to' and 'gather'.

toilet The present meaning of the word is far removed from the original, which was 'cloth wrapper'. The senses evolved in this order: 'cloth wrapper', 'cloth covering a dressing table', 'dressing table', 'act of dressing', 'room for washing and dressing', 'lavatory'. The derivation of the word is thus ultimately in a diminutive of French *toile*, 'cloth'.

toll The word for money paid to use a road or bridge is Germanic in origin, and ultimately relates to Latin *telonium*, 'customs house', itself going back to Greek *telos*, 'tax'.

tombola The type of lottery gets its name from the Italian word *tombolare*, 'to turn a somersault', 'to tumble'. The reference is to the revolving drum in which the tickets *tumble* before being drawn.

tomboy The word for a boyish girl, or one who enjoys 'rough and tumble' activities as boys do, derives from the personal name *Tom*, used as a nickname, and *boy*. The word was originally used for a bold or audacious boy or woman, then came to apply to a girl only.

> ### FALSE
> **tomboy** From Old English *tumbere*, 'tumbler', 'dancer', referring to a girl who skipped and leapt about like a boy. Compare ◊stripling.

tome The word for a volume or large book derives ultimately from Greek *tomos*, 'slice'. A *tome* is usually thought of as forming part of a longer work in several volumes, so that it is a 'slice' or part of the whole.

tomorrow The present word has evolved from the Old English phrase *to morgenne*, in which *to* means 'on' and *morgenne* is the dative case of *morgen*, 'morning'. *Tomorrow* is thus 'on the morn', or 'in the morning'. (*Morn* originally meant both 'the next day' and 'the next morning'. Compare modern German *Morgen*, 'morning', and *morgen*, 'tomorrow'.)

ton The measurement of weight arose as a variant form of *tun* in its original sense of 'large cask'.

tonic A *tonic* is so called since it improves the *tone* of your body. *Tone* itself ultimately derives from Greek *tonos*, 'tension', from *teinein*, 'to stretch'. See also ◊tune.

tooth The word is Germanic in origin, and ultimately derives from an Indo-European root element meaning 'eat'. A *tooth* is thus literally an 'eater'. Related English words are *dentist* (from Latin *dens*, genitive *dentis*, 'tooth'), *tusk*, and even *eat* itself.

topiary The word for the art of shaping trees and bushes into ornamental figures derives, through French, from Latin *topia*, 'ornamental garden work', from the identical Greek word that is the plural form of *topion*, a diminutive of *topos*, 'place'.

topic The word that now means little more than 'subject' has a specific classical origin in the Latin plural noun *topica*, rendering Greek *ta topika*, 'matters concerning commonplaces', the title of a treatise by Aristotle. The basic source of the word itself is Greek *topos*, 'place'.

topsy-turvy   The expression meaning 'upside down' probably evolved from *tops*, the plural of *top*, and *tervy*, an obsolete verb meaning 'to turn upside down'. The idea is of turning an object so that its top is at the bottom.

> **FALSE**
>
> **topsy-turvy**   An altered form of *topside t'other way*.

torch   The modern electric flashlight evolved from the primitive method of lighting one's way by holding a flaming twist of dry grass or other combustible material. Hence the ultimate source of the word in Latin *torquere*, 'to twist'.

tornado   The violent storm probably got its name as a noun formed as a blend of two Spanish verbs: *tronar*, 'to thunder', and *tornar*, 'to turn'. Compare its alternative English names of *cyclone* (referring to its whirling motion) and *twister*.

torpedo   The *torpedo* fired from ships and aircraft derives its name from the *torpedo* that is the fish also known as an electric ray. The fish has an electric discharge that can cause numbness, and the weapon can incapacitate similarly. The ultimate origin of the word is in Latin *torpere*, 'to be numb' (the source of English *torpid*).

tortoise   The shelled reptile probably derives its name from Old French (also modern) *tortue*, influenced by Latin *tortus*, 'twisted', referring to its legs. The French word is said by some to derive ultimately from Late Latin *tartarucha*, 'belonging to Tartary', in turn from Greek *tartaroukhos*, from the belief that the creature originated in *Tartarus*, the underworld of classical mythology.

> **FALSE**
>
> **tot**   From a proverbial remark by the composer Haydn during a visit to England. When bored by visitors, he would say 'Excuse me, I have a thought' (pronounced 'tot'), and retire not to put pen to paper but to refresh himself with a tipple.

tot   The term for a small child or a 'wee drappie' of spirits is of dialect origin and may have arisen as a shortening (applied to the child) of *totterer*. The reference would have been to an unsteady walker. Compare modern *toddler*.

totem   The object or animal that with some North American Indians represents a tribe or family is said to derive from Ojibwa *nintōtēm*, 'mark of my family'.

toupee   The hairpiece derives its name from French *toupet*, 'forelock', the diminutive of an Old French word of Germanic origin that is related to English *top*.

tournament   The sporting competition derives its name from Old French *torneiement*, the noun of *torneier*, 'to turn', This was the term for a medieval tilting match, in which mounted contestants fought for a prize. As they fought, they constantly wheeled or *turned* around each other. Hence the name.

towel   The word came into English, through French, from a Germanic source related to Old High German *dwahal*, 'bath', and Gothic *thwahan*, 'to wash'. A French word *touaille* was formerly used for a roller towel.

> **FALSE**
>
> **towel**   From French *toile*, 'cloth'. Hence the association between *towel* and *toilet*.

toxophilite The formal name for an archer derives from *Toxophilus*, the title of a book by Roger Asham published in 1545. The intended meaning of the title was *lover of the bow*, from the Greek words *toxon*, 'bow', and *philos*, 'loving'.

tractor The literal meaning of the word is 'puller', 'drawer', from the identical Latin word that is the noun of the verb *trahere*, 'to drag'. The agricultural vehicle took its name from a word already in technical use for various kinds of pulling devices.

trade The word is Germanic in origin and is related to *tread*, hence its earliest meaning of 'course', 'way', 'track'. *Trade* winds, which blow in a constant direction, derive their name from the phrase *blow trade*, meaning 'blow in a regular course'.

tradition The literal meaning of the word is 'giving over', from Latin *traditio*, 'surrender', the noun of *tradere*, 'to give up', representing *trans*, 'across', 'over', and *dare*, 'to give'. A *tradition* is passed down or handed over from one generation to the next.

tragedy In its theatrical sense, the word goes back, through Latin, to Greek *tragōidia*, apparently representing *tragos*, 'goat', and *ōidē*, 'song'. If so, the reference is probably to the goat-satyrs that appeared in Peloponnesian plays.

train The public transport sense of the word arose only when the railways themselves did, in the 19th century. The basic sense is of something or someone that pulls or draws. Hence the ultimate source of the word, through Old French *trahiner* (modern *traîner*), in the conjectured Vulgar Latin verb *traginare*, 'to draw', related to Latin *trahere*, 'to drag'.

tram The word for the public transport vehicle was originally used for the shaft of a barrow or cart. Its origin is thus probably in Low German *traam*, 'beam', from an ultimate source that may be related to Latin *trabs*, genitive *trabis* in this sense. The meaning passed from the shaft to the cart itself, then to the wooden track on which it ran, then to a road with such a track, and finally to the modern vehicle that runs on tracks.

> **FALSE**
>
> **tram** From the name of Benjamin *Outram* (1764–1805), the civil engineer who introduced iron railways for colliery traffic.

translate The word has its origin in Latin *translatus*, 'transferred', literally 'carried across', a form of the verb *transferre*, 'to transfer'. If you *translate* a text, you 'carry across' its meaning from one language into another.

transparent Something *transparent* can be seen through. Hence the origin of the word in Medieval Latin *transparere*, 'to show through', representing Latin *trans*, 'across', 'through', and *parere*, 'to show'.

transpire The verb that is now often used to mean simply 'happen' earlier meant (as it still does) 'come to light', 'be made known'. The literal meaning is 'breathe across', from Medieval Latin *transpirare*, representing Latin *trans*, 'across', 'over', and *spirare*, 'to breathe'.

transport The origin of the word is in Latin *transportare*, literally 'carry across', from *trans*, 'across', and *portare*, 'to carry' (English *porter*). If you are *transported* with delight, you are 'carried over' from one emotional state to another.

trapeze The gymnastic apparatus, consisting of a crossbar suspended on two ropes, derives its name, through French, from New Latin *trapezium*. This is properly a geometrical term for a four-sided figure. Hence its own origin in Greek *trapeza*, 'table', literally 'four-footed', from Indo-European root elements related (albeit remotely) to French *quatre* and English *four* (the *tra-*) and French *pied* and English *foot* (the *-peza*). A *trapeze* can be regarded as a four-sided figure if you take the crossbar as one side, the ropes as two others, and the roof from which the ropes hang as the fourth.

travel The verb meaning 'journey' developed from the verb *travail*, meaning 'labour', the concept being that a journey is a laborious business, one requiring effort and possibly discomfort. *Travail* itself derives from Old French *travaillier* (compare modern French *travailler*, 'to work'), in turn from a conjectured Vulgar Latin verb *tripaliare*, 'to torture', formed from the Late Latin noun *trepalium*. This was an instrument of torture constructed from three stakes, and itself represents a blend of Latin *tres*, 'three', and *palus*, 'stake'.

travesty The word for a farcical or grotesque imitation of something derives from French *travesti*, 'disguised', literally 'cross- dressed', from an Italian verb that goes back to Latin *trans*, 'across', and *vestire*, 'to clothe', 'to dress'. (Compare English *transvestite* as a term for a person who dresses in the clothes of the opposite sex.)

treacle The word originally applied to a type of ointment regarded as an antidote for animal bites. Hence its origin, through Old French *triacle*, in Latin *theriaca*, representing Greek *thēriakē antidotos*, 'antidote against wild beasts', ultimately from Greek *thērion*, a diminutive of *thēr*, 'wild beast'.

> **FALSE**
> **treacle** So called because it *trickles*.

treble In its musical sense, as the term for the upper part in a composition or a high singing voice, the word, from Latin *triplus*, 'threefold', may have referred to the *third* part above the *altus* ('high') and *bassus* ('low').

trek The word for a long and difficult journey derives from Afrikaans. It originally applied to the *Voortrekkers*, the Dutch settlers in South Africa who made long journeys by ox wagon during the Great *Trek* of the 1830s, when they migrated from Cape Colony in search of fresh pastures. Hence its origin in Middle Dutch *trekken*, 'to draw', 'to pull', 'to travel'.

trellis The latticework used to support climbing plants derives its name from Old French *treliz*, the term for an open-textured fabric. This in turn evolved from

Late Latin *trilicius*, literally 'woven with three threads', from Latin *tres*, 'three', and *licium*, 'thread'.

trespass The verb used for the act of intruding on someone else's property or privacy literally means 'pass across'. Its origin is in Old French *trespasser*, ultimately from Latin *trans*, 'across', and *passus*, 'pace'.

tress The word for a lock of hair is French in origin, but its original meaning is uncertain. Any link with Greek *thrix*, genitive *thrikhos*, 'hair', is unproven.

> **FALSE**
>
> **tress** From an Old French word related to Latin *tres*, 'three'. *Tresses* were originally made by braiding together *three* locks of hair.

tribe The word for a community of people with a common ancestor derives from Latin *tribus*, itself said to be based on Latin *tres*, 'three'. This presumably related in some way to the three tribes based on kinship into which people were originally divided in ancient Rome.

tribute The word for an acknowledgement to somebody derives from Latin *tribuere*, 'to grant', literally 'to divide among the *tribes*', from *tribus*, 'tribe'.

trifle The word comes from Old French *trufle*, 'mockery', the noun form of *trufler*, 'to cheat'. The word was originally used in English for a false story or idle tale. Hence its modern sense as applied to something slight or unimportant.

> **FALSE**
>
> **trifle** So called because it is *trivial*.

trivial The word, meaning 'unimportant', 'petty', derives from Latin *trivialis*, the adjectival form of *trivium*, 'crossroads', literally 'three roads', from *tres*, 'three', and *via*, 'way', 'road'. The reference is to casual 'chitchat', as between people meeting at a crossroads.

trolley The word probably evolved as a noun form of *troll* in the sense 'roll'.

trombone The large brass instrument derives its name as an Italian augmentative ('big' form) of *tromba*, 'trumpet'. Compare ◊bassoon, which has the same ending.

trophy The object such as a cup that is a symbol of victory derives its name, via French, from Latin *tropaeum*, itself from Greek *tropaion*, a derivative of *tropē*, literally 'turning', meaning a *turn* in fortunes in battle, otherwise a defeat of the enemy and hence a victory.

tropic The two *tropics* of Cancer and Capricorn are the parallel lines of latitude in the northern and southern hemispheres respectively that represent the limits at which the sun can be directly overhead. They are so named from Greek *tropikos kuklos*, 'turning circle', since it was formerly believed that the sun *turned* back at these points at the solstice: at the tropic of Cancer at the summer solstice (around June 21) and at the tropic of Capricorn at the winter solstice (around December 22).

trousers The word was originally *trouse*, a variant of *trews*, now the term for the close-fitting trousers worn by some Scottish soldiers. Its origin is in Scottish Gaelic *triubhas*. The earlier word *trouse* was extended to modern *trousers* under the influence of *drawers*.

> **FALSE**
>
> **trousers** From French *trousser*, 'to bundle up' (English *truss*), referring to the way trousers were tied or strapped in former times.

truant The word for a pupil absent from school derives directly from the identical Old French word meaning 'vagabond'. It is probably ultimately of Celtic origin: modern Welsh *truan* means 'poor', 'wretched', 'miserable'.

truce The word represents the plural of Old English *trēow*, in the same sense. Directly related words are *trow* (an old verb meaning 'believe'), *true*, and *trust*.

truck The road or rail vehicle probably got its name as a shortened form of *truckle*, originally the word for a pulley or a small wheel under a bed or the like. This word itself goes back ultimately, through Latin, to Greek *trokhileia*, the term for the sheave (wheel) of a pulley.

trump The card that ranks higher than all the others in card-playing got its name as an altered form of *triumph*. Shakespeare puns on both meanings in *Antony and Cleopatra* when he makes Antony say: 'She, Eros, has/Pack'd cards with Caesar, and false-play'd my glory/Unto an enemy's triumph.'

Tuesday The third day of the week gets its name from *Tiu*, the Anglo-Saxon god of war. The name translated Latin *dies Martis*, 'day of Mars', since Mars was the Roman god to whom Tiu corresponded.

tulip The flower gets its name, through New Latin *tulipa*, from Turkish *tülbend*, 'turban'. When open, the flower was thought to look like a *turban*. The two words are thus related.

> **FALSE**
>
> **tulip** So called because the flower's petals curve in at the top like *two lips* meeting to kiss.

tummy The popular name for the *stomach* evolved from that word itself, partly as a euphemism.

tune The word evolved as an altered form of *tone*, itself, via Latin, from Greek *tonos*, 'tension', from *teinein*, 'to stretch'. A *tune* is a 'stretched' musical sound or phrase. See also ◊tonic.

tunic Whatever form the modern garment takes, it gets its name from the Roman *tunica*. The Latin word itself is probably from a Phoenician source, although its original meaning is uncertain.

turbine Although now normally a smooth-running machine, its name ultimately derives from Latin *turbo*, genitive *turbinis*, 'whirlwind', from the verb *turbare*, 'to throw into confusion' (as in English *disturb*, *perturb*, etc). The reference is to the whirling and rushing of early water and steam turbines.

turkey The bird is a native of North America. Its name was first given to another bird, the African guinea fowl, apparently because it was brought from New Guinea to Europe through territory belonging to *Turkey*. The name was then mistakenly given to the American bird because that bird's genus name (*Meleagris*) was the name by which the guinea fowl was known to the Greeks and Romans.

turquoise The gemstone has a name of French origin that means *Turkish*. This is because the 'Turkish stone', as it was called, was either first known in *Turkestan* or was brought to Europe through territory belonging to *Turkey*. For a similar history, compare ◊turkey itself.

turtle The shelled reptile has a name deriving from French *tortue*, 'tortoise'. Its present spelling was influenced by that of the other *turtle* that is now known as the *turtledove*.

tuxedo The common American word for a dinner jacket derives from *Tuxedo* Park, New York, where the jacket became fashionable among members of a country club.

tweed The thick woollen cloth was originally known as *tweel*, a Scottish form of *twill*. The word acquired its present spelling by association with the name of the Scottish river *Tweed* (or because the original word was misread as this name).

tweezers The small pincers take their name from the now obsolete word *tweeze*, used for a case of instruments. This itself evolved from the plural of French *étui*, 'case'. The present form of the word arose by association with the names of similar instruments, such as *scissors*, *pincers*, *nippers*, *pliers*, and the like.

twiddle The word probably evolved as a blend of *twirl* and *fiddle*. If you *twiddle* a knob, for example, you both *twirl* it (turn it rapidly) and *fiddle* with it (turn it to and fro or at random).

twilight The *twi-* of the alternative word for dusk represents *two*. This is because the time is a 'half-light', midway between day and night, at a time when the 24-hour day is divided into *two*.

twine The word for thread made by twisting strands together is based on the same word as *two*, since in its most basic form it consists of just *two* such strands.

tycoon The word for a big businessman or 'boss' was originally a foreigners' name for a Japanese ◊shogun. The word itself represents Japanese *taikun*, literally 'great ruler', from Chinese *dà*, 'great', and *jūn*, 'monarch', 'ruler'. Compare ◊typhoon.

typhoon The tropical storm has a name that literally means 'great wind', from Chinese *dà*, 'great', and *fēng*, 'wind'.

typhus The name of the infectious disease derives, through Latin, from Greek *tuphos*, 'stupor', literally 'smoke', 'vapour'.

tyre The wheel covering is probably so called since it serves to *tire* the wheel, that is, *attire* or 'dress' it. The spelling *tire* was common in Britain until the 19th century, and is the regular American form of the word.

ubiquitous In its sense of 'being everywhere' the word has its ultimate origin in Latin *ubique*, 'everywhere'.

ugly The ultimate origin of the word is in Old Norse *ugga*, 'fear'. Its original meaning in English was actually 'fearful', 'horrible'.

ukulele The Hawaiian guitar has a Hawaiian name meaning literally 'jumping flea', from *'uku*, 'flea', and *lele*, 'jumping'. The reference is presumably to the nimble action of the player's fingers.

ultramarine The blue pigment derives its name from Medieval Latin *ultramarinus*, literally 'beyond the sea', from Latin *ultra*, 'beyond', and *mare*, 'sea'. It is so called since it was originally made from lapis lazuli, which was imported from Asia, 'beyond the sea'.

umber The kind of natural brown earth used as a pigment gets its name from French *terre d'ombre* or Italian *terra di ombra*, both meaning 'shadow earth', referring to its colour.

umbrage If you take *umbrage* you are offended because someone has effectively 'put you in the shade'. Hence the origin of the word in Old French *umbrage*, 'shade', ultimately from Latin *umbra* with the same meaning. The original meaning of the English word was 'shade' in the literal sense, as of trees.

umbrella The word came into English from Italian *ombrella*, a diminutive of *ombra*, 'shade'.

umpire An *umpire* is an official who rules on the playing of a game. As such, he is impartial, favouring neither side. Hence the origin of the word in Old French *nomper*, literally 'not a peer', from *non*, 'not', and *per*, 'peer' (in the sense of 'equal'). In Middle English *a noumpere*, from the French, was misdivided as *an oumpere*. This gave the present form of the word. (Compare ◊adder and ◊apron.)

unanimous A *unanimous* descision is one agreed by everybody. Hence the origin of the word in Latin *unanimus*, literally 'of one mind', from *unus*, 'one', and *animus*, 'mind'.

uncouth The word now applies to someone who lacks good manners or refinement. It originally meant 'unknown', 'unfamiliar', which explains its origin in Old English *uncūth* in this sense, from *un-*, 'not', and *cūth*, 'known', 'familiar'. The latter gave former, and modern facetious, English *couth*, related to *know* and *can*.

understand As it implies, the word literally means *stand under*. *Under* here probably has the sense of 'close to', as in 'There was an old woman lived *under* a hill'. If you are close to something, you can appreciate what it actually is, and so *understand* it. The word is Old English (and Germanic) in origin.

undertaker The word was originally used for anyone who *undertook* a task. It then came to apply solely to a person who *undertook* funerals. To *undertake* something is to *take* it *under* one's competence or supervision.

underwriter The term is used for a person who guarantees insurance policies. Such a person literally *writes* his or her name *under* an agreement. That is, he or she *subscribes* to it. Hence the origin of *underwrite* as an exact English translation of Latin *subscribere*, 'to ◊subscribe'.

unicorn The imaginary animal is a white horse with *one horn*. Hence its name, from Latin *unicornis*, 'one-horned', representing *unus*, 'one', and *cornu*, 'horn'. The Latin name itself translated Greek *monokerōs*, from *monos*, 'single', and *keras*, 'horn'.

uniform The word literally means 'one form', from Latin *uniformis*, representing *unus*, 'one', and *forma*, 'form'. As clothing, the reference is thus to *uniform* dress, or garments that all have the same cut or *form*.

unique The word came into English from French, in turn from Latin *unicus*, 'unparalleled', based on *unus*, 'one'.

universe The word for the whole of all created things represents Latin *universum*, the noun of the adjective *universus*, literally 'all turned into one', from *unus*, 'one', and *vertere*, 'to turn'. See also ◊university.

university The institution of higher education is so called since it was originally regarded as representing a ◊universe or collective whole, comprising both students and teachers. The Medieval Latin term for it was *universitas magistrorum et scholarium*, 'society of masters and students'.

unless The *un*- is not the common negative prefix (as in *unreal*) but an altered spelling (influenced by the prefix) of *on*. The literal sense is thus 'on less', with the English phrase modelled on the French, Spanish, or Italian equivalent, respectively *à moins que*, *a menos que*, and *a meno che*, all deriving from conjectured Vulgar Latin *ad minus quam*, literally 'at less than'. The reference is to a condition that is *less* important than another. If I go out *unless* it rains, the rain is more important, since it stops me going out.

upholsterer The word for a person who makes and repairs padded furniture derives from the earlier word *upholster*, used for a dealer or repairer of secondhand articles. His job was to *uphold* or maintain them. The modern word has perhaps been influenced by *holster*, since the leather covering of some furniture resembles the leather casing of a holster.

uproar The original sense of the word was 'uprising', with the *-roar* representing a Germanic word related to modern German *rühren*, 'to stir'. It later became associated with *roar*, and the meaning changed accordingly.

upside down The phrase looks as if it means 'upper side down', ie, top to bottom. It is actually an altered form of *upsodown*, meaning 'up as if down'. Something *upside down* may seem to be right side up but it is actually 'right side down'.

urbane The word now means 'smoothly sophisticated' but originally had the literal sense 'urban'. An *urbane* person was thus regarded as civilized, like someone *urban*, who lived in a town.

urchin The word for a mischievous child, especially a young or poorly dressed one, derives from Old French *heriçon* (modern *hérisson*, 'hedgehog'), and this was the original meaning of the word. (Compare modern *sea urchin*, which resembles a hedgehog.) Hedgehogs were regarded as mischievous animals and thieves, and the sense thus passed to a child of similar nature.

usher The word came into English from Old French (and modern) *huissier*, 'doorkeeper', ultimately from Latin *ostium*, 'door'. Ushers now have many functions but doorkeeping is still one of them.

usurp The verb referring to the act of taking or seizing something without authority derives, through French, from Latin *usurpare*, 'to take into use', itself probably a blend of *usus*, 'use', and *rapere*, 'to seize' (English ◊rape).

utmost The word evolved as an alternate form of *outermost*. A directly related word is *uttermost*, since *utter*, in the sense 'complete', 'total', is itself another form of *outer*.

utopia The term for an ideal state of things derives from New Latin *Utopia*, a word coined by Sir Thomas More in 1516 as the title of his book about an imaginary island that represented the ideal society. The word itself means either 'no place', from Greek *ou*, 'not', and *topos*, 'place', or possibly 'good place', from Greek *eus*, 'good', and *topos*, ie, as if *Eutopia*.

utter In its sense of 'speak', the word derives from Middle Dutch *ūteren* (modern *uiteren*), 'to drive away', 'to announce', related to modern German *äußern*, 'to say'. The word was later influenced by English *out*.

vaccine The original *vaccine* was a preparation of the virus of cowpox, inoculated in humans to produce immunity to smallpox. Hence the origin of the word in New Latin *variolae vaccinus*, 'cowpox', the title of a medical treatise of 1798 by Edward Jenner, its inventor. The ultimate source is in Latin *vacca*, 'cow'.

vagabond The word for a wandering beggar or thief derives from Latin *vagabundus*, 'wandering', itself from *vagari*, 'to wander'. The ultimate Latin source is thus *vagus*, 'wandering', as it is for modern English *vagary* (a 'wandering' notion), *vagrant*, and *vague*.

valance The word for a length of drapery attached to a bed or canopy probably derives from Old French *avaler*, 'to lower', 'to let fall', itself representing Latin *ad vallem*, literally 'to the valley'.

vamoose The colloquial word meaning 'make off', 'decamp', derives from Spanish *vamos*, 'let us go'.

vamp In its sense of 'seductive woman', the word is a shortening of ◊vampire. In its sense of 'improvise a musical accompaniment', it evolved from Old French *avantpié*, the term for the front part of a shoe, from *avant*, 'before', and *pié*, 'foot'. This part of a shoe was often patched up. Hence the use of the word to denote a 'patched up' or improvised accompaniment.

vampire The corpse that rises from its grave at night to drink the blood of the living gets its name from a Hungarian word that is perhaps ultimately related to Turkish *uber*, 'witch'.

van The road or rail vehicle got its name as a shortened form of ◊caravan.

vandal The word for a person who damages or destroys property derives from the name of the *Vandals*, the Germanic people that invaded Western Europe in the 4th and 5th centuries AD.

vanguard The term for the leading position in a particular field derives from Old French (and modern) *avant-garde*, literally 'front guard', from *avant*, 'before', and *garde*, 'guard'. The word originally applied to the leading division of an army.

vanilla The plant is a type of climbing orchid whose long fleshy pods contain seeds used for flavouring (as for ice cream). Hence its name, from a New Latin adoption of Spanish *vainilla*, 'pod', itself from *vaina*, 'sheath', and ultimately from Latin *vagina* in the same sense (the source of the English word).

vaudeville The term for a type of variety entertainment derives from French *vaudevire*, as a particular kind of satirical folk song. This itself is said to come from French *vau de Vire*, 'valley of Vire', from the name of the district in Normandy where such songs became popular. However, there could also be an origin in obsolete French *vauder*, a form of *voûter*, and *virer*, both meaning 'to turn'. Either way, the second half of the word was influenced by French *ville*, 'town'.

> **FALSE**
>
> **vaudeville** From French *voix de ville*, 'voices of the town', originally the title of a collection of songs.

vault In both its senses, 'arched roof' and 'to leap', the word goes back, through French, to a conjectured Vulgar Latin word *volvitare*, 'to turn', itself probably from Latin *volvere*, 'to roll'.

veal Calf meat is so called from Old French *veel* (modern French *veau*), ultimately from Latin *vitulus*, 'calf'.

vegetable The ultimate origin of the word is in Latin *vegetare*, 'to enliven', from *vegere*, 'to excite'. *Vegetables* are plants, whose chief characteristic is their power to *grow*.

vehicle The ultimate source of the word is in Latin *vehere*, 'to carry'. A *vehicle* is a means of ◊transport.

venal The word means 'easily bribed', 'open to bribery'. Hence its source in Latin *venalis*, the adjective of *venum*, 'sale', from *vendere*, 'to sell' (English *vend*).

vendetta The word for a private quarrel originally applied to a feud between Corsican or Sicilian families, in which the members of a murdered person's family sought *vengeance* by killing a member of the murderer's family. Hence the origin of the Italian word in Latin *vindicta*, 'vengeance', from *vindicare*, 'to avenge' (English *vindicate*).

venereal The term for a sexually transmitted disease derives from Latin *venereus*, the adjective of *venus*, 'sexual love', itself from the name of *Venus*, the Roman goddess of love. See also ◊venom.

venison Deer meat gets its name, via Old French *venaison*, from Latin *venatio*, 'hunting', from the verb *venari*, 'to hunt'. For the Normans, hunting was the principal source of meat, and deer provided it.

venom Although long meaning 'poison', the earlier sense of the word was 'love potion', and the word goes back to Latin *venenum* that had both meanings. The sense development was: 'drug', 'magical drug', 'love potion', 'harmful drug', 'poison'. The ultimate source is thus in Latin *venus*, 'sexual love', from *Venus*, the Roman goddess of love. Compare ◊venereal◊.

ventriloquism The art of producing sounds or words as if they came from somewhere else derives from New Latin *ventriloquium*, literally 'belly speaking', from *venter*, 'belly', and *loqui*, 'to speak'. This translated Greek *engastrimuthos*, from *en*, 'in', *gastēr*, genitive *gasteros* or *gastros*, 'stomach' (English *gastric*), and *muthos*, 'speaking' (English *myth*).

verdict The word for a jury's decision derives from Medieval Latin *verdictum*, itself from Latin *vere dictum*, 'truly spoken', from the adverb of *verus*, 'true', and *dicere*, 'to say'.

verdigris The term for the greenish rust that forms on copper is of Old French origin and represents *vert de Grice*, literally 'green of Greece'. The reason for this name is unknown. The German word for it is *Grünspan*, 'Spanish green'.

vermilion The bright red colour derives its name from Old French *vermeillon*, itself from Late Latin *vermiculus*, 'little grub', from a diminutive of *vermis*, 'worm'. The reference is to the insect (of the genus *Kermes*) whose body when crushed yielded a dye this colour.

vermouth The aromatic wine derives its name, through French, from German *Wermut*, ◊wormwood, referring to the herb (also known as absinthe) with which it is traditionally flavoured.

very The word ultimately goes back, through French, to Latin *verus*, 'true'. If something is *very* good, it is *truly* good.

vest The garment, originally a loose outer one, not a brief undergarment as now, derives its name, through French, from Latin *vestis*, 'clothing'. (The *vestry* in a church is the room in which the clergy robe and where their *vestments* are kept.)

vestige In its sense of 'trace', the word has retained some of its original literal meaning, from Latin *vestigium*, 'sole of the foot', 'footprint'.

vet The colloquial word for the 'animal doctor' is short for *veterinarian* or *veterinary surgeon*. The word goes back to Latin *veterinae*, 'draught animals', a word itself related to *vetus*, 'mature', referring to their ability to bear a burden and pull loads. Compare ◊veteran.

veteran The word for an 'old soldier' implies that he or she is an experienced and mature one. The source of the word is in Latin *vetus*, 'old', 'mature'.

veto The formal term for a ban or prohibition represents the identical Latin word meaning 'I forbid', from *vetare*, 'to forbid'. The word was used in Roman times by the tribunes of the people when opposing measures of the senate.

via In its sense of 'through', denoting a route, the word represents the ablative case of Latin *via*, 'way', 'road'. It thus literally means 'by way of'.

viable Although now meaning little more than 'possible', 'capable of happening', the literal sense of the word is 'capable of living'. It derives, via French, from Latin *vita*, 'life'.

vicar The clergyman who is the priest of a parish derives his title, through French, from Latin *vicarius*, 'substitute', 'deputy' (English *vicarious*). A *vicar* was originally the *deputy* of the rector, who had the actual care of the parish. He was thus the equivalent of the modern curate. Hence French *vicaire* for his equivalent, and (misleadingly) *curé* for the equivalent of the rector, as the priest who has the *cure* (care) of the parish.

vicious The word is directly related to *vice*, and so derives from the same ultimate source, which is Latin *vitium*, 'defect'. Hence also *vitiated*, for something faulty or corrupt.

video The word is short for the element *video-* in a number of words and phrases, such as *video cassette*, *video cassette recorder*, *video recorder*, *video tape*, *video tape recorder*, and the like. It ultimately represents Latin *videre*, 'to see', and was modelled on *audio*, from Latin *audire*, 'to hear'.

villain The word for a wicked person derives from Old French *villein*, 'serf', referring to a person who worked for a lord on his *ville*, 'country estate', 'farm' (in modern French, 'town'), from Latin *villa*, 'country house'. (Modern historians use the French word *villein* for a serf of this type.)

vinegar *Vinegar* is a *sour*-tasting liquid made from *wine*. Hence its name, from Old French (and modern) *vinaigre*, literally 'sour wine', from *vin*, 'wine', and *aigre*, 'sour'.

violin The stringed instrument derives its name from Italian *violino*, a diminutive of *viola*, 'viola'. The ultimate origin of the Italian name is uncertain. It is probably related to English *fiddle*.

viper The snake also known as the ◊adder derives its name from Latin *vipera*. This is said to represent a blend of *vivus*, 'living', and *parere*, 'to bear', from a tradition that the snake is *viviparous*, ie, bears living offspring (as distinct from eggs).

virago The word for a violent and ill-tempered woman originally applied to a strong, brave, and warlike one. It represents the Latin word for a manlike maiden, from *vir*, 'man'. It came into currency from its use as the name given by Adam to Eve in the Vulgate (Latin version of the Bible): '*Haec vocabitur virago, quoniam de viro sumpta est*', 'She shall be called Woman, because she was taken out of Man' (Genesis 2:23).

virtue The word ultimately derives, via French, from Latin *virtus*, 'manliness', itself based on *vir*, 'man'.

virus The word came into English straight from Latin, in which it means 'slime', 'poisonous liquid', and its original meaning in English was actually 'venom'.

viscount The nobleman gets his title from Old French *visconte*, from Medieval Latin *vicecomes*, so that it effectively means 'vice-count'. In medieval Europe a *viscount* was the deputy of a *count*. The title has survived in the British peerage even though *count* itself has not.

visit People often make a *visit* to *see* someone. Hence the source of the word in Latin *visitare*, 'to go and see', itself ultimately from *videre*, 'to see'.

vitamin The essential food element was so named in 1913 (originally as *vitamine*) by the American biochemist Casimir Funk, basing the word on Latin *vita*, 'life', and English *amine*, from his belief that vitamins contained *amino* acid. (When he was found to be wrong, the spelling was altered as now, to avoid this association.)

vitriol Although now often used for bitter speech or writing, the word properly applies to a sulphate (for example ferrous sulphate or copper sulphate) or serves as an alternative name for sulphuric acid. Its derivation is in Medieval Latin *vitreolum*, ultimately from Latin *vitrum*, 'glass'. The reference is to the glassy appearance of the sulphates.

vivid The derivation of the word is in Latin *vividus*, 'animated', from *vivere*, 'to live'. The word is now often used of bright colour or a keen imagination, but it can still be used in the Latin sense, as in a *vivid* personality.

viz The word, used before specifying something, is an abbreviated form of Latin *videlicet*, 'namely', 'that is to say', from the base of *videre*, 'to see', and *licet*, 'it is permitted'. The z of the abbreviation evolved from the Medieval Latin character (rather like a figure *3*) that was regularly used to represent a final *-et*.

vodka In origin the word is a Russian diminutive of *voda*, 'water'. The word may have evolved under the influence of Latin *aqua vitae*, 'water of life', used to mean 'alcohol'. For a similar development, see ◊whisky.

volcano The word derives, through Italian, from Latin *Volcanus*, 'Vulcan', the Roman god of fire and metalworking. (The rumbling of a volcano is Vulcan forging metal.) His own name is perhaps of Etruscan origin.

volley Whether used in the military or sporting sense, the word derives from French *volée*, 'flight', in turn ultimately from Latin *volare*, 'to fly'.

volt The electrical unit takes its name from the Italian physicist Count Alessandro *Volta* (1745–1827), who made important contributions to the theory of current electricity.

volume Whether meaning 'mass' or 'book', the word goes back, through French, to Latin *volumen*, 'roll of writing', 'book', in turn from *volvere*, 'to roll' (English *revolve*).

voluntary The word derives, through French, from Latin *voluntarius*, 'willing', ultimately from *velle*, 'to wish'.

voucher The coupon or card that serves as a substitute for cash is so called since it *vouches* for or guarantees the stated amount. The verb *vouch* originally had the legal sense of 'cite as witness'. It derives from Old French *vocher*, 'to summon', itself ultimately from Latin *vocare*, 'to call'.

voyage The word came into English from Old French *veiage* (modern French *voyage*), and ultimately derives from Latin *viaticum*, 'provision for a journey', from *viaticus*, an adjectival form of *via*, 'way', 'road'.

vulgar The derivation of the word is in Latin *vulgaris*, the adjectival derivative of *vulgus*, 'the common people'. The word thus originally meant simply 'ordinary', 'commonplace', and only later came to be used of bad taste.

vulture The large bird of prey has a name that may ultimately relate to Latin *vellere*, 'to tear', referring to its manner of eating.

wade The word is now used of walking through water. It originally meant simply 'go'. Hence its origin in Old English *wadan*, related to Latin *vadum*, 'ford', and *vadere*, 'to go'.

waft If something is *wafted* it is carried gently as if by air or water. The verb was originally used of carrying something by ship. Hence its origin in the obsolete word *wafter*, a term for a convoy ship, itself from Middle Dutch *wachter*, 'guard'. The word is thus ultimately related to English *wait*.

waif The word for a homeless or abandoned child, or someone who looks like one, was originally used for a piece of property found ownerless or abandoned. It is of Anglo-Norman origin and is ultimately related to Old Norse *veif*, 'flapping thing'. Compare ◊waive.

wainscot The word for the wooden panelling in a room derives from Middle Low German *wagenschot*, perhaps representing *wagen*, 'wagon', and *schot*, 'planking' (compare modern German *Scheit*, 'piece of wood').

waiter A *waiter* is someone who *waits*, in the sense that he remains on hand to serve at table, *awaiting* orders from diners.

waive If you *waive* a rule, you do not enforce it. You effectively abandon it, and make a ◊waif of it. The two words are related, and are ultimately of Scandinavian origin.

wake In the sense 'come out of sleep' or 'stay awake' the word is of Germanic origin and ultimately goes back to an Indo-European root element meaning 'be alive'. Related English words are thus *watch*, *vigil*, *vigour*, and even ◊vegetable.

wall The word is of Germanic origin and is ultimately related to Latin *vallum*, 'palisade', itself from *vallus*, 'stake'.

walnut The present name for the tree and its nut has evolved from Old English *walh-hnutu*. This literally means 'foreign nut', and was probably a translation of Vulgar Latin *nux gallica*, 'Gaulish nut'.

> **FALSE**
>
> **walnut** From *wall nut*, referring to the tree's ideal sheltered location.

walrus The aquatic animal, formerly known as a sea horse, has a name that is probably ultimately of Scandinavian origin, with a literal meaning 'whale horse', from words that are themselves directly related to English *whale* and *horse*. The word probably came into English via Dutch.

waltz The ballroom dance derives its name from *Walzer*, its German equivalent. This in turn evolved from Middle High German *walzen*, 'to roll', a word that is related to modern English *welter*.

wampum The colloquial American word meaning 'money', 'wealth', originally applied specifically to money used by North American Indians. This was made of cylindrical shells strung together, especially white shells rather than the more valuable black or purple ones. The word is short for *wampumpeag*, from Narraganset *wampompeag*, representing *wampan*, 'light', 'white', *api*, 'string', and the plural suffix *-ag*.

wander The word is of Germanic origin and is related to other 'going' verbs, such as *wend*, *wind*, and *went* (as the past of 'go').

wangle The verb meaning 'get something by devious means' probably arose as a blend of *waggle* and the dialect word *wankle*, meaning 'wavering', 'unsteady', itself from Old English *wancol*, 'weak', which also gave modern *wonky*. See also ◊wench.

warden A *warden* is basically a form of *guardian*, looking after someone or something. The two words are related, and the origin is in Old French *warder*, 'to guard'.

wardrobe The 'clothes cupboard' derives its name from Old North French *warderobe* (modern French *garde-robe*), representing *warder*, 'to guard, 'to keep', and *robe*, 'robe', 'garment'. The word was originally used not for a cupboard but for a room in which clothes were kept.

warlock The term for sorcerer or magician, especially one who deals in black magic, derives from Old English *wǣrloga*, 'deceiver', literally 'oath-lier', from *wǣ*, 'oath' (related to modern English ◊very), and *lēogan*, 'to lie' (in the sense 'tell an untruth').

warp The word originally meant 'throw', so that the present sense relates to something that has been 'thrown' out of the true, such as *warped* wood or a time *warp*. The source is Germanic. Compare modern German *werfen*, 'to throw'.

warrant A *warrant* gives authority for something or *guarantees* it. The two words are related, and are ultimately, via French, of Germanic origin. Compare modern German *gewähren*, 'to grant'.

wary As a synonym for 'cautious', the word evolved fairly late (in the 16th century) as a more obviously adjectival form of the existing adjective *ware*, meaning 'careful in avoiding'. This word is itself now rarely found on its own, but it survives in modern *beware*.

wash The word is of Germanic origin and goes back to a root element also found in *water*. The correspondence can be seen more closely in German *waschen*, 'wash', and *Wasser*, 'water'.

wasp The stinging insect has a name of Germanic origin that goes back to an Indo-European root element thought to mean 'weave', referring to the 'woven' construction of a wasps' nest. The name is related in many European languages, including Latin and Italian *vespa*, Russian *osa*, French *guêpe*, German *Wespe* and Cornish *guhien*. English ◊weave is also itself related.

water The word is Germanic in origin, and derives ultimately from an Indo-European root element that gave the equivalent in many European languages, including Greek ***hudōr*** (the *hydro-* of many English words), German ***Wasser*** and Russian ***voda*** (see ◊vodka). Related English words are *wet*, ◊otter and ◊whisky.

wayward In its sense of 'capricious' the word is a shortened form of the former word ***awayward***, 'turned away', 'going away'. The present sense was probably influenced by *way*, since a *wayward* child (for example) is one who tries to go his or her own *way*.

weave The word is of Germanic origin and is directly related to *web*, *weft*, and *woof* (the last two words both used for the yarn woven crosswise in a fabric). See also ◊wasp and ◊weevil.

Wednesday The fourth day of the week derives its name from that of *Woden*, the chief Anglo-Saxon god, corresponding to the Norse god *Odin*. Old English ***Wōdnes dæg***, 'Woden's day' translated Latin ***Mercurii dies***, 'Mercury's day' (hence ***mercredi*** as the French name of the day), since *Woden* was held to have many of the attributes of *Mercury*, the Roman god of trade.

wee In its common Scottish sense of 'small', the word is of Old English origin from a source that also gave modern *weigh*. The idea seems to have been that if something is *wee* it has little *weight*. Related *weeny* is probably a blend of *wee* and *tiny*.

weevil The beetle has a name of Germanic origin that probably derives ultimately from a root element, meaning 'move quickly', which also gave ◊weave. Compare *beetle* itself in the colloquial sense 'scurry', 'hurry'.

weird The word was originally a noun meaning 'fate', 'destiny'. (This survives in Scottish *dree one's weird*, 'endure one's fate'.) It then came to be an adjective meaning 'controlling destiny'. Hence *weird sisters* as a name for the Fates of classical mythology. Shakespeare helped introduce the modern sense of 'uncanny' by using this phrase for the witches in *Macbeth*. The word is of Germanic origin and is related to modern *worth*.

welcome The present word evolved from Old English ***wilcuma***, 'welcome guest', itself from ***wilcume***, the greeting spoken to such a guest, and meaning literally 'pleasure comer', from words related to modern *will* and *come*. The first part of this subsequently became associated with *well*, not only from the similarity of the two words but because the expression was seen as a translation of French ***bienvenu***, literally 'well come'.

wench The former name for a girl or woman derives from Old English ***wencel***, 'child', itself from ***wancol***, 'weak', the source of modern *wonky*. See also ◊wangle.

werewolf The word for the person fabled for turning into a wolf derives from Old English *werewulf*, literally 'man-wolf', from *wer*, 'man' (related to Latin *vir* in this sense), and *wulf*, 'wolf'.

wheat The grain *wheat* is so called since it is used for making flour, which is *white*. Both words are Germanic in origin and derive from a common source.

wheatear The small songbird derives its name from words that have their modern equivalent in *white arse*, referring to its white rump. *White* gradually became *wheat* and *arse* became *ears* to produce a new name *wheatears*. This was taken to be plural and so was finally adjusted to its present supposedly 'singular' form.

whisky The Scottish spirit has a name of Scottish Gaelic origin, representing *uisge beatha*, literally 'water of life'. Compare in exactly the same sense Latin *aqua vitae* and French *eau de vie*, both meaning 'brandy' (or some other spirit). The spelling was doubtless influenced by *whisk*, suggesting a drink that invigorates or has a 'nip'.

whist The card game may have got its name as an alteration of *whisk*, from the idea of *whisking* up the tricks. However, Charles Cotton's *The Compleat Gamester* (1674) suggests that the game is 'called Whist from the silence that is to be observed in the play'. If so, the name is associated with the *whist* that is (or was) a call for silence.

whore The word for a prostitute or promiscuous woman is of Germanic origin and ultimately derives from an Indo-European base meaning 'dear' found also in Latin *carus*, 'dear', and Irish *cara*, 'friend'.

wicked The word derives from the dialect word *wick*, itself from Old English *wicca*, 'sorcerer', the feminine of which gave modern ◊witch.

widow The word is of Germanic origin and is ultimately related to Latin *vidua*, the feminine of *viduus*, 'bereft'.

wig The word is short for *periwig*, as an altered form of French *perruque*, itself from Italian *perrucca*. The ultimate origin of the word is uncertain. A blend of Italian *pelo*, 'hair', and *zucca*, 'head' (literally 'pumpkin'), has been suggested.

wigwam The traditional North American Indian dwelling derives its name from Massachuset *wīkwām*, literally 'their house'.

wilderness The word for the wild and deserted region derives from Old English *wildēornes*, from *wildēor*, 'wild beast' (representing *wild*, 'wild', and *dēor*, 'beast', modern *deer*), and the suffix *-nes*, *-ness*.

will-o'-the-wisp The word for a pale flame or 'shining' sometimes seen over marshy ground at night was originally known as *Will with the wisp*, from the personal name *Will* (short for *William*) and *wisp* as formerly used of a twist of hay or straw serving as a ◊torch. Compare its alternative name, *jack-o'-lantern*.

willy-nilly The expression has evolved from the Old English phrase *wile hē, nyle hē*, literally 'will he, will he not', with *nyle* comprising *ne*, 'not', and *willan*, 'to will', 'to wish'.

wind In the sense 'air in motion', the word is of Germanic origin and ultimately derives from an Indo-European root element meaning 'blow'. Related words are Latin *ventus* and French *vent*, 'wind', and, from Sanskrit, English ◊*nirvana*.

windlass The word for the winding machine derives from Old Norse *windáss*, literally 'winding pole', from *vinda*, 'to wind', and *ass*, 'pole'.

window The origin of the everyday word is in Old Norse *vindauga*, literally 'wind eye', from *vindr*, 'wind', and *auga*, 'eye'. The primary function of a window was thus to provide ventilation and offer a view of the external world. The Norse word ousted the Old English one, which was *ēagthyrel*, literally 'eye-hole', from *ēag*, 'eye', and *thyrel*, 'hole' (modern *thrill*). The word *fenester* (modern French *fenêtre*) was also in English use for a while, but did not last beyond the 16th century.

wine The word is immediately Germanic in origin but has its relations in many European languages, such as Latin *vinum*, Greek *oinos*, Russian *vino*, Welsh *gwin* and Armenian *gini*. It is probably ultimately Mediterranean, as are the names of various plants and fruits, such as *fig*, *mulberry*, and *rose*.

winsome The base of the word is Old English *wynn*, 'joy' (modern German *Wonne*), to which has been added *-some*, as in *handsome*. The original sense of the word in English was simply 'pleasant', and the present meaning of 'attractive in looks or manner' did not emerge until the 17th century.

wiseacre The word for a person who wishes to appear *wise* derives from Middle Dutch *wijsseggher*, 'soothsayer' (literally 'wise-sayer'. It is not clear why the second part of this was altered to *-acre*. (The surname of the former German president Richard von *Weizsäcker* originated from this.)

witch The word derives from Old English *wicce*, the feminine form of *wicca*, 'wizard', 'sorcerer', related to modern ◊*wicked*. The ultimate source of the word is unknown. ◊*Wizard* is not related (except in meaning).

witness The word was originally used of an abstract noun meaning 'knowledge', 'wisdom'. It thus derives from Old English *witnes*, in which the first part represents *witan*, 'to know' (the source of modern *wit*), and the second corresponds to modern *-ness*, as in *goodness*. The present sense, referring to a person who bears *witness*, arose only in the 16th century.

wizard The word for the magician or sorcerer arose as an alteration of *wissard*. This represents Middle English *wīs*, 'wise', and the *-ard* suffix, often denoting disapproval, as in *drunkard*, *laggard* or *sluggard*. A *wizard* is (or was) a *wise* man, therefore.

woebegone The word now means 'sad-looking', but originally meant 'afflicted with *woe*'. The form of the word evolved from a medieval phrase such as *me is wo begon*, 'woe has beset me'. This then became *I am wo begon* and finally *I am woebegone*.

wog The derogatory word for a foreigner probably arose as a short form of ◊golliwog.

woman The present form of the word has evolved from Old English *wīfmann*, representing *wīf*, 'woman' (modern *wife*), and *mann*, 'person' (modern *man*). It is not clear why a word that already clearly meant 'woman' added the generic word meaning 'person'.

woo As applied to the seeking of a person's favours or attentions, the word derives from Old English *wōgian*. This is itself of obscure origin, and cannot be reliably linked with any Germanic word or source.

world The present word has evolved from Old English *weorold* or *worold*, representing a combination of *wer*, 'man' (Latin *vir*), and *ald*, 'age' (modern *old*). The literal sense is therefore 'age of man', meaning something that has existed (or will exist) as long as the human race has (or will).

wormwood The plant, also known as absinthe, that yields a bitter extract used as an ingredient of ◊vermouth, derives its name from Old English *wormōd*. The origin of this is not known, but it gained its present spelling by association with *worm* and *wood*, the former because it was used as a remedy for *worms* in the body.

worship The word expressing devotion or admiration for someone evolved from Old English *weorthscipe*, from *weorth*, 'worth', and *-scipe* as the *-ship* in *hardship*, in other words, as if '*worthship*', or the state of being valuable.

wreath The word represents Old English *writha*, directly related to the verb *writhan*, which gave modern *writhe*. Many words beginning *wr-* have the sense of something twisted or distorted. Apart from these two, others are *wrangle*, *wrench*, *wrest*, *wrestle*, *wriggle*, *wring*, *wrinkle*, *wrist*, *wrong*, *wroth*, *wrought*, and *wry*.

wretch The earliest meaning of the word was 'exile', Old English *wrecca*. It is of Germanic origin, and is related to modern (though now obsolete) German *Recke*, 'warrior'. It may also probably relate to English *wreak*, since the original sense of this verb was 'drive away', 'expel'.

write The present word has evolved from Old English *wrītan*, 'to engrave', from a Germanic base meaning 'scratch', related to modern German *reißen*, 'to rip', 'to tear'. The reference is to scratching runes into bark or engraving symbols on stone. Modern *writing* developed from this.

x-ray The English word is a part-translation of the original German *X-Strahlen*. This was the name given the rays by Wilhelm Röntgen, the German physicist who discovered them in 1895, from *X*, denoting their basically unknown nature at the time, and *Strahl*, 'ray'. Some languages now call the rays by Röntgen's own name, such as German *Röntgen*, Russian *rentgen*, and Japanese *rentogen*.

yacht The sailing boat or ship derives its name from obsolete Dutch *jaghte* (modern Dutch *jacht*), short for *jaghtschip*, literally 'hunter', 'chaser', from *jagen*, 'to hunt', and *schip*, 'ship'.

yard The word is Germanic in origin, from a base meaning 'enclosure' that also gave English ◊garden and ◊orchard and that is related to Russian *gorod*, 'town' (the *-grad* in Volgo*grad* and the former Lenin*grad*).

yarn The word is Germanic in origin, and is related to Old Norse *görn*, 'gut'. Outside Germanic it is related to the first part of Latin *haruspex*, 'diviner of entrails' (literally 'gut-looker'), Greek *khordē*, 'intestine', 'guts' (English *chord*), and Sanskrit *hirā*, 'vein'. The sense of 'story' came from the nautical phrase *spin a yarn*.

yell The word is Germanic in origin, and ultimately comes from a root element meaning 'sing', as found in the last syllable of ◊nightingale.

yeoman The rank and title, as in '*Yeomen* of the Guard', perhaps evolved as an alteration of some form of *youngman*.

yes The word evolved from Old English *gēse*, representing the phrase *iā sīe*, 'may it be'. As such, it was an affirmative reply to a question, as distinct from *yea*, from Old English *gēa*, which was simply an affirmative word, not used to answer a question.

yesterday The word is Germanic in origin, and some modern Germanic languages simply have the first part of the word in this sense (without *day*), such as German *gestern* or Dutch *gisteren*. The *yes-* represents an Indo-European root element that itself means 'yesterday' and that is seen in Latin *heri*. The *-ter-* represents a comparative ('more') meaning, as in the second syllable of *interior*. The overall meaning of *yesterday*, therefore, is effectively a double one: 'yesterday (as) another day'.

yoga The Hindu system of philosophy derives its name from the identical Sanskrit word meaning 'union' (English *yoke*). *Yoga* involves the *union* of the self with the Supreme Being.

yokel The word for a 'country bumpkin' perhaps derives from the identical dialect name of the green woodpecker. If so, it would have been used as a derisory nickname for a person who had 'more sound than sense' (like the noisy tapping of the woodpecker).

zany The word for a clown or buffoon derives from Italian *zanni*, itself from *Zanni*, a dialect pet form of the personal name *Giovanni*, 'John'. This was a traditional name in the theatre for a comic actor who played a servant and imitated his master.

zenith The word for the highest point or peak of something derives ultimately, through French and Latin, from Arabic *samt*, 'way', 'path', as in the phrase *samt ar-ras*, 'way over the head', representing *samt*, 'way', *al*, 'the', and *rās*, 'head'.

zigzag The word is unusual in that it is not only meaningful but both sounds and looks like its sense. It is a reduplication of a word that gave modern German *Zacke*, 'point', 'jagged projection'. When spoken it has the sound of a sharply alternating course, and when written its sense is expressed visually by its repeated letter *z*.

zodiac The imaginary belt in the celestial sphere, divided into 12 signs (each named after the constellation that once lay in it), derives its name, via French and Latin, from Greek *zōidiakos kuklos*, 'circle of animal signs', from *zōidion*, 'animal sign' (ie, a carved figure of an animal), and *kuklos*, 'circle'.

zone The word came into English, via French or Latin, from Greek *zōnē*, 'girdle', 'belt'.

zoo The word arose as a colloquial short form of *Zoological Gardens*, a name originally applied to what is now the London *Zoo* (opened to the public in 1827). *Zoology* is the study of animals, from Greek *zōion*, 'animal', and *logos*, 'word'.

LANGUAGE GUIDE

The following is a guide to the language names used in the entries. It does not include obvious names, such as French and German, but it does explain the more specialized terms, such as Old French and Germanic.

Anglo-French The dialect of French introduced into England by the Normans after the conquest of 1066.

Anglo-Latin The form of ◊Medieval Latin used in England.

Anglo-Norman The same as ◊Anglo-French.

Aramaic An ancient ◊Semitic language of the Middle East, still spoken in parts of Syria and Lebanon.

Celtic The branch of ◊Indo-European that includes Irish, ◊Gaelic, Welsh, Breton, and Manx.

Church Latin The written form of ◊Vulgar Latin that was adopted by the Christian church from the 4th century AD.

Etruscan The language of the ancient people who inhabited Etruria (modern Tuscany), Italy, from about 600 BC to 100 BC.

Frankish The West ◊Germanic language spoken by the Franks who lived along the Rhine.

Gaelic The ◊Celtic language of Scotland, also known as *Scottish Gaelic* to be distinguished from ◊Irish.

Gaulish The ◊Celtic language of the people of Gaul, an ancient region corresponding to modern northern Italy, France, Belgium, part of Germany, and the southern Netherlands.

Germanic The branch of ◊Indo-European that split into ◊Gothic (East Germanic), ◊Scandinavian (North Germanic), and English, Frisian, Dutch, and German (West Germanic).

Gothic The language of the Goths, the ancient people who settled mainly in eastern and southern Europe and who invaded the Roman Empire from about AD 200 to AD 400.

Hebrew The ancient ◊Semitic language of the Jews, a modern form of which is spoken in Israel.

High German The West ◊Germanic dialect of central and southern Germany (where the terrain is *higher* than the north). Modern German developed from this. Compare ◊Low German and see also ◊Old High German.

Hindi The language of northern India that is the official language of India as a whole. It is closely related to ◊Urdu.

Indo-European The conjectured (assumed) prehistoric language family from which many of the modern languages of India, western Asia, and Europe are derived. Branches include ◊Iranian, ◊Italic, ◊Slavic, ◊Germanic, and ◊Celtic.

Iranian The branch of ◊Indo-European that includes Persian, Avestan, Pashto, and Kurdish.

Italic A branch of ◊Indo-European that includes ◊Latin and other ancient dialects of Italy, such as Oscan and Umbrian.

Late Greek The Greek language from about AD 300 to AD 700.

Late Latin The ◊Latin language from about AD 300 to AD 700.

Latin The ◊Italic language of the ancient Romans, and the ancestor of the ◊Romance languages.

Low German The German dialect of northern Germany (where the terrain is *lower* than the south). Compare ◊High German.

Low Latin The same as ◊Vulgar Latin.

Medieval Greek The Greek language during in medieval times, from about AD 700 to about 1500.

Medieval Latin The ◊Latin language in medieval times, from about AD 700 to about 1500. It was the language of European intellectuals during this period.

Middle Dutch The Dutch language from about 1100 to 1500.

Middle English The English language from about 1100 to about 1500, when the influence of French was beginning to make itself felt.

Middle French The French language from about 1350 to 1600.

Middle High German The ◊High German language from about 1100 to about 1500.

Middle Low German The ◊Low German language from about 1100 to about 1500.

Modern English The English language from about 1500 to the present day.

Modern French The French language from about 1600 to the present day.

Modern German The German language from about 1500 to the present day.

New Latin The ◊Latin language after 1500, with many words formed from classical Greek and Latin. It was the language used by the Roman Catholic Church and is the source of many modern scientific words.

Norman French The same as ◊Anglo-French.

Old Dutch The Dutch language before about 1100.

Old English The English language before about 1100.

Old French The French language from about AD 800 to about 1400.

Old High German The ◊High German language before about 1200. Modern German developed from it.

Old Latin The ◊Latin language before about 100 BC.

Old Low German The ◊Old German language before about 1100.

Old Norse A joint name for Old Icelandic and Old Norwegian, as representing the North ◊Germanic language before about 1300.

Old North French The dialect of northern France before about 1500.

Old Provençal The form of ◊Provençal before about 1500.

Old Saxon The form of ◊Low German spoken by the Saxons in northwestern Germany before about 1100.

Old Welsh The Welsh language before about 1150.

Phoenician The language of Phoenicia, an ancient kingdom in the eastern Mediterranean.

Pidgin English A language that blends the vocabulary of English with the structure of Chinese or some other language.

Provençal The ◊Romance language of Provence, in southeastern France.

Romance The group of European languages that developed from ◊Vulgar Latin. They include French, Spanish, Italian, Portuguese, Romanian, and ◊Provençal.

Sanskrit The ancient sacred and literary language of India.

Scandinavian The historic and modern North ◊Germanic languages of Denmark, Iceland, Norway, Sweden, and the Faeroe Islands.

Scottish A dialect of English spoken in Scotland, mainly in the Lowlands.

Scottish Gaelic The same as ◊Gaelic.

Semitic A group of non-◊Indo-European languages that includes Arabic, ◊Hebrew, ◊Aramaic, Amharic, and such ancient languages as ◊Phoenician.

Slavic A branch of ◊Indo-European that includes modern Russian, Polish, and Czech.

Urdu the official language of Pakistan, also spoken in India.

Vulgar Latin The spoken or popular form of ◊Latin during the later period of the ancient Roman Empire (from about the 3rd century AD). The ◊Romance languages developed from it.